Conscience
Over
Mind

By

Faith

The First Step Toward **Salvation**

And

The Perfection Of **Character**

In Jesus **Christ**

Amen

Written by Stephen H. Sergeant

Dedicated to my mother, Wilhelmina Forskin

Faith is the Word and will of God, the inspiration of both spirit and truth to cultivate love and hope in our hearts toward Jesus Christ, whereby we say...

The Lord

Is

My Helper

Conscience

Over

Mind

By

Faith

To Rule Over the Senses

The Word of God is quick, and powerful, and sharper than any two–edged sword, piercing even to the dividing asunder of soul and spirit, and of joints and marrow, and is a discerner of the thoughts and intents of the heart. *Hebrews chapter 4:12*

The Vindication

Of

God the Father

By

Christ the Son

&

The Holy Spirit

The Tabernacle of Shiloh came and dwelled among mankind. In the volume of the book, it is written of Him: Jesus Christ the only begotten Son, Who was the express Image of God in the Likeness of a man, whereby He vindicated His Father's name and paid the penalty for our sins. And there was silence in heaven as the universe bears witness unto His death at the cross. Every mouth was shut including the accuser of the brethren, namely Satan. For he accuses the brethren day and night, namely those that are written in the book of life; at which point the entire world was pronounced guilty in front of God. After Jesus was resurrected God gave His Holy Spirit the authority to reproduce the moral law, which is the circumcision made without hands.

The outpouring of His Holy Spirit rained on the just and the unjust alike. **John chapter 3:16** tells us that God so loved the world, that He gave His only begotten Son, that whosoever believes in Him would not perish, but have everlasting life. For He that is faithful and merciful will not leave us nor forsake us, neither in trials nor in tribulations. For when Christ was tried, He was found not guilty. Furthermore, He overcame the world, and made us heirs to His Kingdom. **Acts chapter 14:22** tells us that as believers we are commissioned to discipleship, and that we should inspire new believers to continue in faith, edifying them with the gospel of Jesus Christ that we must go through many tribulations in order to further personify our journey of entering the Kingdom of God. **Isaiah chapter 53:5** tells us that Jesus Christ gave mankind a second chance by paying the penalty for sin. He was wounded for our transgressions, He was bruised for our iniquities: the chastisement of our peace was upon Him; and by His stripes we are healed. **Psalm chapter 58:3** tells us that everyone is born sinful or self-centered, because everyone is born separated from God. The wicked are separated from the womb; they go astray as soon as they are born, speaking lies.

God doesn't hold us accountable for being born sinful. We sin because we are sinful. We are not sinful because we sin. **Ezekiel chapter 18:20,21** tells us that the person who sins will die. The son shall not bear the punishment for the father's iniquity; neither shall the father bear the punishment for the son's iniquity. Everyone's righteousness is accredited to himself. It is the same for the wickedness of the wicked; it is charged against the wicked person. However, if the wicked turns from all his sins that he has committed, and keep all My Commandments, and does that which is lawful and right, he shall surely live, he shall not die. Jesus refers to us as an adulterous generation. **Matthew chapter 16:4** tells us a wicked and adulterous generation seeks after a sign; and there shall be no sign given unto it, except the sign of the prophet Jonas.

Our lives are sinful no matter how well balance it may seem. **Romans chapter 3:23,24** tells us that all have sinned, and come short of the glory of God; being justified freely by His grace through the redemption that is in Christ Jesus. **Philippians chapter 2:5-8** tells us that Jesus Christ was selfless and made Himself of no reputation by being a servant, even though He was a King, and the Son of the Father in heaven. Let this mind be in you, which was also in Christ Jesus: Who was God, and is God, but thought it not robbery to be stripped of all privileges and rightful dignity: but made Himself of no reputation, and took upon Him the form of a servant, and was made in the likeness of men: And being found in the fashion as a man, He humbled Himself, and became obedient unto death, even the death of the cross. Amen

Prayer for Wisdom

Dear, heavenly Father Who created all things unto Your glory. You are the God of David and the God of Solomon. How excellent is Your name throughout the universe. I have seen the works of Your hands in the days of our forefather Abraham, and in the days of Your beloved Son Jesus Christ. And today O Lord my God I have seen the works of Your Holy Spirit upon the human soul. Strengthen me by the words of Your mouth, so that I may hate sin and forsake evil; and that I may learn to love Your ways of righteousness. When I consider all things that are done under the sun I say to myself, what is man that You are mindful of him? The ways of man are deceitful, who can know it except You O God.

Your Holy Spirit dwells in me, and Your Holy angels stand by my side protecting me day and night. I am steadfast in Your Word, ever learning Your ways and getting understanding from Your wisdom. Moreover, O Lord I thank You for Your mercy and grace. As I open Your Word I see the multitude of Your selfless love toward humanity. You are a God of perfect love, and perfect peace. Apart from You there is no other. I praise You O God for Your Holy Spirit that has united me with You in spirit and in truth, so that in glory You are glorified; and in honor Your name is magnified to the fullness of Your Character that we may know that You are God. And apart from You there is no other. "Let the words of my mouth and the meditation of my heart be accepted in Your sight, O Lord You are my strength and my redeemer." Amen

Focus

From creation until now the earth groans like a woman in travail. The indication of the end being near, and the time for repentance is now. As the angels are sent forth into the Lord's harvest, will you not answer to the last call for repentance? **Matthew chapter 9:13** tells us that the Son of man did not come to save the righteous, but to call sinners unto repentance. As we approach the beginning of the sixth millennium, we are faced with many challenges. However, let us consider all things that are true and holdfast to our faith. For we have an advocate with the Father in heaven, namely Jesus Christ, Who is merciful unto us. As it is written the just shall live by faith, but woe unto him that finds pleasure in the tree of knowledge of good and evil. For no place shall be found on the earth for the sinner who rejects the gospel of Jesus Christ. **John chapter 14:1-3** tells us that Jesus said, "Let not your heart be troubled, if you believe in God, believe also in Me. In My Father's house are many mansions; if it were not so, I would have told you. I go to prepare a place for you. And if I go and prepare a place for you, I will come again and receive you unto Myself, that where I Am, there you may be also."

The tree of knowledge of good and evil comes down to choice. The daily self–sacrifice of every true disciple is centered on Christ, whereby the Word of God feeds the spiritual man. True faith is surrendering moment–by–moment unto His Holy Spirit. However, many will refuse sound doctrine, whereby leaving their faith behind for the contemporary life of the world: holding their breath, and dying prematurely, unable to let go of lust, and finally being consumed by the cares of the world.

The path to redemption is made straight by the blood of the Lamb. However, the discernment of the truth isn't in the world and the road to destruction may first seem appealing to the eye, but then comes guilt, humiliations, and obstacles at every turn. Is there any value or purpose to the things, which have brought us so much grief? So often you will hear of someone's journey from rags to riches hoping that Jesus Christ is the final result, but only to hear of their downfall. More money more problems is the theme of the world. The principalities of the world will not allow us to find serenity, but instead lust and greed, which will plunge even the most well balanced individual into chaos and destruction.

Jesus Christ is my Lord and Savior, and He grants serenity unto all who seeks after Him. We all share the same weakness when it comes to rebellion and disobedience. And personally I haven't accomplished anything that I can take to the grave except the free gift of grace. The success of our Lord and Savior Jesus Christ was based upon His obedience unto God the Father. The sinner isn't condemned for his sin, neither is he accredited for his own righteousness. However, if we choose to turn away from His unconditional love: the Holy Spirit bears witness to our rebellion as disobedience. Take into consideration that time well spent is like money saved; meanwhile time wasted is like money borrowed with interest. Those that are of a carnal mind find pleasure in the world. We are not of a carnal mind, but of the Spirit of the Word of God. Remember whatever you do in life, do it to the best of your ability and also unto the glory of Him that is worthy to be praised. Amen

Truth versus a Lie

What is truth? And who told the first lie? God is the Spirit of truth. Before Lucifer left heaven he started a war by accusing God of being unfair. Lucifer was the first person to tell a lie, and he is the spirit of lies.

Here is an analogy of a man accused of raping a woman. After the man was sentence to prison, the woman that accused him of raping her decided to confess after forty years that she had consensual sex with him, instead of being raped. The woman implied that it was very difficult for her to tell the truth about the relationship between her and her adopted son. All who break the law are subjected to punishment. And a mother having sex with her own son would be something to lie about. In many cases a lie would seem more conventional than the truth. What then, should we lie about everything to avoid punishment? Justice is the fulfillment of God's law, whereby Jesus took our place on the cross and paid the penalty for our sins.

Have you ever had a friend, or a child that confessed to you about doing something wrong, but it made things worse simply because it indicates that they are at fault. And you felt that they needed to be punished with some sympathy of course for telling the truth. But who wants punishment regardless of how loving, or considerate the punisher is? God doesn't take the same approach: He shows the sinner mercy, whereby we don't get what we deserve, which is death; but instead, He grants us grace, which is pardon without punishment. Furthermore, He rewards us with power to overcome sin by granting the sinner the opportunity to live a life of purpose and value according to His glory. Truth and fact isn't the same thing! The Word of God reveals the truth about His great plan for saving humanity. Fact is the evidence of our current situation, which is a life of sin, which leads to the death of our soul.

The Origin of Sin (Desire)

There are three types of love: Agape, Philia, and Storge. The Agape love is God's unconditional love toward humanity, and Philia love is brotherly love toward one another, and Storge is compassion toward our biological family members. Imagine that the heart is the center of everything that is good: faith, hope, and Agape love, whereas Eros, the desire to satisfy self has become the primary pursuit of humanity. I suppose for some the counterfeit has benefits?

God created mankind in His Own Image and Likeness, and called them Adam. However, God foreseeing the future of humanity, He took one of the man ribs and made a woman. The woman being the weaker vessel illustrated the separation of light and darkness in the Garden of Eden. In other words she relied on her sensual knowledge, instead of exercising faith and obedience unto God for spiritual discernment. Eros, which is human desire, or lust. **Genesis chapter 3:6** tells us that when the woman <u>saw</u> that the <u>tree</u> was <u>good</u> for <u>food</u> and that it was <u>pleasing</u> to her <u>eyes</u> and a tree to be <u>desired</u> to make one <u>wise</u> she took of the <u>fruit</u> thereof, and did <u>eat</u>, and gave also unto her husband Adam, and he did eat.

We all share the same pitfall of wanting to create something out of rebellion. However, we don't have the ability to create our own destiny, we can only embrace the one that God has already set in motion. The predestination of our soul salvation was already in place from the foundation of the earth. Are we hand puppets? God forbid! He gave us free–will. The abundance of life comes down to one single choice, and that is choosing Christ. We can choose to surrender our free–will unto Christ or take the bull by the horn, which is the same as the tree of knowledge of good and evil. Jesus Christ is the right choice for me, which is why I have placed my entire life into His hands. Amen

About the Author

My name is Stephen Howard Sergeant, and I believe in Jesus Christ, because He took my place on the cross at Calvary, so that through His sacrifice I may have life abundantly. My early teenage years were a challenge, and I felt as if I was placed at the back of the bus. I became rebellious, and my heart was led away by the cares of the world. I tried to convince myself that God wasn't real, and Christianity was more or less a myth. However, the truth is always staring us in the face whether we choose to believe it or not. Most people don't recognize the truth when it presents itself, but instead a lie finds more room in the hearts and minds of many who have made a choice to reject the truth about soul salvation.

About ten years ago I was in the world, but today I am in the Word. My story is very simple, I hated life, and I hated God for giving it unto me. I did not attend law school. However, if they had an award for manipulating the truth, I would be one of the most qualified recipients. I didn't make up lies; I only use the ones that were already available to support the result that I wanted. The summary of a lie is broken down into three categories: seduction, manipulation, and deception of the heart, whereby pride has become the substitute of the moral law. Pride is the seed of rebellion, which leads to disobedience. Pride suppresses the truth, and hardens the heart by means of which our entire life becomes a lie. False accusation is the same as giving ones' opinion, whereby it contradicts the truth about God's great plan for soul salvation. A judge may say, "Guilty or not guilty" but the only thing that the human race is guilty of is not spending enough time worshiping God. Never confide in another, especially when you are feeling guilty. The only person that you can trust is God. He has made me trustworthy, and He is able to do the same for you. Truth is the Word of God, the unseen faith without any trace of evidence to support that which we already believe in our hearts. Amen

What is Our Destiny?

Should we observe life through our five senses and then come to the conclusion that we are in charge of our own destiny? The human race is not as knowledgeable as one would like to believe. Furthermore, living a balance life in this day and age is very difficult. The repetitive cycle of man's wickedness can be seen throughout the history of his generations. And the knowledge of how to accomplish character perfection is not a part of our DNA.

Personally, I consider the human race to be somewhat incompetent including myself. And no matter how we spin the dice death is the final result. When I was about seven years old, an angel appeared unto me in a dream and said, surely it would have been better if you had not been born rather than not to trust in the Lord. A few years later I had a second dream. However, I had the opportunity of asking, what was in store for my future? The answer that I got was not what I expected or wanted to hear. Consequently, I did what any normal teenage boy would do; I rebelled and withdrew myself from the presence of the Lord.

In the year 1989 I visited the United States of America for the first time. My classmates and I went to Disney World. And after returning home to Jamaica, I spent the following two years finishing high school. After graduation, I decided to visit my aunt Zelta that lives in Allentown, Pennsylvania. I remembered that cold winter as if it were yesterday. My first experience of snow was not as joyful as I thought it would be. The only thought that came to mind was how could people endure such harsh weather conditions? But since it was my first Christmas away from home, I wasn't about to let the cold weather ruin my vacation. After four months of seeing snow, I finally had enough of it, so I decided it was time for me to go home. It was the beginning of spring and the temperature on the island was about eighty-five degrees. And since it wasn't hurricane season, the beaches were open. Thirteen Sabbath was coming up and the local Seventh-day Adventist Church was getting ready for Communion.

That very Sabbath I had a third dream. I saw the greatness of the Lord's salvation coming down from heaven during His Passover. Everyone dressed in white, which is the righteousness of Christ. And I was numbered with the saints to preach the gospel unto the four corners of the world. As my feet march toward His redemption I stumbled and fell. I awoke from the dream, and I told my mother that I was certain that I wanted to be baptized. I was seventeen years old at the time of my baptism. And likewise of the revelation of the dream, after one year I left the church to follow my own selfish desires. I spent more than two-thirds of my life chasing shattered dreams that led to a life of sin. And after a long road of disappointments and regrets, I heard the voice of the Holy Spirit calling my name three times like a gentle whisper, saying, Stephen it is time. My Savior had returned to redeem the one lost sheep that was left behind. God gave me a second chance and the assurance of hope in His salvation. I was raised from a sedated lifestyle to a spiritual journey that would bring glory and honor to His name, Jehovah Jireh, Jehovah Nissi, and Jehovah Shalom. Amen

Prayer of Mercy

Dear Father God, You are my going out, and my coming in; have mercy on my soul. I am weary, and my burden is heavy. My true friends have given upon me; the world has turned its face against me. O Lord my God will You turn away from me? My soul is sour vex with sorrow, and my heart has fainted in pain. My tears have left me dry, and my very thoughts betray me. Who can I trust, or where can I hide from the oppression that I feel? O Lord my God, I beg You not to turn away from me. I will seek You early in the morning, and I will stay up late at night to find You, I will walk quietly by the still waters, and fast for many days till my God return unto me. How precious You are to me; I miss the days when Your love filled my heart with joy, and Your peace rest upon my shoulders. How I love those quiet moments where You shared Your thoughts of wisdom with me, so that I may have knowledge to discern Your will, and have hope in Your eternal salvation. O Lord my God in You I put my trust, turn to me again and never depart from me. I thank You O God for hearing my cry. Amen

Contents

"Faith Love and Hope"

Part I

"Separation of Light and Darkness"

Part II

"Jesus is the Lord of the Sabbath"

Part III

Introduction

After Adam fell, the face of God was hidden from mankind, because of our sinful nature. Since then, no one has met face to face with the Creator of the universe. However, we were given a glimpse of Jesus Christ: Who is the express Image of God, but yet He humbled Himself in the likeness of a man and became a servant unto many. As we all share the same atmosphere of faith and hope, we acknowledge that the Agape love *(Unconditional love)* of Christ is the primary factor that will help us to bear the fruit of the Spirit and overcome the things that will deprive us of our joy and peace.

The human heart has become a wall of stone, lacking compassion for others. The fulfillment of Eros *(Romantic love)* has become the primary pursuit of humanity. As many times as we have heard and used the words I love you, but only to discover that Philia love *(Brotherly love)* is becoming more and more of a rarity in our society. And the Agape love that we share with Christ has become more or less of a one–way street, namely Christ's divine love for humanity. An apology has become the norm to every social aspect of the entire human race. I am so sorry, I don't know how it happened; please forgive me. The fulfillment of the Agape love needs no apology, only the sacrifice of self to glorify God by being a servant unto others, as did Christ: our Lord and Savior.

In the past, I was among those who found no joy in nurturing faith for God, and having no compassion for others. I was also guilty of breaking promises. I was ignorant and destitute of the truth, and if it weren't for the conviction given unto me from the Holy Spirit, I would still be on the same destructive path of unbelief and rebellion today.

Life can be burdensome for the individual. And without the divine attributes of Christ the human heart has a distinctive way of becoming more and more condescending as it becomes entangled in the world. Many will find themselves in a state of hopelessness as the success of the elite surpasses those that are left behind. Today, the opportunity of getting ahead is the next lottery winner. Everyone wants to become his or her own god, as opposed to being perfect and complete by surrendering to Christ selfless love. God Himself is perfect and complete: and He bears witness that I am a human being by means of which, I am His creation; and therefore I have surrendered my entire life to Him, so that I am perfect and complete! We are all created in the Image and Likeness of God. However, pride has become the downfall of humanity.

The intent of this book is to provide simple and practical ways of how to relieve you of unwanted stress. If you are completely happy there is something very wrong. Personal happiness is achievable, unlike the omniscient joy and peace that comes through the divine intervention of our Lord and Savior Jesus Christ. In this chaotic world only a selfish person would be naive to believe in happiness, which lacks joy and peace.

God gave us faith, and from faith sprang hope to believe in Him that was raised from the dead. At the cross we saw the Agape love of God manifesting itself through the sacrifice of His beloved Son Jesus Christ. The barren tree is dwarf in the knowledge and hope of our Lord Jesus Christ, because of unbelief. However, if we believe in our hearts that Christ was raised from the dead, we must surrender all unto Him. As hope without faith is dead, so is faith without surrendering to the unconditional love of God. The primary principle of faith and hope is to love God and your brethren as yourself. Brotherly love is a daily self-sacrifice by means of which our primary focus is on Christ's divine love, the instrument of every true Christian faith and belief. God's mercy and grace can be seen through the works of faith, whereby loving one another and having the spirit of empathy and compassion even as much as Christ Himself died to save us.

Many will preach, "Love, love" but yet find it difficult in their hearts to make the sacrifice of helping their brother. However, with great ease and laxity the hypocrite makes an excuse; please come again at another time, its not convenient for me to help you right now. When the rich young ruler spoke to Jesus about what he needed to be saved; he was told to sell all his possessions and give it to the poor. Many have disobeyed the commandment, but yet claiming to serve, and follow not in the steps of our dear Lord and Savior Jesus Christ. **Matthew chapter 25:45** tells us that Jesus will answer them, saying, surely, I say unto you, as you did it not to the least of these, you did it not to Me. How does one fulfill the will of God and the needs of others without feeling obligated to do so? Self–denial is the key to surrendering to Christ selfless love, which He, Himself manifested at the cross; whereby partaking of the heavenly current that unites us with Him in Spirit and truth. On the contrary, if we choose not to surrender unto Christ, Satan becomes the victor and our seared conscience remains entangled in the world by means of which we carry our own burden. I write this not to be critical, but by conviction. The greatest commandment is to love God, because without the unconditional love of God, we can do nothing. Be a blessing unto others by fulfilling their needs, for by doing so we are the children of God. Amen

Write a prayer of faith to personalize your book...

"Faith Love and Hope"

Chapter 1

Faith

Hebrews chapter 11:1-40 gives us a summary of faith, whereby letting us know that faith is the substance of things hoped for without any physical evidence to support that which we believe. Faith is given to the believer to discern the spiritual things of God, which are invisible to the world. Faith is the unseen heavenly current that descends from God the Father through Jesus Christ His beloved Son. Furthermore, sanctification is the preparation of the believer to live in heaven, whereby His Holy Spirit unites with our spirit as one. **Psalm chapter 15:1,2** tells us that David asked the Lord, who would live in His temple? Who will dwell in Your Holy presence? They that keep the faith of Jesus Christ: and walk upright, he that do right and speak the truth in his heart. **Revelation chapter 14:12** tells us here is the patience of the saints: here are they that keep the commandments of God, and have the faith of Jesus. **Hebrews chapter 12:2** tells us that the margin between the tree of knowledge of good and evil comes down to one denominator; namely, Jesus Christ Who is the author and finisher of our faith. **Genesis chapter 1:1** tells us that in the beginning God created the heaven and the earth. Therefore since God is the Creator of all things, and there is nothing hidden from Him, He would also be the most suitable person to consult on every matter. The Holy Spirit is the combination of faith mixed with hope to reproduce the Agape love of God in us, whereby the believer progressively becomes more and more like Christ. Amen

Agape Love

Those that God foreknew before the foundation of the earth, He also predestinated them to take on the Image and Likeness of His only begotten Son, so that through Him all would be saved. Justification gives us access to God the Father through the communication that we have with Christ Jesus our Lord and Savior. Sanctification is the preparation of the believer, whereby His Holy Spirit unites with our spirit as one. God is love and apart from Him there isn't any other source that can reproduce the Agape love in us. The Agape love is the first and greatest commandment, which Christ Himself illustrated at the cross toward humanity. The works of faith is better understood as the discernment of both good and evil. Faith enables the believer to discern the will of God, whereby we labor in love toward one another, and by the hope that we have in Christ Jesus we are called as a witness unto the world in the patience of His coming.

Even though God is everywhere and His work can be seen in everything, we can only relate to Him in spirit and truth. **Romans chapter 2:14,15** tells us that when the Gentiles, which have not the law keep the law, it is our conscience who bears witness, and our thoughts are made perfect to discern both good and evil toward each other. The Agape love is the first commandment of the Bible, and Philia love is the second of the great commandment, which shares the same equal value as the first. The manifestation of true repentance is the Agape love of God. God's love is unconditional, and all love including: Brotherly love and Storge, which is compassion toward our biological family comes from God.

The combination of faith, love, and hope is the fulfillment of Jesus' retroactive work upon the human soul. The relationship that we share with Christ empowers us to do all things through His Holy Spirit. **John chapter 15:12,13** tells us that Jesus commands us to love one another, as He has loved us. There is no greater way to show love for a friend, than to give your life for his. The moral law comes from the Agape love of Jesus Christ, whereby Philia love is the relationship that we share with Him in our daily walk. The Bible reveals the retroactive work of His Holy Spirit upon the human soul, whereby the believer becomes submissive unto Christ by means of which a daily self–sacrifice is made in order to consecrate our hearts in doing His will. Getting to know the Father through Jesus Christ empowers us to trust and obey Him, whereby our spirit is renewed daily. **Matthew chapter 4:4** tells us that man shall not live by bread alone, but by every word that proceeds out of the mouth of God. **Matthew chapter 4:7** tells us that we should not tempt the Lord our God. **Matthew chapter 4:10** tells us that we should worship the Lord our God, and Him only should we serve. **Matthew chapter 4:17** tells us to repent: for the kingdom of heaven is coming soon. **Matthew chapter 4:19** tells us that Jesus wants us to follow Him, and He will make us fishers of men.

The Sermon on the Mount fills the hearts of every sincere born–again Christian with joy and peace, which is the result of our righteousness in Him. However, the rebellious heart is filled with bitterness, whereby guilt stops the sinner from enjoying the promises of our beloved Lord and Savior Jesus Christ. **Matthew chapter 5:3-16** tells us blessed are the humble in heart: for theirs is the kingdom of heaven. Blessed are they that have their focus on God: for they will be comforted. Blessed are the humble: for they will inherit the earth. Blessed are they that seek after God: for they will be filled. Blessed are they that forgive their debtors: for their debts will be forgiven also. Blessed are they that have been cleanse by the blood of Christ: for they will see the face of God. Blessed are the peacemakers: for they will be called the children of God.

Blessed are they, which are persecuted for righteousness sake: for theirs is the kingdom of heaven. Blessed are you when men will provoke you, and persecute you, and will say all manner of evil against you falsely for My sake. Rejoice, and be exceedingly glad for great is your reward in heaven: for they also persecuted the prophets, which were before you. You are the salt of the earth: but if the salt loose its taste, wherein its not salted then it has lost its purpose, and therefore has become good for nothing, but to be thrown out, and be trodden under the feet of men. You are the light of the world. A city that sits on top of a hill cannot be hidden. No one lights a candle and cover it with a basket, but instead it is placed on a candlestick, so that it may give light unto the entire house. Let your light so shine before men that they may see your good works and glorify your Father, which is in heaven. **Galatians chapter 5:13,14** tells us that God has called us to liberty, but not for our own purpose to satisfy ourselves, but to be of service unto each other. Furthermore, the law of God is fulfilled in one word: love your neighbor as yourself.

Galatians chapter 5:22 tells us that the fruit of the Holy Spirit is the Agape Love of God, which are these: Philia love, joy, peace, longsuffering, gentleness, goodness, faith, meekness, temperance. If anyone has these qualities in them, you are perfect in love, and you are not under the law of sin. The Holy Spirit of God works through faith, whereby love becomes the primary focus of the believer. True faith is love toward one another. Likewise on this matter, it is God Who grants us the capacity to love one another, whereby His Holy Spirit reproduce the Agape love inside of our hearts.

The moral law is the declaration of hope that we have in Christ Jesus if we surrender unto His will. God wants to reconcile us unto Himself through Jesus Christ His beloved Son; and renew the relationship we once shared with Him. The indwelling of His Holy Spirit allows us to draw near to Him with sincerity. Also knowing that He loves us and forgave us from the foundation of the earth. There are only two words, which are suitable to describe God's law: unconditional love. Love God, and love your neighbor as yourself, this is the whole law. The Ten Commandments is the knowledge and letter of the law. However, God gave the command to obey while manifesting the true power of His unconditional love toward us, which is Christ Jesus Who is the Spirit of the law.

Lucifer was envious of Jesus, whereby revealing his pride and ambition to become his own god. And not realizing that the law can only be kept by having a sincere relationship with Christ. The Pharisees also manifested the attributes of their father the devil whose children we are by the works of the human nature: law breakers, high-minded, unbelief, malice; having a guilty conscience; and meanwhile provoking the Holy Spirit. I tell you, whosoever you are repent of such evil deeds. Learn to do good, and good will follow you, this brings God great pleasure. Doing good deeds come after having a relationship with God through Christ, and not before. In other words it is impossible to keep the law without the indwelling of His Holy Spirit. **James chapter 2:18** tells us that you have people that will say, that they have faith and does nothing to show their love for God, and then you have those that will say, that they don't need faith in order to show love unto their neighbors: but I say unto you, show me your faith without brotherly love, and I will show you my faith by loving my neighbor as much as I love myself.

The Agape love points away from self, whereby the retroactive work of the Holy Spirit can be seen in the lives of everyone that believes. By faith we labor in love toward one another, holding onto the hope of His salvation to come. **Hebrews chapter 13:6** tells us that the Word of God is transpired through the works of faith, so that we may boldly say, the Lord is my helper, and I will not fear what man shall do unto me. **1 Corinthians chapter 13:1-13** tells us that if we had the ability to speak every language known to man and angels, and we didn't have the Agape love of Jesus Christ in us, we would sound like a squealing noise, or a clanging symbol. Furthermore, if we had the ability to see into the future and understand all things, and have endless knowledge, and enough strength to move mountains, but didn't have the Agape love we are nothing. And even if we gave all our substance to feed the poor and sacrifice our lives for theirs, and we didn't have the Agape love of Christ in our hearts, it gains us nothing. Love is patient, love is kind, love and not hate; love is without envy, love is not selfish, love is not conceited, love doesn't seek its own reward, love has no anger, love has no evil thoughts. Rejoice not in hate, but rather in truth. Love bears all things, and believes all things. Surrender all things to Christ, and our patience in Him will enable us to endure all things through Him.

For the love of Christ will never fail. Eventually prophecies will come to an end, languages will cease, and knowledge as we know it will vanish away. For we know so little, and prophecy only gives us a glimpse of the future, but when our characters are made perfect in Him that is to come, then our personalities which are imperfect will fade away. When we were children, we spoke as children, we understood as children, we thought as children: but now that we have obtained obedience through His righteousness, we must put away our rebellious attitude. Now we see things obscurely as in a dark mirror, but then we will see things as they really are. Now we know God through His Word, but then we will know Him face to face, even as He knows us. And now these three things that will last forever: faith, hope and love in perfect peace and harmony, but the greatest of these is love. Amen

Philia Love

Who is Our Neighbor? Is it just the man and the woman on the right or on the left of our homes? The answer goes beyond the city block, but rather the entire civilization of the universe. **Hebrews chapter 13:1,2** tells us that we should let brotherly love continue, and forget not to entertain strangers: for by doing so some have entertained angels. **Genesis chapter 18:1-5** tells us that while Abraham was living in the plains of Mam—re the Lord visited him. And the Lord appeared unto Abraham in the plains of Mam—re. Abraham was sitting in the doorway of his tent around noon time when he raised his head and saw three men standing afar off, so he ran to meet them and bowed himself toward the ground, and said, I welcome you, and if now I have found favor in your sight, I beg you to accept my hospitality. I wish to offer my service unto you by washing your feet, and allowing you to rest under the shade of the tree. And I will bring you a loaf of bread, and after you have rested you may leave.

Abraham was unaware that it was the Lord that stood afar off, but by faith he showed his hospitality unto strangers. How many of us today can be sociable to someone we have never met before? The story of Cain and Abel comes to mind? God was getting ready to sacrifice His only begotten Son in order to save the world, but in order for Jesus' sacrifice to be made known an invitation had to be sent to those that were in need of soul salvation. **Genesis chapter 4:4** tells us that Abel brought a sheep according to the commandment of God. And the Lord had respect unto Abel and his offering. Abel surrendered himself unto the will of God and brought the correct offering, but Cain the rebellious one, did things his own way. God is a giver, and He wants us to participate in sharing with others as well. Think of tithe and offering as an exchange. Whenever we tithe out of obedience God blesses us with His unconditional love. We don't tithe to receive His love, but because His Agape love dwells inside of us; we tithe to show our brotherly love toward one another. We give up selfishness, so that we may receive selflessness to the glory of His name.

Tithing is God's way of inviting us to participate in something extraordinary. **Genesis chapter 14:18-20** tells us that Melchizedek King of Salem was the Priest of the Most High God, and He brought forth <u>bread</u> and <u>wine</u>. And He blessed Abraham, and said, blessed be Abraham of the Most High God, possessor of the heaven and earth. And blessed be the Most High God Who delivered your enemies into your hands. And Abraham gave Him tithes of all.

Tithing is a test of faith. Melchizedek is a type of Christ; He was a direct representative of the Most High God Who brought Spiritual bread and wine to Abraham who gave tithes of all. **Genesis chapter 28:22** tells us that Jacob made a pledge to God with a stone, which he had used for a pillar. And he said this shall be God's house. And of all that God shall give me, I will surely return the tenth unto Him. We know that God established His righteousness through the Stone, which was Christ Jesus, but it was through the willingness of tithing that God Himself gave His only begotten Son.

Tithing is something that God takes seriously. **Leviticus chapter 27:30-32** tells us that tithing is Holy unto the Lord. And all the tithe of the land, whether of the seed of the land, or of the fruit of the tree, it belongs unto the Lord. And if a man wants to buy back his tithe, he must add five percent more than its value to redeem it back. Concerning the tithe of the herd or the flock, whatsoever passes under the rod, the tenth one shall be Holy unto the Lord. **Exodus chapter 35:4-9** tells us that God spoke unto Moses, saying, speak unto all the congregation of the children of Israel, saying, this is the thing, which the Lord commanded, saying: take from among you an offering unto the Lord. Whosoever is of a willing heart, let him bring it as an offering unto the Lord: gold, silver, bronze, blue, purple, scarlet thread and fine linen. And goat's hair, ram skins dyed red, badger skins, acacia wood and oil for the light. And spices for the anointing oil, for the sweet incense and onyx stones to be set in the priest's apron and breastplate.

Numbers chapter 18:25-28 tells us that the Lord spoke unto Moses, saying, speak unto the Levites, and say unto them, whenever you receive tithe from the children of Israel, which I have given unto you for your inheritance, you will offer unto Me a fellowship offering of it, even the tenth part of the tithe. And your fellowship offering will be recognized as though it were corn from the field, and as if it were the choice grapes from a winepress. You will also offer your fellowship offering unto the Lord of all your tithes, which you have receive of the children of Israel, and you shall give the Lord's fellowship offering unto Aaron the priest.

The Fellowship Offering

The person that has all the resources doesn't need anything, but to him that is in need God wants to share. Furthermore, God creates an exchange for our sinful life, where He gives us mercy, whereby we don't get what we deserve, which is death; and grace is something better, the opportunity to have eternal life with Him in heaven. Whenever I spend money I feel as if I am robbing the other person by giving them my useless dirty money. We live in a society that cherishes money more than people, whereby it is the price of our labor. **Deuteronomy chapter 14:28,29** tells us that at the end of every three years, bring all the tithes of that year's harvest and store it in your towns, and give to the Levites who neither have part nor inheritance with you. Furthermore, give to the foreigner, and the fatherless, and the widows who live in your neighborhood, and let them come and eat and be satisfied. And the Lord your God will bless you in all the work of your hands. **Deuteronomy chapter 15:1,2** tells us that at the end of every seven years you shall make a release. And this is the manner of the release: every creditor that lend unto his neighbor shall forgive the debt owed. He shall not exact it of his neighbor or of his brother: it is the Lord's release. (Debt cancelation)

Matthew chapter 5:42-45 tells us to give to him that ask of us, and from him that would borrow turn him not away. It was said, that you should love your neighbor, and hate your enemy. But I say to you: love your enemies, bless them that curse you, do good to them that hate you, and pray for them which despitefully use you and persecute you that you may become the children of your Father which is in heaven. Amen

The Ransom

Imagine that you owed a debt and you had no alternate way of settling it: Jesus Christ paid for such on our behalf. **Matthew chapter 19:16-23** tells us behold, a young man came and said unto Jesus, Good Master, <u>what good thing shall I do that I may have eternal life?</u> And Jesus said unto him, why call Me good? <u>There is none good but one, that is, God.</u> <u>However, if you will enter into life,</u> keep the commandments. The young man said unto Him, which? And Jesus said, you shall do no murder, you shall not commit adultery, you shall not steal, you shall not bear false witness, honor your father and mother, and <u>love your neighbor as yourself.</u> The young man said unto Him, all these things have I done from my youth up: what lack I yet? Jesus said unto him, <u>if you want to be perfect, go and sell that which you have and give it to the poor.</u> And you shall have treasure in heaven: and come and follow Me. But when the young man heard the saying, he went away sorrowful: for he had great possessions. And Jesus said to His disciples, <u>for certain I say to you, that a rich man shall hardly enter into the Kingdom of heaven.</u>

In the beginning Lucifer was perfect, but instead of nurturing love for Christ in his heart, he chose to nurture pride, whereby self became his downfall. The rich young ruler's heart was harden by his material wealth, and therefore he needed to surrender himself unto Christ in order to let go of his pride, so that he could have treasure in heaven. **Matthew chapter 16:24** tells us that Jesus said to His disciples, if any man will come after Me, let him deny himself, and take up his cross daily, and follow Me.

Surrendering is the hardest part of being a Christian. **Luke chapter 22:42** tells us that in the Garden of Gethsemane Christ spoke these words so that we may have life in Him. Father, if You are willing, remove this cup from Me, yet not My will, but Yours be done. Jesus Christ our Lord and Savior surrendered His entire being unto God the Father at the cross. Therefore, you and I have an advocate with the Father in heaven, namely Jesus Christ Who has passed through the heavens, and now sits at the right hand of God as our Mediator. Amen

First hand experience is something that money can't buy. The harshness of life has taught me many things. And after considering all the facts I came to one conclusion, that apart from Christ I am nothing. God is offering a relationship that has many benefits. Soul salvation came at a price, which no one can afford. The most patriotic person throughout the ages was Jesus Christ Who not only had faith to believe in His Father, but also trusted Him enough to be obedient unto death, even while He was nailed to the cross. The relationship that Christ shares with His Father means more to Him than His own life. He believed that God was able to raise Him from the dead: and also save the world from certain destruction to come. As believers prepare themselves for the Second Advent, unbelievers speculate on whether the matter is true or false. However, since we all started out as unbelievers, lets not forget the second commandment of the law: to love one another even as Christ loves us.

From the Agape love of God sprang faith to believe in Him that was raised from the dead, whereby through Christ we labor in love toward one another. **Genesis chapter 1:26** tells us that God said, let us make man in Our Image, after Our Likeness, and let them have dominion.

Conscience over mind by faith to rule over the senses is the retroactive work of Christ Holy Spirit upon the human soul. Image refers to the Spiritual Character of God the Father; meanwhile Likeness is the express conduct of Jesus Christ Who is the moral law. The privilege of being a Christian is having faith in God, and surrendering to the hope that we have in His soul salvation by means of which conscientious decisions are made to glorify Him as the Creator of all things, whether principalities or dominions. The indwelling of His Holy Spirit becomes the activist of our conscience to rule over the mind by pacifying the senses. The conscience is the power of perception and belief, so that we may have hope in His eternal salvation to come.

Born–again is our faith being renewed by the work of the Holy Spirit, whereby the Agape love of Christ is transcendentally engraved into the hearts and minds of everyone who accepts Him as their Lord and Savior. **Hebrews chapter 9:13,14** tells us that Moses used the blood of bulls and goats, and the ashes of a heifer to sprinkle the people who were unclean, sanctifying them so that they are outwardly clean. How much more will the blood of Christ Who through the eternal Spirit offered Himself without spot unto God, purge our conscience from dead works to serve the living God? Born–again is the inward man coming to life: the entire soul, conscience, and mind to rule over the senses, whereby our spirit is made perfect in the Image and Likeness of Christ's Character. God created man with free–will. However, free–will doesn't give us the right to disobey. Whenever a commandment or promise is made void, the conscience becomes seared and things always take a turn for the worse. Rebellion leads to disobedience and a seared conscience destroys the moral law. Guilt is the burden of sin by means of which demonic agents of the devil are given access to our spirit; whereby the sinner is held captive. **Genesis chapter 2:16,17** tells us that the Lord God commanded the man, saying, of every tree of the Garden you may freely eat, but of the tree of knowledge of good and evil, you shall not eat of it.

After Adam disobeyed the commandment of God, the plan of salvation went into effect immediately. **Genesis chapter 3:14,15** tells us that the Lord God said unto the serpent, because you have done this, you are cursed above all cattle, and above every animal of the field: upon your belly you shall go, and dust you shall eat all the days of your life, and I will put opposition between you and the woman, and between your generation and her offspring; I will bruise your head, and you shall bruise His heel. **Romans chapter 16:20** tells us that Satan's treachery and betrayal came to an end at the cross, where Christ became victorious. The God of peace shall bruise Satan under Your feet shortly. The grace of our Lord Jesus Christ be with you.

After the fall of Adam, the face of the Creator was hidden from mankind, because of our sinful nature. However, through faith, which is the retroactive work of Christ, our conscience has been renewed by the power of His Holy Spirit to cultivate the Agape love. The mind of the believer is circumcised by the influence of His Holy Spirit, having the senses subdued and cleansed from the pollutions of the world, so that we may bear fruit unto God. **Hebrews chapter 10:22-24** tells us that we should draw near with a true heart in full assurance of faith, having our hearts sprinkled from an evil conscience, and our bodies washed with pure water. Let us holdfast the profession of our faith without wavering, for He is faithful that promised. And let us consider one another to provoke unto love and to good works. Amen

Hope

Psalm chapter 71:5 tells us that God is our hope. For you are my hope, O Lord God: and my trust since my childhood. The decisions that we make today are the outcome of tomorrow. We are married to every decision made right or wrong. **Romans chapter 8:18** tells us that our present sufferings are hard to bear, but they are nothing when compared to the glory that will be revealed in us when Christ comes. **Romans chapter 8:24,25** tells us that true hope doesn't pertain to prosperity, but rather the conversion of the heart unto the hope of soul salvation; whereby we are justified by faith if we continue in the hope and patience of Jesus Christ. **Hebrews chapter 10:19-22** tells us that we should have boldness to enter into holiness by the blood of Jesus, by a new and living way, which He consecrated for us. Also He separated the curtain of the sanctuary and removed the veil. Christ sacrificing His own body, so that He could become our High Priest over the house of God. Let us draw near with a true heart in full assurance of faith, having our hearts sprinkled from an evil conscience and our bodies washed with pure water.

The human race is given the freedom of choice to surrender all emotions unto the will of God. We are spiritual beings living inside of a physical body and can be subjected to spiritual oppression like: insomnia, stress, and various forms of oppressions. Compulsive behavior is exasperating, and also leads to hopelessness by means of which the final result is death by sin. After sin separated Adam from God, the law of love was broken; and their conscience became seared. Therefore, He Who established the law of love also renewed our conscience, so that by faith we could learn obedience unto Him in Whom we now trust and obey, namely Christ Who is set as an example for us to abide in. **John chapter 4:24** tells us that our thoughts and our heart are connected to God Who is a Spirit: and we who worship Him must worship Him in spirit and in truth.

The complexity of the human brain goes beyond modern science and technology, and basically I don't know of anyone who would want to get into the cockpit of a Boeing 747 passenger airline without knowing how to fly. Jesus has given us joy and peace, so that we could glorify God the Father. The Word of God is life evermore; meanwhile the cares of the world bring forth death. Many have labored in vain by placing their trust into the things of the world. God wants believers to labor in love, and thereby giving access to the Holy Spirit. A broken spirit, and a humble heart is the work of the Holy Spirit upon the human soul, which was meant for good. However, the adversary has manipulated the hearts of many unbelievers to reject the gospel that God gave unto us for soul salvation.

Personally, I believe that God created man in His Own Image and Likeness to have dominion over his mind and senses. God never intended for man to die or else He would have not predestinated the plan of soul salvation. For without life there is death, and clearly not even the wicked hope to die. Beholding doesn't bring satisfaction nor does gain sustains our joy and peace.

Our minds are unique in the sense that we have the ability to make conscientious decisions without any physical evidence to support what we believe. The human brain shares two spiritual components: conscience and mind. The conscience is the retroactive work of the Holy Spirit upon the human soul by means of which faith is transpired into the mind to discern both good and evil. There are only two courses of action that the mind can process and conclude: fact and faith. For example: it has been proven that the earth is round, cold is the absence of heat, darkness is the absence of light, and hate is the absence of love. However, If I told you that I have an elephant in the trunk of my car; you could choose to believe it or not. Speculation is the same as guessing, and should never be allowed to take root in the mind. Our senses are not subjected to the Word of God, but they're of the cares of the world. The mind is a vehicle, which accumulate and transport information to the brain. However, without a clear conscience it's impossible for us to make the right choice. The Holy Spirit works through our conscience to help us make wise decisions.

44

Our senses are like back seat drivers, they will sidetrack the mind every chance they get. The deception of sin works through the senses to bring about condemnation of the soul. In many cases we are deceived by what we hear, feel, see and smell, but yet no one has ever tasted salt and mistaken it for sugar. The contrast between fact and faith is belief, whereby the believer surrenders his freedom of choice unto the will of Christ in every decision that is made. **Romans chapter 4:3-7** tells us that Abraham believed God, and it was counted unto him for righteousness. No one receives a wage as a gift or favor, but to him who labors not by the works of his own strength, but believe in God Who justifies the sinner, his faith is counted for righteousness. Even as David also describes the blessedness of the man, unto whom God credits righteousness without him working to secure his own salvation, saying, blessed, are they whose iniquities are forgiven, and whose sins are covered.

For even though we witness the challenges of life through our senses, we can't overcome the world by taking a psychological approach. **2 Corinthians chapter 10:3-6** tells us that the solution to the situation is not sensual, but spiritual, and mighty through God, being able to remove, and eliminate strong holds; casting down the imagination and every immoral act that exalt itself against the knowledge of God by surrendering every thought captive to the obedience of Christ; whereby having the discernment and obedience made perfect to crucify every disobedience. Furthermore, having the discernment of wisdom, knowledge and understanding by means of which a clear conscience enables us to move forward in faith, whereby the mind is subdued by the conscience to crucify the senses, and bringing them to the hope of surrendering unto the will of Christ. **Hebrews chapter 5:14** tells us that you have those who by reason of use have their senses exercised to discern both good and evil.

2 Corinthians chapter 4:7-10 tells us that we are treasures in earthly vessel, so that the supernatural power of God may be seen in our mortal bodies, whereby we are oppressed in everyway, yet not consumed, we are perplexed, but not hopeless; persecuted, but not abandoned, struck down, but not destroyed. Always staying focus on the death and life of Jesus, so that through the hope that we have in Him we may have the fullness of His righteousness manifesting itself in our mortal bodies. **1 Timothy chapter 1:18-20** tells us that Paul the Apostle reassures young pastor Timothy of the importance of holding onto his faith, and also having his hope directed into the love of Jesus Christ. Timothy, my son I lay this charge before you, according to the prophecies which were made about you, so that by them you may fight a good warfare; holding onto faith, and a good conscience. There are some concerns about those who have rejected their faith and have made shipwreck: among these are Hymenaeus and Alexander; whom I have delivered unto Satan that they may learn not to blaspheme.

Every now and then out of curiosity someone will say to me, does God really exist and how do you know, can you prove it? Then I'll simply reply, don't be ridiculous! No one needs proof of God, only faith to believe. The ultimate pursuit in life for many is to find complete happiness. However, joy and peace is God's goal for everyone who seeks after Him. Most individuals refuse to believe anything than the norm. The natural man lives a life of unbelief; he doesn't believe in anything that he can't prove intellectually, but instead he is deceived into taking the bull by the horn. The average person carries the weight of the world by himself without any hope of ever finding joy and peace. And at the end of their physical life, they die without having anything to hope for. Many have come to the conclusion that there isn't a God, when the evidence shows that a child needs the love of a mother and father to guide them through their infant years.

Here is an analogy of a chicken and an egg, which came first the chicken or the egg? Well it depends on the Creator Who made them both. I bear witness that God made all things, whereby the law of God testifies of His mercy and grace toward humanity. Personally, I am one of the wealthiest men on the earth, not because I have money, but because I have surrendered my free-will unto God by means of which His mercy and grace is more than sufficient for me to overcome the sins of the world. The life that I live testifies of my faith in God the Father through Jesus Christ His beloved Son. My personal relationship with Him becomes my hope in His eternal salvation. Therefore, what can I say that will glorify my God? My own life changing experience is the only testimony I have to offer unto you. I can say with absolute assurance that God is in charge of my destiny. For which is greater, giving a testimony or the Mediator, which is Christ Jesus Who testifies of our righteousness in Him? Amen

Prayer of Surrendering and Thanksgiving

Father, I am more than grateful for the life that You have given unto me. I am forever in Your debt, and I know that I can never repay Your Son Jesus Christ for what He has done; I can only surrender my life unto the glory of His name. Jesus is sinless and I am sinful, and He is merciful unto those that call upon His name. You have given us faith, and hope to labor in love toward one another, whereby Your commandment is fulfilled in one word, even this: thou shall love thy neighbor as thyself. I call You Father from this day forward, because of Your dear; Son Jesus Christ Who is my Lord and Savior. I am looking forward to His return, whereby through the adoption that we have in Him, I am Your son. Grant me this day O God and strengthen me by Your Word that I may stand in the days to come. Heaven is Your Kingdom and the earth is Your footstool. Remember me O Lord, for my days are numbered and evil is standing at my door. Who will deliver this generation from the snares of the wicked? I am but a sinner standing at Your door O God, I beg that Your mercy and grace not be taken away, but that Your Holy Spirit remain and sanctify me that I may know kindness and goodness. I surrender in the name of Jesus Christ unto the will of God that I might be saved. Amen

"The Fulfillment of His Promises"

Chapter 2

Surrendering by Faith

For many years I socialized and associated myself with people who drank alcohol, because the liquor gave me a false sense of comfort. I thought I had it under control, but when it came time for me to surrender it unto Christ, I found myself drinking twice as much. I imagine the devil was making one last attempt to use the liquor to kill me. However, God didn't take the bottle from me, I gave it to Him, but soon after I went back to drinking; then I realized that I wasn't completely surrendered. If you are waiting for the right time and place to surrender to Christ that may never happen. **Romans chapter 10:12,13** tells us that there is no difference between the Jew and the Greek. Christ is the same Lord over all, and He distributes the same blessings unto all who call upon Him. For whosoever shall call upon the name of the Lord Jesus Christ shall be saved.

There is no appropriate time like the present moment for us to surrender to His Holy Spirit. Conscience over mind by faith to rule over the senses is where the believer makes a conscientious decision to surrender one time and for all, without going back and forth to the particular sin that we have grown accustom. Faith without belief is dead, even so belief without surrendering to Christ Agape Love. **Galatians chapter 2:20** tells us that we are crucified with Him, and by His Spirit we shall live. It is no longer I who live, but Christ Who lives in me, whereby we live by faith outwardly showing the Son of God Who loved us and gave Himself up for us. Faith in Christ is my belief. However, surrendering to Him is a challenge for me. Believe it or not, no one can surrender without the work of the Holy Spirit.

Matthew chapter 9:17 tells us that no man put new wine into old wine bottles. The soul of the believer is understood as being like an empty vessel, whereby the attributes of Christ's selfless love is poured out into the hearts of those who have surrendered unto the influence of His Holy Spirit. Remember God has no delight in vain obligations. **Proverbs chapter 21:27** tells us that the sacrifice of the wicked is an abomination unto the Lord: how much more when he brings it with a wicked mind.

Love and forgiveness can only be cultivated, after surrendering unto Christ. The plan of soul salvation was centered on Christ, but it was the Father Who sent Him unto us. **John chapter 3:16** tells us that God so love the world, that He gave His only begotten Son, that whosoever believes in Him would not perish, but have everlasting life. Even though we are saved by His grace: it's our choice to choose to believe in Him. Sanctification is the preparation of the believer to meet God the Father. Sanctification can only be administered to those who have surrendered to His Agape love, which enables us to love Him and our neighbors as much as ourselves. Trust and obedience comes after we have made a conscientious decision to surrender unto His unconditional love. Think of someone you trust, and then ask yourself why do I trust this person? You can't have trust and obedience without true love. Jesus loved His Father, and therefore He trusted Him to be obedient unto death. Our forgiveness comes through the love that Christ shares with His Father.

Since God is the one that first loved us, He made it easy for us to receive forgiveness. Sin separated us from God; therefore by accepting Christ as our Lord and Savior it renews the relationship between us, and the Father. Accepting Christ becomes the apparatus of our justification and sanctification before God, and therefore we are forgiven of our sins no matter how many times we sin from now until we die. However, intentional sin leads to blasphemy, and there is no forgiveness. Amen

"The Fear of the Lord"

Chapter 3

Trusting by Faith

The fear of the Lord is the first of the three–angel's message. **Revelation chapter 14:6,7** tells us that John saw another angel flying in the middle of heaven, having the everlasting gospel to preach unto them that dwell on the earth, and to every nation, and families, and language, and people, saying with a loud voice fear God, and give glory to Him; for the hour of His judgment is come: and worship Him that made heaven, and earth, and the sea, and the fountains of waters.

There are two types of fear: Spiritual light, and spiritual darkness. Spiritual light is given unto the true disciples' of Christ to discern both good and evil. However, spiritual darkness overshadows one–third of earth, and all who dwell in the world. The fear of the Lord our God, is the love that we share in our hearts toward Him, and mankind. **Proverbs chapter 1:7** tells us that the fear of the Lord is the beginning of knowledge, but fools despise wisdom and instruction. **2 Timothy chapter 1:7** tells us that God did not give us the spirit of fear, but of power, and of love, and of a sound mind.

Humanity has one of two things in common: ignorance, meaning, we don't know everything that is to know about living a perfect life, and therefore, we are going to make mistakes. The fear of the world is the manifestation of hate, whereby ignorance becomes rebellion, and from thereon disobedience becomes guilt among unbelievers who say there is no God.

The fear of the Lord is the spoken Word of faith, whereby God is neither audible nor visible. One of the many attributes of the Holy Spirit is the circumcision of our hearts, which is made without hands, whereby the Holy Spirit gives light to our conscience, so that we may discern both good and evil. The Holy Spirit is the activist, and power of the conscience moving our mind forward in faith; meanwhile the senses are standing still. **John chapter 3:5** tells us that Jesus said, verily, verily; I say unto you, except a man is born of water, and of the Holy Spirit, by means of which our spirit is lifted up by His Holy Spirit, we cannot enter into the kingdom of God. The fear of the Lord is a direct result of His Holy Spirit indwelling in us. If we choose to abide in Him, He will abide in us. **Job chapter 1:1** tells us that there was a man in the land of Uz whose name was Job; and he was blameless, and upright, for he feared God, and abstained from sin. Pure religion, and Christianity is abiding always in the Spirit of God by staying focus on Christ. The Holy Spirit unites us with Him in spirit and truth, whereby He keeps the believer from the blemishes and spots of the world.

1Timothy chapter 3:2-4 tells us that soul sanctification empowers the believer to become more like Christ Who is the Husband of the church: avoiding gossip, holy and blameless, husband of one wife, vigilant, sober, longsuffering, given to hospitality, apt to teach, not a drunkard, not violent, but gentle, not quarrelsome, not a lover of money. Furthermore, being able to manage his own family, making sure that his children are in subjection unto the Lord, or how else will he rule over the church. **Exodus chapter 20:12** tells us that we should honor our Father and mother: that our days may be long upon the land, which the Lord our God has given unto us. At the cross Jesus cried, Abba, Father it is finished, and gave up the ghost. God made Adam, the first man out of clay, therefore, God is our Father; and the earth is our mother. Eve the first woman came from Adam, her father. Furthermore, God also gave us the health message, which is the edenic diet that our days may be long upon the earth. **Deuteronomy chapter 6:13** tells us to fear the Lord our God, and serve Him only, and make our vows in His name, do not follow other gods, for the Lord our God is a jealous God.

From Jesus' death at the cross until now, the plan of soul salvation is the ongoing seven-fold ministerial work of the Holy Spirit upon the human soul, and the message of hope that we have in Christ Jesus, whereby through Him we have access to the Father Who sent Him. **Mathew chapter 22:35-39** tells us that the one lawyer who wanted to tempt Jesus, asked Him, which is the greatest commandment in the law? Jesus said unto him, love the Lord your God with all your heart, and with all your soul, and with your entire mind. This is the first, and greatest commandment. And the second is like unto the first, you shall love your neighbor as yourself. **Amen**

"Faith and Faithfulness"

Chapter 4

Obedience by Faith

Everyone has a measure of faith even the devil. However, faith without love is dead. Words cannot define true faith. **Hebrews chapter 11:6** tells us that without faith no one can please God. True faith is the Word of God working from within the conscience to rule over the mind and senses, whereby we are united with Christ in love. **John chapter 14:9** tells us that Jesus replied, if you have seen Me, you have seen the Father Who sent Me.

The unbelieving soul is filled with rage, and the imaginations of the world; and without the divine attributes of Christ his heart is given over to a degenerate mind. But Who is He that is faithful? For the contrast between the tree of knowledge of good and evil is faith, and faithfulness. **James chapter 1:23,24** tells us that anyone who hears the Word of God, and does it not, he is like a man beholding his natural face in a mirror, and after taking a good look at himself, he turns around and forgets his own reflection. The catchphrase mind over matter is used loosely, but on the contrary without faith our spirit is dead, and our conscience is seared. Faith empowers the believer to surrender to the obedience of Jesus Christ, so that through Him our hope becomes faithfulness to the glory of God the Father. **Hebrews chapter 5:8** tells us that even though Jesus was God's Son, He learned obedience by the things He had to suffer.

Suffering is common among believers and unbelievers alike. However, through the power of Jesus Christ, the fruit of the Spirit is given unto us, so that we may bear fruit unto God the Father, whereby, longsuffering and temperance will produce patience and self–control in every believer who has surrendered self to the obedience of Jesus Christ. It is very difficult for any believer to walk in the Spirit of obedience. Rebellion is a part of our personalities, which came from Adam. And in many cases you and I as believers of Christ, rebels against the commandments of God. How much more the Holy Spirit finds no room in the heart of the unbelieving soul. **Galatians chapter 5:16-18** tells us that if we choose to surrender to Christ: His Holy Spirit will renew our dead spirit, so that we can become obedient unto Him. God is love, and He is the one Who bestowed His love into our hearts by faith to bring us a greater measure of inner peace and sanctification.

Psalm chapter 58:3 tells us that the wicked are separated from the womb: they go astray as soon as they are born, speaking lies. From embryo to fetus, and from newborn to toddler: a child's first reaction to any given command is rebellion, because of sin. However, God created mankind in His Own Image and Likeness, whereby giving us free–will to claim His promise of soul salvation. Christ's object lesson is the best training tool for any child to live by. Character perfection and obedience should be taught as early as possible by means of which the child will develop a Christ–like Character of love, joy, peace, longsuffering, gentleness, faith, meekness, and temperance. **Luke chapter 6:40** tells us that the pupil is not above his teacher: but perfection is learned from the lesson taught by our Lord and Savior Jesus Christ.

Rebellion and disobedience are like peas in a pod, wherever you find one: all manner of evil is present. Think of rebellion as the road traveled, and disobedience is the life lived up until the close of probation. After many years of practice most people have perfected their pride to the point where God isn't allowed to enter their thoughts. The Holy Spirit finds no access in the unbelieving soul who will not surrender to Christ; therefore making it impossible for them to be sanctified. The reproduction of a child–like faith can only take root in the heart of a person who has surrendered their will unto Christ. God knows the motive behind every willful act, and will only accept the work of true faith that comes from a willing heart. **Matthew chapter 19:14** tells us that Jesus said, permit the little children to come unto Me, for of such is the kingdom of heaven. For only a child–like faith will produce the faithfulness of a Christ–like Character.

The frontal lobe of the brain is the location of the mind and the birthplace of faith. Conscience over mind is the work of the Holy Spirit by means of which we labor in love toward one another. The resisting of the Holy Spirit is common among believers and unbelievers alike, in the manner of which, relying on self leads to spiritual blindness. Rebellion leads to disobedience and from thereon pride becomes the fulfillment of guilt, and sin that oppresses, whereby oppression leads to death. Spiritual adultery is the suppressing of the conscience by choice: whereby the tree is separated from the vine, which is Christ Jesus, and the branches are broken off. **Matthew chapter 21:19** tells us that when Jesus saw the fig tree in the way, He came to it, and found no fruit thereon, but leaves only. And He said unto it, let no fruit grow on you from now until forever. And immediately the fig tree died. The fig tree of itself had no power to cultivate fruits. The Pharisees lost their faith when they took their eye off Christ. The word (eye) refers to our mind and faith: whenever we take our mind and faith away from God Who is our first love: spiritual blindness leads to spiritual darkness and Satan becomes the victor.

Today many have labored, but not in faith according to Christ recommendations. **Revelation chapter 3:15-17** tells us that Jesus said, I know your works, that you are neither cold nor hot, but I would rather if you were cold or hot. But because you are lukewarm: neither cold nor hot, I will spit you out of My mouth. You say that you are rich, and increased in merchandise, and have no need of nothing, and know not that you are: despicable, unhappy, poor, blind, and naked.

In order for us to live a perfect life of faith the mind must enter into dormancy, and spiritual transcendence becoming as one with Christ by surrendering to His unconditional love, which is the promise of hope that we have in His eternal salvation to come. The old saying goes without a doubt, the mind is a terrible thing to waste. **Matthew chapter 6:21-23** tells us that whatever the mind is focus on, our heart's will pursue. The mind is the eye of the soul: if the eye is single then the whole heart is focus on God, and the soul is full of light. However, if the eye is focus on the world, the whole body is in darkness, and how great is that darkness?

God has given us a measure of faith, and the capacity to handle our fair share of trials and tribulations according to His glory. However, oppression will break even the unbreakable. **Mark chapter 15:34** tells us that Jesus Christ cried, Abba, Father, why have You forsaken Me? Say with me out loud, and believing that God answers prayers; I am in Christ, and He is in me, whereby, I surrender my mortal body unto You O Lord my God to be crucified moment–by–moment, and adding to my longsuffering temperance to maximize the coping mechanism of my mind by means of which, I surrender completely unto You my Lord Jesus Christ through the power of Your Holy Spirit. Amen

Rebellion became our second nature after sin entered the earth, whereby we prioritize the senses over the conscience. The imagination can only be defined as self–motivated desires and thoughts projected into imagery. Furthermore, having a seared conscience gives access to demonic spirits by means of which the mind is held captive, and fully sedated under their influence. Selfish desires and demonic agents will then create a veil over the mind, whereby they will wrestle and contradict the Spirit of truth in the sense that two spirits can't dwell peaceable in one place at the same time. For either we will surrender our hearts unto the Holy Spirit or unto the spirits of devils, and satanic oppressions. **Genesis chapter 6:5** tells us that God saw that the wickedness of man was great in the earth, and that every imagination of the thoughts of his heart was only evil continually.

Imaginary thoughts and opinions may seem random in most cases. However, they all give access to the seat of the mind by means of which evil thoughts can be generated through sight and sounds, whereby making the senses become reactive, and thereby wrestle against the conscience and mind, so that it is impossible for us to make good judgments. A double-minded person will observe the law of love, but finds no joy in doing that, which is right. **2 Peter chapter 2:22** tells us that it happened unto them according to the true proverb, the dog is turned to his own vomit again, and the pig that was washed to her wallowing in the mud. **Mark chapter 3:28,29** Jesus tells us that without a doubt, I say unto you, all sins will be forgiven unto the sons of men, including whatsoever perverse words they might have spoken. But whosoever turn away from the Holy Spirit will not be forgiven; but is subjected to eternal condemnation.

The mind is the heart of every living soul, and consists of over a billion thoughts per lifecycle. The mind can become overwhelmed with the cares of the world. Individually, we have to make a conscientious decision to surrender to Christ in order for His Holy Spirit to sanctify us before the close of probation. God doesn't force anyone to serve Him.

Furthermore, oppression and guilt isn't from God. The accuser of the brethren, namely Satan accuses us day and night, whereby guilt becomes oppression, the work of demonic spirits: forces of evil, and darkness, principalities in high places gaining access to the mind, and creating strong holds. Individuals who are self–motivated by the cares and pleasures of the world find it difficult to surrender, because of sin. Many have made a choice to embrace the contemporary life, instead of surrendering to Christ, so that they may bear the fruit of the Spirit unto God. Spiritual adultery and self–motivation are alike, they lead to a sedated lifestyle of habitual sin, whereby our own opinion brings us to the conclusion that our lives are of little value, and soul salvation has nothing to offer.

Life wasn't meant to be spontaneous. The fantasy will last, but for a moment. However, the tree of knowledge of good and evil will continue to blossom into chaos and destruction. Pride, which is self–motivation will produce a soul filled with disappointments, guilt, and regrets. And for the most part it would seem easier to commit suicide, but don't be persuaded by guilt. No matter how negative the situation might become; always remember to exercise faith followed by surrendering to Christ's selfless love. Surrendering to Christ is the key for overcoming sin. Staying focusing on Christ gives us power to turn away from self, whereby we become single eye; being able to surrender to Him completely. **Romans chapter 12:2** tells us not to be conformed to this world: but be transformed by the renewing of our mind, so that we may prove what is good, and acceptable, and perfect will of God. By turning the other cheek, we are surrendering, and allowing God to take control of every situation. The number one factor is self–surrender when it comes to exercising faith in God. Furthermore, trials and tribulations is the work of the Holy Spirit, so that we may overcome sin.

So often, we miss out on those miracles waiting at the next intersection. Life is a journey and the means by which we get there makes a difference. Jesus made it to the end of His journey by staying focus on His Father in heaven. And He is now sitting down at the right hand of power and eternal salvation. Even while Christ was yet suffering on the cross, He received a greater measure of love from His Father to give to His people by surrendering. Likewise, I am compelled and convicted in my heart to say, righteousness apart from surrendering to Christ is simply not achievable. The divine attributes of Christ can be seen through the gift of humility, whereby sanctification through faith will strengthen even the feeblest believer to overcome the sins of the world. I don't know of anyone including myself that would want to suffer, much more longsuffering in a situation that is agonizing. Most Christians talk a good game, but when it comes down to it, no one wants to suffer. The Nike commercial just do it, has more of an impact on the world, than the free gift of soul salvation. However, Jesus Christ on the other hand not only suffered from birth, but also endured forty days, and forty nights of fasting in order to have enough strength to offer up Himself as sacrifice unto the glory of Him Who is worthy to be praise.

So often, we don't realize how much we have to be thankful for until after it's taken away; only then we find ourselves consumed with grief. Ninety percent of the time people who end up suffering from cardiovascular disease weren't born with birth defects. However, without proper nutrition, exercise, water, sunlight, temperance, fresh air, rest, and trusting God: even the healthiest person on the planet can become a victim of various illnesses. Lets just say for argument sake your 1971 Ford Pinto runs on 87 regular, but you decided to go with 93 octane instead, it might not improve the quality or performance of the car in one way or another. However, it will definitely have an impact on your wallet.

Making a conscientious decision is not a theory, but rather a conviction from the Holy Spirit by means of which our conscience becomes the activist over the mind to rule over the senses. God created mankind in His Own Image and Likeness for one specific reason, to display His moral Character, whereby the attributes of Jesus' love is poured out into our hearts. The mind is the vehicle of faith, whereby the Holy Spirit gives us the discernment to discern both good and evil, which the prince of darkness has cast a veil to overshadow the eye of those that are in the world. The ministerial work of the Holy Spirit upon the human soul removes the veil of unrighteousness, whereby the conscience gives us spiritual light both in wisdom, and knowledge to subdue the senses, and bring them to the understanding of surrendering to the hope and glory of Christ's salvation to come. Amen

The Rod of Correction, which is Christ

- **Ephesian chapter 6:1-4** tells us that children should obey their parents in the Lord: for this is right. Honor thy father and mother: which is the first commandment with promise that it may be well with you, and you may live long on the earth. And fathers, provoke not your children to anger, but bring them up in the nurture and admonition of the Lord. **Colossians chapter 3:20,21** tells us that children should obey their parents in all things, for this is well pleasing unto the Lord. Fathers, provoke not your children to anger lest they be discouraged. For we are but children in the eye of our heavenly Father, even as Christ obeyed His Father unto death. Spare not the rod and spoil the child. **Proverbs chapter 13:24** tells us that he that spares the rod hates his son, but he that loves him instructs him early.
- **Proverbs chapter 15:1** tells us that a soft answer pacifies anger, but grievous words fuels rage.
- **Proverbs chapter 15:2** tells us that the tongue of the wise speak knowledge, but from the mouth of fools comes foolishness. The words of a true friend are sweeter than honey, but the jokes of fools fill the mind with foolishness.
- **Proverbs chapter 3:7** tells us not to be wise in our own eyes: fear the Lord, and depart from evil. Amen

Chapter 5

Spiritual Adultery

The Bible reveals the history of creation of the earth, and mankind. **Genesis chapter 1:1-4** tells us that in the beginning God created the heaven and the earth. Before God created the earth it was without form and void; and darkness was upon the face of the deep. And the Holy Spirit of God moved over the surface of the water. And God said, let there be light: and there was light. And God saw the light, that it was good: and God divided the light from the darkness. **John chapter 8:12** tells us that Jesus is the light of the world. "I Am the light of the world: he that follow Me shall not walk in darkness, but shall have the light of life."

Before sin, time stood still as mankind walked the earth in peace and tranquility, they lived in harmony with God. The light that is spoken of is Christ Jesus Who is the light of the world, whereby mankind is given free–will to surrender unto the unconditional love of God. However, after the woman was deceived by the devil: I saw great darkness overshadowing one third of the earth's atmosphere with chaotic events. **Genesis chapter 2:8,9** tells us that the earth is a Garden, and mankind is illustrated as a tree that was planted in the Garden of Eden by the Lord God. "And the Lord God planted a Garden eastward in Eden; and there He put the man whom He made. And out of the ground the Lord God made every tree to grow that is pleasing to the sight, and good for food: the tree of life also in the middle of the Garden, and the tree of knowledge of good and evil." **Genesis chapter 2:15** tells us that the Lord God took the man, and put him into the Garden of Eden to dress it, and keep it.

Isaiah chapter 5:1,2 tells us that the Lord God had a choice vineyard on fertile ground; He plowed it, and pruned it. Furthermore, He planted it with the best grapevines, and built a watchtower in the center of it. He also made a winepress therein: and He looked that it should bring forth good grapes, but instead it brought forth wild grapes. **Matthew chapter 3:10** tells us that the ax is laid to the root of the trees, which bring forth not good fruits; they will be cut down and cast into the fire.

The tree of knowledge of good and evil illustrates the sinful nature of humanity. Sin has reached its fullness: as death sweeps across the globe claiming millions of lives, but yet the world continues with its flamboyant attitude toward our Creator. I have seen the works of the wicked, those that find pleasure in the tree of knowledge of good and evil. So then, I pondered to myself, "How long will God allow the wicked to prosper, and evil to descend upon us like rain?" O Lord God, What is man that You are mindful of him, or even the Son of man Who was righteous in all His deeds? The unbroken relationship between God and Christ that I desperately seek!

God foreseeing the future and fall of mankind, He predestinated the plan of soul salvation on the Seventh Day. This was foretold that during the first millennium good and evil would become discernable in mankind spirit. **Genesis chapter 3:22** tells us behold, the man has become as one of us, to know good and evil. **Jeremiah chapter 17:9** tells us that the hearts of men being deceitful above all things, and desperately wicked: who can know it? **Psalm chapter 14:1-3, 53:1-3** tells us that the fool has said in his heart there is no God. They are corrupt, they have done abominable works, and there is none that do good. The Lord looked down from heaven upon the children of men, to see if there were any that did understand, and seek God. They are all gone aside, they are all together become filthy: there is none that do good, no not one. **Romans chapter 3:10-12** tells us that there is none righteous, no not one. There is none that understand; there is none that seek after God. They are all gone out of the way; they are all together become unprofitable; there is none that do good, no, not one.

John chapter 3:19,20 tells us that Jesus said men love darkness rather than light, because their deeds are evil. For everyone that is evil hate light. **Luke chapter 23:31** tells us that while Jesus was nailed to the cross, He said, will I find faith on the earth when I return? For if they do these things while the tree is yet green, what shall be done when the tree is dry? Jesus spoke of the fullness of the ministerial work of the Holy Spirit upon the human soul. **Ephesians chapter 6:12** tells us that we wrestle not against flesh and blood, but against principalities, against powers, against the rulers of the darkness of this world, against spiritual wickedness in high places.

The composition of the heart is fearfully and wonderfully made in the Image and Likeness of God. We are all spiritual beings sharing the same breath of life, whereby the Word of God oxygenates the soul and spirit of the believer. God's divine love unites us with Him in spirit and truth. However, if we choose to rebel and disobey His commandments, whereby our conscience become seared; our senses will become the primary objective toward every decision made. After Adam sinned, the covenant was broken, whereby it led to the separation between him and the Father. After the separation sin didn't stop there, but instead it became sinful unto death. If we choose to continue in a life of sinning, the soul shall surely die. Spiritual adultery is the defilement of the spirit that dwells within our soul by means of which the rejection of God's moral law leads to the second death.

The Pharisees were guilty of spiritual adultery; they lived apart from Christ. The spirit of man is the Son of man, whereby we are all connected to Christ in spirit and truth. We are justified by our thoughts and motives in front of God; therefore let no one think evil of his neighbor. Spiritual adultery is where the believer ignores the commandment of Love, love, which is the primary factor that will help us to bear fruit of the Spirit. Rebellion leads to disobedience and from thereon the habitual practice of sinning leads to the close of probation. Pride is sinning, plural, which leads to sin, singular.

Spiritual Darkness

The battlefield is the mind, and we have the ability to discern both good and evil. **Genesis chapter 3:22** tells us behold, the man has become as one of us, to know good and evil. God is good, and He gave us Spiritual light, which is Christ Jesus, whereby we have hope in His eternal salvation to come. The devil is evil, and he gave birth unto the world through the deception of the serpent. Spiritual adultery separated us from God the Father, whereby spiritual oppression became the downfall of humanity. The world is contrary unto the Word and faith of our Lord Jesus Christ. Furthermore, imaginary thoughts and desires will quench our faith and our hope if we focus on the world. People enjoy having a false sense of comfort in their hearts for many different reasons. However, the most common is pleasure from the things of the world.

The devil shows no mercy, and after sin reaches maturity it blooms into chaos and destruction. Spiritual darkness weakens our ability of reasoning, whereby making it impossible for us to discern the will of God; evil will then manifest selfish desires through which Lucifer envied our Lord Jesus Christ: wanting to be his own god. Satan has thousands of demonic agents working in the shadows trying to manipulate our hearts with selfish motives to fulfill his evil plan, which is the death of humanity. **Romans chapter 7:25** tells us that Paul the Apostle discern that they are two laws: one spiritual, and the other sensual. Therefore he thank God through Jesus Christ our Lord, so then with his mind he served the spiritual law of God, whereby he had discernment to rule over the sensual law of sin. Disobedience unto God's law is the primary reason why oppression is so rampant. The broken relationship between God and mankind has left us struggling with sin. Everyone struggles with sin in someway or another. The world is in complete chaos due to the lack of spiritual discernment, which is the opposite of exercising faith in God. The frustration of the once beloved church came through rebellion, which led to unbelief. Moneychangers and those that sold doves using the gospel as a bargaining chip to win souls for their own personal financial gain; meanwhile trampling upon Christ's divine love for His people.

Now that our hope is mixed with unbelief: soothsayers and astrologers are in demand. Fortune-tellers have made their way into the church that was once sanctified by His blood, and set a part for holiness, and gifts of a divine nature. The Word of God is the tree of life springing forth like a well. God's Word is hope unto all who abides in Jesus Christ. True faith doesn't rely on evidence, but rather on the conviction, and revelation of Jesus Christ Who is blessed forever and ever. Amen

The Pride of Life

Galatians chapter 5:19-21 tells us that spiritual adultery will manifest the works of the human nature, which are these: selfishness, pleasure seeking, orgies, hatred, fighting, malice, envy, temper tantrums, rage, accusations, division, speculations, fault finding, premeditated killings, drunkenness, and merry making.

Genesis chapter 11:1 tells us that in the beginning the entire earth spoke one language. Today you'll find that a conversation is nothing more than meaningless gibberish. Multilanguage, culture, and race separates people into groups, whereby the color of the human skin has become the agenda for white supremacy groups that find comfort in hate and racism. Even the most inconsiderate person on the planet knows the difference between right and wrong. A child doesn't need to have a full understanding of the entire Bible when it comes to the basic principle of obedience. Furthermore, Astronauts have made it to the moon and back; apparently the sky no longer limits us. I don't believe that we have to travel to the furthest point of the universe to find love. Most likely you'll find people on this very planet who have not heard the gospel of Jesus Christ, but yet they will show brotherly love toward one another. "As it is written the just shall live by faith." Obedience is from faith to faith: the indwelling of the Holy Spirit working from within our conscience to cultivate faith in the mind to rule over the senses. **Romans chapter 2:14** tells us that when the Gentiles, which have not the law, do by nature the things pertaining to the law, they not having the law, are a law unto themselves.

God knows that I am not perfect and this world is far from it. However, God finds no pleasure in the hearts of the foolish. Speculating is the same as guessing, whereby theories infused the mind with opinions that are controversial to the gospel of Jesus Christ. If I have to convince you of the truth then I am wasting my time. The choice is yours to surrender to Jesus Christ or else false belief becomes the replacement of sound doctrine. I lived a lie for many years until I experience Jesus for myself. Most unbelievers have one or two things in common: ignorance when it comes to the truth and a false sense of pride. Many will freely give their opinion about something they know nothing about. If it's not broken don't fix it they'll say. We live in a society where a lie carries more weight than the price of gold. Ignorance and pride means more to the world than the truth.

Pride and arrogance is the downfall of humanity, and sin is the final result before the close of probation. Pride is confidence in one's self to bear his own cross; meanwhile crucifying Christ afresh by laying claim to His promises by the works of the human nature. An atheist will exercise faith when it comes to breathing fresh air, but on the contrary he will not believe that God created all things for His good pleasure. The pride of life is the basic purpose and value of things, which are visible in the world. However, faith is the invisible current that comes from above and beyond the norm of the earth's atmosphere. The cosmic supply of sunlight, water and oxygen produces life how? The facts might reveal evidence to support evolution, but on the contrary mankind has yet to conclude our purpose and value without faith.

God revealed His love unto us by His law, and thereby exposing pride and arrogance as destructive power, which is contrary to knowledge and truth. And even with our most sincere efforts the human race is powerless when it comes to restoring love and hope to a dying planet. An atheist will not be convinced even if someone came back from the dead, but rather finds pleasure in speculations that are far from the truth. Rebellion leads to disobedience, and from thereon the tree of knowledge of good and evil blossoms into pride, whereby producing every inconceivable thought to gratify the lawlessness of sin.

71

God created mankind, and called them Adam. Furthermore, He gave them the ability to exercise free-will by faith in the conscience of their mind. However, after the wife urged her husband to disobey, his mind became rebellious against God, and he was found guilty with sin. Faith mixed with hope will produce obedience unto Christ, but hope by itself is dead. Free-will is the power of hope to surrender unto Christ, but on the contrary if we choose not to surrender we no longer have free-will: only rebellion, which hardens the heart, so that we cannot please God. Rebellion is the misconception of pride, whereby everyone that is self-motivated is of the devil. Even though mankind was created with free-will, free-will doesn't give us the right to disobey the commandments of God.

Faith and obedience is the garment of the faithful, which gives us hope in His eternal salvation; meanwhile rebellion and disobedience is the nakedness of pride, which leads to unbelief and condemnation of the soul. **Genesis chapter 3:7** tells us that after Adam realized that he was naked his pride wouldn't allow him to exercise free-will to surrender unto the Lord God, but instead his pride became sinful unto death. There are three main reasons why we choose to disobey: deception, seduction, and manipulation. The enemy of good attacks the mind through the senses by means of which self-motivated ideas are spawned to give access to demonic spirits, whereby evil thoughts enters the heart and defile the spirit that dwells within. Sensual knowledge has no positive effect on our spiritual growth. Lucifer was in heaven and had nothing to gain by disobeying Christ, but yet he was unable to discern his point of error. Even though Eve was ignorant, she gained nothing in the end by disobeying the Commandment of God.

My son is six years old, and he is unaware of the tree of knowledge of good and evil. However, he has sensual knowledge to hear, feel, see, smell and taste, but his personality will not allow him to develop a spiritual character. Disobedience is the sacrifice of sin, and pride is the practicing of wickedness in the eye of the Lord. **Proverbs chapter 30:20** tells us that such is the way of an adulterous woman; she eats, and wipes her mouth, and says, I have done no wickedness. We are all born with a sinful nature, which separates us from God. We disobey because we are sinful, whereby spiritual adultery becomes the fulfillment of sin.

Romans chapter 7:14-23 tells us that the law of love is spiritual, but we are sinful, born into sin. I find myself doing things that I wouldn't normally do. And the things that I want to do, I cannot. But the things I hate, that I do. Now if I find myself breaking the commandment of God, then clearly I must surrender to the law of love. However, it is no longer I who do the deed, but the sinful nature I inherited from Adam. We are all born with the sinful human nature, and no good deed comes from our selfish desires. I know what's right, but how to preform that which is good, I know not. For the good that I want to do, I cannot. But the evil that I hate that I do. If I behave not according to the law of love, it's because of the law of sin that dwells in me. So then, I see two laws within my own body that when I try to do good, selfishness and pride would raise its ugly head and take control of my mind and bring me into captivity unto the law of sin. Spiritual adultery is the same as having a seared conscience. **Isaiah chapter 59:1,2** tells us behold, the Lord's hand is not shortened that it cannot save; nor His ear heavy that it cannot hear. However, our sinful nature has separated us from Him; and our sins have hidden His face from us, so that He will not hear. **Jeremiah chapter 5:25** tells us that our disobedience has turned away these things, and our sins have withheld good from us.

Overcoming Spiritual Adultery

Spiritual adultery was illustrated in the Garden of Eden when the man and the woman rejected the commandment, which came from their Creator. **Genesis chapter 2:21-25** tells us that the Lord God caused a deep sleep to fall upon Adam, and he slept. And God took one of his ribs, and closed up the flesh of his skin. And the rib, which the Lord God took from the man, He made a woman and brought her unto the man. And Adam said, this is now bone of my bones, and flesh of my own body: and she shall be called <u>woman</u> because she was taken out of <u>man</u>. Therefore a man shall leave his father and his mother, and get <u>married</u> to his <u>wife</u>: and they shall be of <u>one mind</u>. And they were both naked, the man and his wife, and were not ashamed.

The story of Adam and Eve bears the wounds of mankind up until the cross where Christ Himself carried our sins in His own body. After the separation between God and Adam, the woman became the glory of the man; whereby she was called Eve, the mother of all living unto whom the redemptive work of Christ was made known through the power of His Holy Spirit concerning childbearing. **Genesis chapter 3:16** tells us that God said unto the woman, I will greatly multiply your sorrows, and out of pain you shall give birth to children. And you shall be in subjection unto your husband, and he shall be the head of you, even as Christ is the head of the church.

The emotional-cycle can be seen in women of all language, nationality, culture and race. However, a good woman is of great value to a loving husband that will nourish and cherish her. Husbands have the duty of loving their wives as themselves. And wives must show respect unto their husband, whereby the commandment of marriage unites the man and woman not only in body, but also in spirit and truth making them of one mind: even as God the Father, Jesus the Son and the Holy Spirit are one.

Adam was the first born from Christ; even so, Eve was the first born from Adam. God gave the man someone to love as himself. However, after Adam disobeyed the commandment, he was separated from God, and *Eros*, which is romantic love, replaced the Agape love, which binds the Father and us together in spirit and truth. **1 Corinthians chapter 7:1-6** tells us that Paul the Apostle wrote to the church of Corinthians concerning sexual immorality, saying, It is best for a man not to get involved with an adulterous woman. However, to avoid sexual immorality, let every man seek a wife of his own, and every woman a husband of her own. Spouses should be committed to each other in the sense of benevolence. The wife should give herself unto her husband, and let the husband give himself unto his wife. Do not withhold physical affection from each other without consent, and only for a period of time that you may give yourselves to fasting and prayer; and come together again, so that Satan doesn't tempt either of you with sinful desires. This was only a recommendation, and not a commandment.

Ephesians chapter 5:21-33 tells us that both the man and the woman should give themselves one to another in the fear of God. Wives, give yourselves unto your own husbands, as unto the Lord. For the husband is the head of the wife, even as Christ is the head of the church: and He is the Savior of the body. Therefore as the church is in subjection unto Christ, let the wives also honor their husbands in everything. Husbands, love your wives, even as Christ also loved the church, and gave Himself for it; that He might sanctify and cleanse it with the washing of water by the Word, that He might present it to Himself as a glorious church, not having spot, or wrinkle, or any such thing; but that it should be Holy, and without blemish. God commanded the husbands to love their wives as their own bodies. He that loves his wife loves himself. Conscientiously, no man has ever hated his own body; but nourish and cherish it, even as the Lord nourishes the church. Therefore as we are a part of Christ body: flesh and bones joined together by water, blood and spirit, so shall a man leave his father and mother and get married to his wife, whereby there are joined together in body and spirit in the sight of God.

This is a great mystery: but I speak concerning Christ and the church. Furthermore, let every man purposely love his wife even as himself: and the wife should make a sincere effort to give respect unto her husband. **1 Peter chapter 3:1-9** tells us that wives should give respect unto their husband; by doing so, if the husband obey not the law of God, then her conduct may convince him of the truth; whereby the husband beholding the holiness of his wife unto the Lord with reverence: whose outward appearance isn't about fancy hairstyles, jewelry and expensive clothing; but let it be the act of humility from the heart, in which there are no corruption, even the outward appearance showing meekness with a quiet spirit, which in the sight of God is glory and honor. This particular example goes back centuries, whereby devoted women also, who trusted in God, and accepted the family leadership of their husband. Sara, also honoring her husband Abraham by calling him lord. If you do as she did, then you're Sara's daughters, as long as you do well.

Be not unfaithful in your relationship with God. Also husband love your wives according to the knowledge of the gospel of Jesus Christ: giving honor unto the wife, because she is the weaker vessel; knowing that we are heirs together in the Kingdom of grace and life. If husbands abuse their wives God will not answer their prayers. Finally, be of one mind, having compassion for each other; love as sisters and brothers of Christ. Be pitiful, be courteous: not doing evil for evil, or being spiteful, but instead love; knowing that you are called to inherit blessings. Furthermore, Paul expanded on the importance of Philia love, and how loyalty to each other is of great value. **Ephesians chapter 4:31,32** tells us that we should let all bitterness, and rage, and anger, uproar, and evil speaking be put away from us, with all malice. And be kind to one another, tenderhearted, forgiving one another, even as God the Father on Christ's behalf forgave us. God the Father never intended for humanity to sin. However, we have hope in Jesus Christ our Lord and Savior if we choose to surrender unto Him. Amen

Avoiding the Adulterous Woman

God is the author of faith; therefore God's Word cannot return void. Many will confess Christ as their Lord and Savior, but find no joy in keeping His commandments. The adulterous woman illustrates the broken relationship between Christ, and His beloved church. Adam was made in the Image and Likeness of Christ; therefore it's not good for husbands to give their opinions unto their wives, but to love them as Christ Himself loves the church; neither should wives criticize their husbands, but respect the man, because he is the Image and Likeness of Christ. The root word for adultery is Adullam, or Adullamite to live voluptuously in pleasure and delight.

The pitfall of any relationship starts with rebellion, and with the lack of trust comes disobedience and lies, which leads to guilt. Covetousness is one person wanting to gain from another through deceit. We are drawn to the world by our senses, whereby we conform to what we hear, feel, see, smell and taste. Physical emotions will blossom into desire, and from thereon lust becomes the burden of life, which leads to sin. When Adam ate from the tree of knowledge of good and evil, it was the relationship that he had with his Father that was put in jeopardy. The evidence showed that God already had the plan of soul salvation in place. Relationships that are anchored to self will not allow us to grow spiritually nor produce faith, so that we may do the will of God.

Many people believe that love is an emotion, but true love is a commitment to God, whereby conscientiously we enter into a covenant, which is an agreement between us, and Christ with one common interest of serving God out of obedience. The relationship that we share with Jesus Christ involves spiritual discernment, which leads to trust and obedience. Trust is of a necessity in order to grow spiritually. Love is a two-way street between God, the Father and us: by means of which we grow closer to Him, if we abide in Christ. Whenever we show love unto each other it's the same as showing love for God. **Galatians chapter 5:14** tells us that all the law is fulfilled in one word, even in this; you shall love your neighbor as yourself.

If you have experienced the complexity of a bad relationship then you know how to avoid the next person that doesn't have the disposition of Jesus Christ. Sex and romance might be the appetizer of your delight, but the wounds of a broken heart will damage even the most well balanced believer. When my daughter was about four years old, she came home from school one day and said, dad I am in love and I want to get married. It's just the kind of thing that a father wants to hear! So, I told her to go and clean her room, when she hesitated; I asked her, what's wrong? She replied, what does being in love have to do with cleaning my room? **Ephesians chapter 6:1** tells us that children should obey their parents in the Lord, for this is right. **Colossians chapter 3:20** tells us that children should obey their parents in everything, for this pleases the Lord. Giving my four-year-old daughter a reasonable explanation wasn't something that I was prepared to do. **1 Corinthians chapter 7:27-29** tells us that if a man is married don't get divorce, and if you are a single man seek not a wife; and if you are a single woman seek not a husband. However, if a man gets married it's not a sin; and if a virgin marries, she has not sinned. Paul the Apostle wanted to let us know that marriages can be a challenge in our spiritual walk with God.

Ecclesiastes chapter 7:26-29 tells us that King Solomon searched for a good woman, and found none. I find more bitter than death, the woman's heart which is like snares and nets, she can bind a man with her hands like a chain: whosoever please God shall escape from her; but the sinner shall be taken by her charm. Furthermore, I searched for a good man among a thousand, and found one; but a good woman was even harder to find. **Proverbs chapter 2:16-19** tells us that wisdom will save you from the adulterous woman with her seductive words, who has left the marriage of her youth to pursue another, and ignored the covenant she made before God. Surely her house leads to hell. Furthermore, after she seduces you, your life becomes meaningless.

Proverbs chapter 5:3-6 tells us that the lips of the adulterous woman drips honey, and her speech is smoother than oil; but in the end she is bitter as vinegar, and leave wounds like a double–edged sword. Death follows her; she gives no thought to life, she wonders aimlessly and doesn't know it. **Proverbs chapter 6:24-35** tells us to keep far from our neighbor's wife, from the smooth talk of a seductive woman. Do not lust in your heart after her beauty or let her captivate you with her eyes. For a prostitute can be had for a loaf of bread, but another man's wife will provoke death. Can a man scoop fire into his lap without his clothes being burned? Can a man walk on hot coals without his feet being scorched? A man that sleeps with another man's wife will not go unpunished. People do not despise a thief if he steals to satisfy his hunger when he is starving, but if he is caught he must pay seven times more than the value. However, a man who commits adultery has no sense: whoever does so destroys himself. Blows and disgrace are his reward, and his shame will never be wiped away. The fury of an angry husband shows no mercy, he will not accept an apology, no matter how sincere it is.

Proverbs chapter 19:13 tells us that a quarrelsome wife is like the constant dripping of a leaky roof. **Proverbs chapter 22:14** tells us that the mouth of an adulterous woman is a deep pit; a man that has no discernment will fall into it. **Proverbs chapter 25:24** tells us that its better to live on the rooftop of a small house, than to share a mansion with a quarrelsome wife. **Proverbs chapter 27:15** tells us that a quarrelsome wife is like the dripping of a leaky roof in a rainstorm; restraining her is like trying to hold back the wind, or gathering oil by hand. Spiritual adultery is the same as rebellion and witchcraft in the eye of the Lord. The adulterous woman is rebellious, and her husband finds no comfort in her. Christ is our husband, and the adulterous woman is the church; and He wants us to become His faithful wife, so that we might be saved. Amen

Self–denial & Repentance

Self–denial is the road to redemption if we have our entire life centered on Christ Jesus. The opposite of self–denial is rebellion, which leads to the rejection of the Holy Spirit, whereby intentional sin leads to the close of probation. Furthermore, blasphemy is the final result for many who have left the church in pursuit of the world. The pig returning to the mud is a true saying; if we become entangled again in the same situation that Christ had cleansed us from. Intentional sin is where the believer becomes presumptuous in front of God. Remember God has the power to throw lightening bolts, why would anyone want to tempt Him? But you would be surprised of how many souls will be lost because of their presumptuousness.

Intentional sin, or presumptuousness goes beyond rebellion and disobedience. My six–year old son throws a tantrum whenever he doesn't get his own way, but yet he has righteousness in Christ. After being born–again we become more like Christ by relying upon His Holy Spirit moment–by–moment. Presumptuous sin is knowingly doing something wrong. Think of the reasons why we pray, then imagine not praying at all. A Christian who doesn't pray is like a doctor that doesn't practice medicine. Praying and believing in Jesus Christ is the entire relationship between us, and the Father. Jesus prayed more than any other person in the universe, and He recommends that we do the same.

Every so often you'll hear of someone switching from one church to another or getting remarried to someone else. Now what does switching from one church to another has in common with getting remarried? Church hopping and spouse swapping becomes a revolving door, which leads to the world. The church represents a person or a group of people, and people aren't righteous. Therefore no matter which church or spouse you get involved with you'll have trouble. It's more important to stay focus on God than anything else. Here's my point, soul salvation only comes through obedience unto Christ.

The Apostle Paul was a sinner like you and I. However, he repented and God was able to turn his life around. Glory and honor belongs to God our Father for saving us from a multitude of sin. The Word of God is Jesus Christ Who became human, whereby His Holy Spirit grants us wisdom to discern the knowledge of good and evil, and bring us to the understanding of the hope of His soul salvation. Repentance comes after self–denial. **Jeremiah chapter 13:22,23** tells us that if we say in our heart, why have these things come upon me? Because of our pride our sin has been revealed and our heels made bare. Can the Ethiopian change the color of his skin or the leopard its spots? Neither can you change yourself to love goodness when you are accustomed to doing evil. Christ is sinless, and I am sinful. The sinner has not the power to change himself; he can only surrender to Christ's unconditional love. **Deuteronomy chapter 30:17-19** tells us that God call heaven and earth to record the day after which the Israelites cross over Jordan to go into the promised land, whereby He set before them life and death, blessing and cursing; therefore choose life that both you and your children may live.

The uneducated man is foolish and ignorant of the knowledge of Jesus Christ. However, God is able to have compassion upon the sinner who is willing to repent of his sins by means of which we are all called unto repentance. However, the highly esteemed educated man is proud, arrogant and boastful: he will not accept the truth even if someone came back from the dead. The uneducated man can be admonished in the ways of the Lord: unlike the educated man who is a stumbling block to the church and also the enemy of our Lord and Savior Jesus Christ. Many have already committed blasphemy in their hearts, and their probation has already ended even while they're yet alive. Spiritual adultery leads to blasphemy by means of which the close of probation is the end of grace, and the alternative becomes damnation. **John chapter 3:18** tells us that he who believes in Jesus Christ is not condemned; but he who believes not is condemned already, because he does not believe in the name of the only begotten Son of God.

Probation is the time given to the individual to surrender to Christ unconditional love. However, many will reject Him and their soul salvation will be lost because of rebellion. Blasphemy is the continual rejection of the Holy Spirit by means of which rebellion and pride becomes the road traveled and disobedience is the life lived. The close of probation is where the tree is completely separated from the vine, and the branches are broken off at which point the Holy Spirit is withdrawn from the spirit of the sinner and his soul salvation is lost eternally!

The Moral Law

The basis of the written law is the knowledge of good and evil. However, the written law did not have the power to cultivate the moral law, which is the unconditional love of Christ. The Ten Commandments was added, because of transgression of the law. The written law was the first half of the two-edged sword. Jesus took away the first and made the second with endless power to give life to our dead spirit. Furthermore, He added truth to knowledge to set us free from the bondage of sin, whereby we are all convicted by the power of His Holy Spirit. Conscience over mind by faith is the fullness and witnessing of the ministerial work of the Holy Spirit upon the human soul. Born-again is the renewing of our dead spirit, the circumcision of the heart, which is made without hands: our mortal bodies being crucified, and nailed to the cross at Calvary. After the believer has completely surrendered himself to the will of Christ: abating the old-man by means of which the Holy Spirit is given authority to reproduce the moral law in the hearts of everyone who accepts Jesus Christ as their Lord and Savior. **James chapter 1:12** tells us that blessed is the man that has the moral law: for when he is tried, he shall receive the crown of life, which the Lord has promised to them that love Him.

Morality by itself doesn't make us righteous, but our righteousness in Christ justifies us in front of God the Father, whereby it is His righteousness that makes us moral. In other words doing right doesn't make us righteous; likewise doing wrong doesn't make us bad. Christianity is the fruit of the Holy Spirit, whereby we walk with God moment-by-moment carrying our cross daily and abiding in Christ continually for spiritual growth, which will not allow us to remain in sin. However, life apart from Christ is sin no matter how well balance it may seem. Did you know that we only sin when we go against the conviction given unto us by the Holy Spirit? God wants Christians to abide in Christ, so that we may live and enjoy life to the fullest.

A true believer doesn't take the bull by the horn, but instead surrender every thought captive unto the will of God through the power of His Holy Spirit. His unconditional love becomes the primary focus of every believer who wants to bear fruit of the Spirit. Everyone who accepts Christ will get to know God the Father: even as He foreknew us from the foundation of the earth. No man who has truly repented will draw back, whereby the dog returning to his own vomit becomes a true saying for those who choose to live life apart from Christ.

In order for us to become perfect the key component is "faith" which is the discernment given unto us from the Holy Spirit. Judge no man according to sin, or else you will be judged by whatever measure you measure unto others. God is righteous, but yet He condemns no one, but mercy and grace is granted unto all, so that through Jesus Christ all might be made perfect in the law of love. For God bears witness that I was condemned in the world, but now wherein I judge, not I, but the Holy Spirit that dwells in me. God is the one Who exposed pride and arrogance as being sinful unto death, even the death of the soul. Life apart from Christ leads to sin; therefore apart from Christ I am nothing. He who rejects Christ has become his own judge: whereby judging ourselves leads to condemnation becoming more and more like Satan who wanted to be his own god. Good judgment is the result of the Holy Spirit by means of which we overcome every obstacle.

Judgment is a conscientious decision made from the heart of every Christ–like believer who has surrendered self unto the unconditional love of Him, Who is a righteous judge in all things, whether it be kingdoms, dominions, or principalities. The Pharisees were rebuked for not having good judgment of God's mercy and grace, which reflects the Image and Likeness of our Lord and Savior Jesus Christ. Morality by itself doesn't make us righteous, but instead a legalist in front of God. Philia love without the Agape love of Christ will not bring us to the point of repentance. For without the Lord's mercy and grace there is no remission of sin. The Pharisees kept the written law, and rejected Christ Who came to fulfill the moral law, so that all who believed upon Him would be saved.

Romans chapter 5:14-19 tells us that death reigned from Adam to Moses, even over them that had not sinned after the disobedience of Adam's transgression, who was made in the Image and Likeness of Christ to come. However, our Lord did not come to punish sinners, but as the free gift of grace unto all. If the disobedience of Adam will cause many to die, then how much more can be saved by the grace of God, and the free gift of soul salvation through Jesus Christ?

Now as Adam's sin brought forth condemnation to all, so will the free gift of grace bring justification to all those who will accept Jesus Christ as their Lord and Savior. By the disobedience of one man, death came upon all; even so shall grace be given in abundance unto all. After Adam sinned, condemnation came upon all; even so by the righteousness of Jesus Christ, the free gift came upon all, and the justification of life.

Although salvation is a free gift: we have to want to surrender our free-will unto Christ. **Romans chapter 6:2-23** tells us that we are dead to sin, living no longer therein. Knowing that we are baptized into Jesus Christ, and also into His death. Furthermore, we are buried with Him by baptism into death, and as Christ was raised up from the dead by the glory of the Father, even so we are to walk in the newness of life. Furthermore, if we are planted together in the likeness of His death, we are also in the likeness of His resurrection: knowing this, that our old man is crucified with Him, so that the body of sin might be destroyed, and moving forward give no desire to serve sin. He that is dead is free from sin. Therefore, if we are dead with Christ, we believe that we shall live through Him: knowing that Christ was raised from the dead, and death had no more dominion over Him. Jesus died once for our sin, but now He lives in heaven with His Father. Likewise, we are also dead to sin, but alive unto God through Jesus Christ our Lord. Furthermore, we have been given strength to overcome the sinful nature and evil desires of our mortal bodies. Give no access to sin by offering yourself as instruments of unrighteousness, but instead present yourselves to God, knowing that you are born—again and your body is the temple of righteousness unto God.

The law of sin has no control over you, because you are under the protection of God's mercy and grace. What then? Should we continue to sin by convenience, because we have grace? God forbid! Whosoever we surrender to as servants to obey becomes our master; whether you are slaves to sin, which leads to death, or obedience unto God for righteousness. God is the one to be praise for delivering us from sin. Obedience by faith came from the heart, the Holy Spirit convicting us through the gospel of Jesus Christ, which was given unto us. Now that we are free from sin: and we are the servants of righteousness. I speak as a man, so that you may understand the weakness of our mortal bodies. Likewise as we were once practicing evil, which led to sin, even so we have to surrender ourselves as servants of righteousness, which leads to sanctification and holiness. For when we were partakers of sin, we did not know righteousness and evidently we received no reward for those things that we are now ashamed of. The reward of sin is death, but now that we are free from sin and have become the servants of God, we have the reward of holiness unto everlasting life. The reward of sin is death, but the free gift of God is eternal life through Jesus Christ our Lord. Amen

Apart from Christ it is impossible for anyone to keep the law of God. However, after Christ died for our sins mankind was given a second chance; and we were no longer in subjection unto the written law, but unto Him Who died for us. The bond that we share with Jesus Christ is like a marriage between a man and a woman. **Romans chapter 7:1-17** tells us that the physical laws of nature have control over a person as long as he lives. A husband and wife are united by marriage until death. However, if the husband dies the wife is a widow and she is free to marry someone else, but if she remarries another while her husband lives, she is an adulteress. However, if her husband is dead, she is free to get remarried, so then she is not an adulteress. Likewise, brethren we are separated from the law of sin after baptism by means of which we get married to Christ. Baptism, which is immersion under water, is symbolic for being buried, and also a spiritual awakening through the eternal salvation of Jesus Christ, so that He may present us as fruit unto God.

Before we became spiritual, we relied on our sensual knowledge, and sin used the appearance of the law that was meant for holiness to bring about desires, which led to sin. Now that we are free from the appearance of the law: being born–again, so that we can serve in the newness of the spirit, and not in the previous of the letter, which is works without faith. Why was the law that was meant for good seem so harsh unto me, was that God's plan? God forbid! If it weren't for the instructions from the Bible, I would have not known the truth about soul salvation. How could I have known lust, if the Bible had not said, you shall not covet.

The Old Testament of the Bible would seem to contradict the New Testament. However, it was sin that brought the controversial by using the commandments of God to work evil in humanity: and all manner of lustful desires. If you take notice where there are no posted laws, there are no violations. For without the tree of knowledge of good and evil the law of sin was inactive, but after God gave the commandment not to eat of it, sin became active. Wherever you find good evil is present. People that are lawless lived without the law, but as soon the commandment came from God to trust and obey: sin saw it as an opportunity to revive its ugly head; and used the law, which is good, and was meant for righteousness to destroy the moral hope that we have in Christ Jesus. God's commandments are always meant for good and they're ordained unto life, but they became evil unto death, because of sin using them as a weapon of destruction. The law is Holy, and the commandment is Holy, and just, and good. Why is the earth in such chaos, and why is the commandment of love so hard to keep, was it God's intention from the beginning? God forbid! It was the law of sin working through our senses to destroy that, which is Holy and true! God revealed the harshness of sin unto us by His commandment of love, so that it would expose the law of sin as being sinful unto death.

Spiritually we are all connected to God the Father through the hope and love of Jesus Christ, which is obedience through faith. Let us have our hope centered on His eternal salvation through His Agape love. Furthermore, I have to conclude that loving people as ourselves is the only solution. For we have yet to see anything made perfect by the written law. Life can be a mystery especially when it comes to oppression. However, faith is the key for unlocking joy and peace, whereby the spirit will sustain the body, but the body by itself is dead. Amen

"The Knowledge of Good and Evil"

Chapter 6

The Mark of the Beast

Genesis chapter 2:16 tells us that the Lord God commanded Adam, saying, of every tree of the Garden you may freely eat, but of the tree of knowledge of good and evil, you shall not eat of it, for in the day that you eat thereof you shall surely die. This was foretold that after Adam sinned, he would surly die, whereby death came upon all humanity. Furthermore, the earth was given six thousand years of probation by means of which Satan was sentence to death. The great controversy, and the battle of good and evil can only be seen through the discernment given unto us by the Holy Spirit. The conflicts of the ages are explicitly illustrated in the stories of the Bible. **Genesis chapter 3:14,15** tells us that the Lord God said unto the serpent, because you have done this, you are cursed above all other animals, and above every beast of the field; upon your belly you shall go, and dust you shall eat all the days of your life. And I will put enmity between you and the woman, and between your children and her children; and Jesus shall bruise your head, and you shall bruise His feet. **Romans chapter 16:20** tells us that the God of peace shall bruise Satan under Christ feet shortly. The serpent was a medium used by the devil to deceive the unsuspecting Eve. The restoration of mankind came through the victory of the cross, which our dear Lord and Savior Jesus Christ was crucified for our sins by means of which soul salvation was granted unto all humanity.

After Lucifer sinned, he became the devil, and Satan, that old dragon who is Christ greatest adversary. The Bible tells us that he was the most glorious created being, but instead of nurturing love, and thanksgiving, and praise toward our Lord, he became envious of Christ position and privileges. Sin originated from Lucifer's desire to become his own god, which progressively plunged his heart into self-exaltation. We are all tempted by sin, whereas self-motivation and giving access to demonic agents of Satan will captivate our minds with sinful thoughts and desires, which will eventually plunge our heart's into a life of hopelessness. Every now and then, I get the feeling that I have the power to achieve whatever I set my mind to, but on the contrary positive thinking will not produce faith. It wasn't meant for us to be self-seeking, but instead to be thankful in all things by giving thanks unto God. The war between Christ and Lucifer started in heaven, after he became self-seeking. The son of perdition: meaning, everyone who hates God will become more and more like the devil. The angelic being known as Lucifer was the first of his generation that was created by Jesus Christ unto the glory of the Father in heaven. Before Lucifer became the enemy of good, he stood beside Christ.

The Hebrew/Aramaic word for Lucifer is Heylel, meaning, brightness of the daystar, or light bearer. Lucifer's body was made from every precious stone that you could think of: rubies, topaz, diamonds, beryl, onyx, jasper, sapphire, emerald, turquoise and gold. Lucifer was perfect in beauty, and his beauty became his vanity. Furthermore, his wisdom limited him as a created being, whereby he was unable to discern his downfall. One of his divine purposes was to harmonize sounds and praise unto God. Lucifer was the anointed angel that was set above the other angels; he was given the opportunity to stand in the presence of God on the Holy Mountain. He was able to perform his duties without flaw, until pride was found in him. **2 Corinthians chapter 11:14,15** tells us that Satan can transform himself into an angel of light; therefore it is a simple thing for his ministers also to be transformed as the ministers of righteousness; whose end God will judge according to their wicked acts.

Lucifer took thought of his own beauty, and it filled his heart with violence and sin. Furthermore, he was found guilty of sowing discord among the angels in heaven, whereby criticizing God's Character. Christ gave him numerous opportunities and counseling to repent. However, he did not, which led to God the Father casting him out of the Holy Mountain. **Ezekiel chapter 28:14-16** tells us that Lucifer was once the anointed cherub that covers; and I have put you on the Holy mountain of God; you walked in the midst of the stones of fire. You were perfect in your ways from the day you were created, until iniquity was found in you. By the multitude of your merchandise it filled you with violence, and you sinned: therefore I will cast you out as profane. I will cast you out of the Mountain of God from the midst of the stones of fire. And I will destroy you, O covering cherub. **Isaiah chapter 14:12-14** tells us that Lucifer has fallen from heaven. O Lucifer, son of the morning; you are cut down to the ground. Furthermore, you did weaken the nations. You said in your heart, I will ascend into heaven, I will exalt my throne above the stars of God, and I will also sit upon the mount of the congregation in the region toward the north. I will ascend above the heights of the clouds. I will be like the Most High.

After, Lucifer was cast out of heaven: he used the serpent to deceive Eve; and took control of the earth for four thousand years. Christ victory at the cross gave Christians, non–Christians, and Jews hope in His eternal salvation. However, until Christ return mankind weary soul will never truly find peace and harmony with each other, because of Satan working in the shadows to deceive as many as possible. Today, we are holding onto our faith and hope as true believers of Christ, whereby God's Agape love unites us with Him in the name of Jesus Christ Who has blessed us in times pass with blessings of joy, and peace. Furthermore, we have to acknowledge the work of the Holy Spirit in the final days of Judgment by means of which, we must surrender our life and spirit into the hands of our Lord Jesus Christ before the close of probation that we might be saved. Amen

Christ Investigative Judgment

Genesis chapter 1:26 tells us that God made man in His Own Image and Likeness, and gave them dominion, whereby the man and the woman was one: even as Christ and the Father are one.

However, after the great controversy between God and Lucifer, Adam fell at the hand of his deception, and he was appointed to rule over the earth for six thousand years. Diplomacy was no longer the theme of the earth, but chaos and destruction became the attributes of the dragon's empire, whereby he created the proverbial world system to establish himself.

In the year *4,000 BC*, the Virgin Mary gave birth to Jesus, Who came as the second Adam from God, whereby He had victory over Satan at the cross by taking dominion away from the devil. After, Jesus was born the countdown was put on pause, because Christ walk the earth for *33* years without sinning. Furthermore, He instructed His disciples to spread the gospel to the entire earth, before He returned to heaven in *34 AD*. After, Christ left the earth most of mankind went back to their old ways of sinning, whereby the countdown for His return to judge the earth began. **Revelation chapter 17:1-5** tells us that the Lord spoke unto John His beloved in the year *95 AD*, saying, Satan would take control of the Church of Thyatira by *538 AD*. And there came one of the seven angels which had the seven vials, and talked with me, saying unto me, come closer, and I will show you the judgment of the false church, which teaches the whole world to sin. And with whom the leaders of the world practice immorality, and the people are deceived by her false teachings, and her lies. So, the angel carried me away in the spirit into the wilderness: and showed me a woman who sat upon a bright red dragon, fill of names of blasphemy, having seven heads, and ten horns. And the woman was clothed in purple, and red, and gold, and precious stones, and pearls, and having a golden cup in her hand filled with abominations, and the filthiness of her fornication. And upon her forehead was the name written: **Mystery, Babylon the Great, the Mother of Harlots, and Abominations of the Earth.**

The devil's advocates are in action the same way in which the serpent deceived Eve in the beginning. His goal is to take control of the minds of the leaders of the world, and eventually he will reveal himself unto everyone. **Revelation chapter 17:9-11** tells us to him that have wisdom. There are seven mountains, on which the false church sits. And there are seven political leaders all together; and five of them already died, and the one that's alive now is number six. And he will reign up until its time for number seven to take office, and after he takes the devil's seat, he will reign for a short period of time. And the devil that was from the beginning, and still to come, he would become the eight before the close of probation of the earth.

Revelation chapter 3:15,16 tells us that the church is compromised, and Christ is making one final request to the Laodiceans, saying, I know your works that you are neither cold nor hot: I would rather you were cold or hot, but instead you are lukewarm. The fulfillment of Nebuchadnezzar's dream of the statue made of gold, silver, brass, iron, and clay has come to pass. Furthermore, we are given the discernment of the Holy Spirit that the motive of the church has been changed from the spreading of the gospel, and apart from the collection plate the focus has now turned toward the recruiting of new members, whereby the church has become a snare for the righteous. The pews are filled with moneychangers, and those that sold doves. **Revelation chapter 3:19,20** tells us that as many as Christ love, He will reprimand, and discipline: therefore be zealous, and repent. Behold I stand at the door and knock: if anyone hears My voice, and open the door, I will come in, and I will drink with him, and he with Me. Amen

Who is the Church?

The word church was first mention in the gospel of Matthew for the first time, and the total of eighty times throughout the New Testament. The word church derived from the Greek word ekklesia, meaning: a group of people called out for a special purpose. As the fig tree that was from the beginning grew until it touched the sky, whereby its branches reached across the globe, but when the Son of man came thereof, at the appointed time of figs, He found the tree barren.

Today you'll find churches all across the globe filled with people singing songs of praise, and having a form of worship. However, the testing of our faith and the love for our God can be seen through the trials and tribulations that we bare as believers. Faith is the seed of hope that was planted in the middle of the Garden of Eden: that magnificent tree of life that stood next to the tree of knowledge of good and evil. And while the tree of knowledge of good and evil brought forth sin and death, the tree of life brought forth the fruit of the Spirit for the healing of the nations; whereby God illustrated Christ as the tree of life that would reunite the church with Him as one spiritual body to fulfill His good pleasure of joy, peace and salvation unto all. Therefore now that we have drank of that Spiritual Rock, let us be as bold as lions, praying under the influence of the Holy Spirit, where unto we are called to witness unto the world on Christ's behalf. Brethren, I appeal to you, let us preach the everlasting gospel, meanwhile bearing much fruit and living a life of purpose and value to the glory and honor of His name, Jahovah Shalom.

Even though we are born sinful by nature, the heart of every sincere believer belongs unto the Lord. God not only gave us faith to believe in His only begotten Son, but He also gave us hope, so that we might surrender unto His unconditional love and eternal salvation. In the Most Holy Place we see the lampstand with seven candlesticks reminding us of God's sovereignty and divinity, for He is an omniscient God, and apart from Him there is no other Rock. The Seventh Day Sabbath is the coming of our Lord and Savior Jesus Christ. Adventism is the rediscovery of the Bible and the Word of God, whereby the individual accepts Christ as Lord and Savior; apart from Christ the Christian faith doesn't exist. Adventist faith differs from other religions and denominations in many aspects. Adventism shares the protestant belief of the Word of God over the church: the believer standing on his or her own two spiritual feet. The death and resurrection of Jesus Christ gave us hope in His salvation to come. God resist the proud and reward the humble with eternal life. If one does not value the gift of salvation, God has no delight in him. **Romans chapter 6:23** tells us that the wages of sin is death, but the gift of God is eternal life through Jesus Christ our Lord.

Many churches today have very little faith in spiritual gifts, but with all arguments aside without the Holy Spirit it is impossible for us to discern the will of God for our lives. For only through the power of God and the resurrection of Jesus Christ can a man be saved. Therefore, he who lacks wisdom, knowledge and understanding will fall. **Proverbs chapter 29:18** tells us that where there is no vision the people perish, but happy is he that keeps the law of the Lord.

We have all heard the good news of Jesus Christ, and the testimonies of the patriarchs. For we have creation as a witness that life without purpose is sin. Now that the death of Jesus Christ on the cross gave us hope in God by means of which faith is given to believe in Him, Who is bless forever and ever. What then? Should we continue to try everything except Christ Who is willing and able to do it all? God forbid! Let us put our trust in the Lord Jehovah: for in Him there is everlasting strength. Amen

The Glory of God's Church

Christianity was never something that I had any love for, but after I was told that works without faith is dead, it got me thinking about a story that involved three blind men who lived in the same town. The first man, who was a talebearer, went from house to house sowing discord among his brethren, and likewise the second stole from the rich to satisfy the needs of the poor. However, the third man was highly esteemed in his own righteousness, but in the darkness of his seductive heart, there was deception. For a good man is but a shiny tool in the hands of the devil. **Luke chapter 18:10-14** tells us that two men went into the temple to pray: one man was a Pharisee and the other a tax collector. The Pharisee stood by himself and prayed saying, God, I thank you that I am not as other men are: extortionist, unjust, adulterers, or even as this tax collector; I fast twice a week, and I give tithes of all that I possess. But the tax collector stood at a distance, he would not even look up to heaven, but put his hand across his chest, and said, God have mercy on me, for I am, but a sinner. Jesus replied, I tell you that the tax collector, rather than the other, went home justified before God. For all those who exalt themselves, will be humbled, and those who humble themselves will be exalted.

Since the foundation of our righteousness is Jesus Christ; and there is only one God, and one Salvation. How do we determine, which church is right for us? **Matthew chapter 16:13-19** tells us that when Jesus came into the region of Caesarea Philippi, He asked His disciples, saying, who do men say that I, the Son of man, Am? And they said, some say John the Baptist, some Elijah, and others Jeremiah, or one of the prophets, Jesus said unto them, but who do you say that I Am?

Simon Peter answered and said, You are the Christ, the Son of the living God. Jesus answered and said unto him, blessed are you, Simon Barjona, for it was not revealed unto you by people, but My Father Who is in heaven. And I also say unto you that you are Petrous: little rock, and I Am Petra, the mighty Rock. And on this Rock I will build My church, and the gates of hades shall not prevail against it. And I will give you the keys of the kingdom of heaven, and whatsoever you bind on earth shall be bound in heaven, and whatsoever you loose on earth shall be loose in heaven.

The diversity of religions has made it difficult for churches to unite as one spiritual body in Christ according to God's great plan for saving humanity. Many will argue that the yearly Sabbath, and appointed feast days were given unto the Israelites as a memorial, and not unto Christians. In the Ten Commandments the Sabbath wasn't a weekly Sabbath, but instead a reminder of the Lord's Passover, Feast of unleavened bread, First fruits harvest, Pentecost, Blowing of trumpets, Atonement of sin, and the Feast of tabernacle. **Mark chapter 2:27-28** tells us that the Sabbath was made for man, and not man for the Sabbath: therefore the Son of man is Lord also of the Sabbath.

Jesus is the fulfillment of the Sabbath, whereby He reconciled us to the Father, Who sent Him. Many believers refer to the Sabbath as the Lord's Day. Six days was given unto the prince of darkness, but the Seventh Day was reserved for mankind, whereby Jesus is the Lord of the Sabbath. Getting to know God is the retroactive work of the Holy Spirit, whereby truth becomes belief. **Numbers chapter 23:19** tells us that God is not a man, that He should tell a lie. If we believe with all our heart, and continue in His Word, then we are His disciples in deed. **John chapter 21:15-17** tells us that when the disciples had eaten breakfast, Jesus said to Simon Peter, Simon, son of Jonah, do you Agape Me above your brethren? He answered and said, yes, Lord; You know that I Philia You. Jesus said, feed My sheep. Again a second time, Jesus said, Simon, son of Jonah, do you Agape Me above your brethren? He replied, yes, Lord; you know that I Philia You. Jesus said, tend to My sheep.

And again a third time Jesus said to him, Simon, son of Jonah, do you Agape Me above your brethren? Peter was grieved because Jesus said to him the third time; do you Agape Me above your brethren? And he said to Jesus, Lord, You know all things; You know that I Philia You. Jesus said, feed My sheep. Jesus ask Peter if he Agape Him as Lord and Savior and if you do you will keep My commandment of Philia love by feeding My sheep three times to restore him, because he had denied Christ three times. Christ gave Peter the keys to the Kingdom of heaven to grant access to those who would Agape Him, as their Lord and Savior. Peter was not the owner of the keys; he was only the servant doing his Master's will. Faith is the Word of God, whereby the believer surrenders unto the hope of soul salvation. Furthermore, sanctification is the perfecting of our character in Christ Jesus. The Protestant belief is the Word of God over the church: the individual standing on his or her own two spiritual feet. This belief not only supports Jesus Christ as the Messiah, but also Him being God in human form, whereby righteousness is by faith.

America was founded without a king or church, whereby the pilgrims wanting to escape from the servitude of oppression came to this free land in the year *1620*. The constitution is a beacon of hope, and freedom to the entire human race. In the year *1789*, George Washington became the first American President, and the constitution was established not long after based upon equality of freedom, and religion. Two hundred and twenty-six years later, President Barack Obama is the forty fourth President of America, and as a country she is three hundred and ninety-seven years old. The constitution must be upheld to the letter——for it is the liberty of our nation that is at stake. America stood for freedom long before church and state by means of which her liberation came at such a high price that if the forefathers knew about the present condition of their once beloved country, they would roll over twice in their graves. For the constitution that was established for freedom is now being abolished, and the very things that they fought against are being promoted into law.

Now that our privileges are made void, and our freedom has been taken away, we realize that apart from raising our eyebrows we can do nothing to overcome the financial burden we all share as Americans. Conformity is another word for globalism, and hopelessness is the final result of the American dream. Imagine that you were on a highway that had no speed limit, and your car had no speedometer, you wouldn't have any idea of how fast you were traveling.

However, God gave us the Ten Commandments by faith, whereby the heart is circumcised with the love of Christ. For it was God Who wrote the commandments by hand, and then gave them unto Moses. As our sinful desires are revealed unto us, we realize that we have a greater need to have God in our lives. In the pass, rebellion has led us to disobedience, but now that our minds are renewed it is clear that only Jesus Christ has the power to bring us to repentance that will result in His righteousness. **James chapter 4:17** tells us that to him that knows the right way of pleasing God, and does it not, to him it is sin. Jesus Christ was a free man that exercised faith in doing His Father's will. A man that is free from sin, think and live as a free man to the glory of God, but on the contrary the thoughts of the wicked are an abomination unto the Lord. God detest the sacrifice of the wicked and finds no room in his wicked mind, for even though the shackles are not seen around his hands and feet, his heart is nonetheless a prisoner of Satan. I am a sinner, who will deliver me from this life of sin. A slave has many masters, but I have one God, and one Mediator My Lord and Savior Jesus Christ. For this particular reason, I pray for you, that your life be filled with joy and peace. For the righteousness of our Lord Jesus Christ is poured out upon all humanity. Jesus Christ was willing to die to save humanity: even so every true believer will lay down his life for his brethren. Amen

The Revelation of Jesus Christ

Revelation chapter 1:1 tells us that the revelation of Jesus Christ which came from God the Father unto His Son, to show unto His servants, things, which must shortly come to pass. And Christ sent and signified it by His angel unto His servant John. **Revelation chapter 1:8-20** tells us that He that is holding the Seven Stars in His right hand, and walks in the middle of the Seven Golden Candlesticks, spoke unto the church of Ephesus by His servant John as well as unto us, saying, I Am the Alpha and the Omega, the Beginning and the End, says the Lord, which is, and which was, and Who came in person, and I shall return, the Almighty.

The Apostle John who is our brother, and companion in tribulation, and in the Kingdom and patience of Jesus Christ. John was imprisoned on the island of Patmos in the year *95 AD*, for preaching the Word of God, and for sharing the gospel, and testimony of Jesus Christ. John was in the Spirit on the Lord's day when he heard a great voice like a trumpet, saying, I Am the Alpha, and the Omega, the First, and the Last, what you see, write in a book and send it to the seven churches which are in Asia Minor: Ephesus, Smyrna, Pergamos, Thyatira, Sardis, Philadelphia, and Laodicea. John turned to see where the voice was coming from. As he turned he saw Seven Golden Candlesticks, and in the middle of the Seven Golden Candlesticks one like the Son of man clothed with a robe down to His feet, and a belt made from fine gold wrapped around His waist. His head and His hair were as white as snow, white like wool, and His eyes like a flame of fire; His feet were like fine brass, as if they were burned in a furnace; and His voice was like the sound of a great waterfall.

The illustration identifies Christ in all His Glory. And He had in His right hand seven stars, and out of His mouth went a sharp two-edged sword, and His appearance was as the sun times seven in brightness. And when He got close to me, I collapsed at His feet as if I was dead. And He laid His right hand upon me and said, fear not; I Am the First and the Last. Furthermore, I Am He Who lives, I was once dead, and behold now I Am alive forevermore, Amen; and I have the keys to hell and death. Write the things, which you have seen, and the things, which are, and the things, which shall soon come to pass.

The mystery of the Seven Stars, which are seen in Jesus' right hand: and the Seven Golden Candlesticks. The Seven Stars are symbolic for the seven-fold ministerial work of the Holy Spirit given to each church age, and the Seven Candlesticks are seven literal churches. The seven churches of Asia Minor began during the apostolic church age: after Christ ascension in *34 AD*.

The Church of Ephesus *34–100 AD*

The first letter to the church of Ephesus, which means: desirable, also known for its purity in doctrine. The Church of Ephesus was the first apostolic church, which started in *34 AD*, after Christ ascended. These seven churches represent a type of church that existed literally; and also carries a prophetic meaning for us as well.

Correction, Counsel and Restoration

Revelation chapter 2:1,2 tells us of the clerical error of the church of Ephesus. Unto the angel, or messenger of the church of Ephesus write these things says He that holds the Seven Stars in His right hand, and walks in the middle of the Seven Golden Candlesticks. I know your works, and your labor, and your patience. Christ identifies their works, and labor, and patience. Ephesus began with a zeal for God. The young church was growing vigorously, but soon became consumed by works, and labor. As you can see Christ was evaluating their efforts and good deeds. However, they weren't spending enough time with Him. **Romans chapter 10:1-4** tells us that Paul's prayer to God was for the Israelites to be saved. I testify that they have a zeal of God, but not according to the knowledge of Jesus Christ. Them not knowing the righteousness of God, and being ignorant of the truth going about to establish their own righteousness: and therefore they have not surrendered themselves unto the righteousness of God. And not knowing that Christ is the end of the law, whereby, He Himself made us righteous by dying for everyone that believes.

Revelation chapter 2:2 tells us that Christ implied, that they have not tolerated them, which are evil. And you have tested them, which say they are apostles, and are not, and have found them to be liars. False apostles are in every church, and Ephesus was no exception. **1 Timothy chapter 1:3** tells us that Paul urged young Pastor Timothy to stay at Ephesus while he travel to Macedonia that he might instruct others not to teach any other doctrine apart from Christ.

Revelation chapter 2:3 tells us that Christ had some positive things to say about the church of Ephesus. You have persevered, and have endured hardships for My name, and have not grown weary. Paul urged the Ephesians, as well as the church today that our grace and peace came through the adoption, which was made possible by the Father in Christ. **Ephesians chapter 1:1-10** tells us that Paul became an apostle of Jesus Christ by the will of God. And he wrote to the saints, which were at Ephesus, saying, to the faithfulness in Christ Jesus grace be unto you, and peace from God our Father, and from the Lord Jesus Christ. Blessed be the God and Father of our Lord Jesus Christ, Who has blessed us with all spiritual blessings in heavenly places. God chose us to be with Him before the foundation of the world, that we should be holy, and blameless before His sight, laboring in love. Furthermore, He also predestinated us to become His sons and daughters through the adoption that which is made possible by Jesus Christ, according to the good pleasure of His will.

Praise and glory to God the Father for His grace, which He freely gives unto us through His beloved Son; In Whom we have redemption by His blood and forgiveness of sins, which came by the multitude of His grace. God also lavished us in the abundance of all wisdom and understanding by making His plan of salvation known unto us, according to His good pleasure, which He established for the glory of Himself. So, that when the right time comes, He will bring all things together both heaven and earth under the leadership of Christ. Amen

Revelation chapter 2:4-6 tells us that Christ is making us aware of some of the negativity of the church of Ephesus. Nevertheless, I have some things against you, because you have left your first love. Remember therefore from where you have fallen, and repent, and do the first works, or else I will come unto you immediately, and remove your candlestick out of his place, except you repent. I know how much you hate the deeds of the Nicolaitanes, (false doctrine) which I also hate.

Acts chapter 20:28-30 tells us that Paul expanded on the importance of watching over the church of Christ. Take heed therefore unto yourselves, and to all the flock, over which the Holy Spirit of Christ have put you in charge of, to teach the church of God, which Christ Himself has purchased with His own blood. I know that after I leave Satan will enter in amongst you, not sparing the flock. Even amongst yourselves you will have disputes, speaking perverse things to draw away disciples unto false beliefs.

Promise and Encouragement to Persevere

Ephesians chapter 4:1-8 tells us that Paul encourages his readers to surrender unto Christ by exhibiting himself as a prisoner of the Lord. Therefore I, the prisoner of the Lord, beg you to walk in a manner worthy of the calling of which you have been called, with all humility and gentleness, with patience, showing benevolence one to another in love. Make every effort to keep the unity of the Spirit in the bond of peace. There is one body, and one Spirit, just as you were called to one hope in your calling, one Lord, one faith, one baptism; one God and Father of all, Who is over all, and through all in all. But unto every one of us is given grace according to the measure of the gift of Christ. Therefore it is said, when He ascended on high, He led the captives in captivity, and gave gifts unto mankind.

Revelation chapter 2:7 Christ reminds us to hold on: he that has an ear let him hear what the Spirit says unto the churches. To him that overcome (holdfast) will I give to eat of the tree of life, which is in the middle of the paradise of God. **Ephesians chapter 6:10-18** tells us to be strong in the Lord, and in the power of His might. Today, the power of Paul's message brings new rival, and hope unto us, as it did unto the church of Ephesus centuries ago; whereby it is of a necessity that we put on the whole armor of God, that we may be able to stand firm against the persecution of the devil. Life seems harsh and sometimes controversial, and we think that people are behind the scene. However, there are principalities, and powers, and rulers in dark places of this world, and spiritual wickedness in high places.

Therefore, let us put on the whole armor of God, so that we may stand in the day of evil, and having done everything to stand firm, let us stand with the belt of truth wrapped around our waist: even as Christ Himself had a golden belt wrapped around His waist. Furthermore, take the breastplate of righteousness, and your feet fitted with the preparation of the gospel of peace, and above all take the shield of faith, whereby you may extinguish all the flaming arrows of the wicked. And take the helmet of salvation, and the sword of the Spirit, which is the Word of God by means of which making all prayers and petition always in the Spirit, stay alert, watch with all diligence and perseverance, and remember to petition for all the believers. Amen

The Church of Smyrna *100–313 AD*

The second letter to the church of Smyrna, which means: sweet aroma when crushed. The worshiping of Domitian Caesar, Cybele, Apollo, Aesculapius, Aphrodite, and Zeus was the tradition of the people living in the city of Smyrna, which is now called Izmir, Turkey.

Praise and Acknowledgment

Revelation chapter 2:8 Christ introduces Himself as the First and the Last: reminding us of His victory over death, and the promise of His salvation to come. Unto the angel, or messenger of the church in Smyrna write these things says the First and the Last, which was dead, and is alive. **Revelation chapter 2:9** Christ identifies some key points: I know your works and tribulation and poverty, but you are rich, and I know the blasphemy of them, which say they are Jews and are not, but are the synagogue of Satan. **Acts chapter 13:42-45** tells us that when the Jews were gone out of the synagogue, the Gentiles beg that the same words might be preached to them the next Sabbath. Now when the congregation was broken up, many of the Jews and religious proselytes of Judaism followed Paul and Barnabas, and urged them to continue in the grace of God. And the next Sabbath day came almost the whole city together to hear the Word of God. But when the Jews saw the multitudes, they were filled with envy, and spoke against the Word of God contradicting and blaspheming those things, which were spoken by Paul. **Acts chapter 18:4-6** tells us that Paul reasoned in the synagogue every Sabbath, and persuaded the Jews and the Greeks. And when Silas and Timothy came from Macedonia, Paul was convicted in his spirit, and testified to the Jews that Jesus was Christ. And when they resisted and blasphemed, he shook his garment, and said unto them, your blood is upon your own heads; I am clean: from now on I will go to the Gentiles.

Promise and Encouragement to Persevere

Revelation chapter 2:10 tells us that Christ encourages the church of Smyrna to stay focus. Fear none of those things, which you will suffer. Behold, the devil will cast some of you into prison that you may be tried; and you will have tribulation ten days, be faithful unto death, and I will give you a crown of life. **Revelation chapter 2:11** Christ reminds us to hold on: he that has an ear let him hear what the Spirit says unto the churches. He that overcome (holdfast) shall not be hurt of the second death. From *98–313 AD*, Satan began to move the hearts of many Roman emperors to persecute God's people whose religion was then made illegal.

- Emperor Trajan *(98–117 AD)*
- Emperor Hadrian *(117–138 AD)*
- Emperor Antonine *(138–161 AD)*
- Emperor Marcus Aurelius *(161–180 AD)*
- Emperor Septimius Severus *(193–211 AD)*
- Emperor Decius *(249–251 AD)*
- Emperor Valerian *(253–260 AD)*
- Emperor Diocletian *(284–305 AD)*
- Emperor Galerius *(305–311 AD)*
- Emperor Constantine *(306–337 AD)*

From Emperor Trajan to Constantine the great many Christians became a martyr like Polycarp who was the head minister of the church of Smyrna for more than forty years, whereby the Jews eagerly gathered firewood on the Sabbath to burn him at the stake. **1 Peter chapter 1:3-9** tells us blessed be the God and Father of our Lord Jesus Christ, Who according to His abundant mercy caused us to be born–again to a living hope through the resurrection of Jesus Christ from the dead. We obtain an inheritance which is imperishable, undefiled and will not fade away: reserved in heaven for us, which is protected by the power of God through faith, a salvation ready to be revealed at the end. In this we should eagerly rejoice, even though we suffer various trials for a season, so that the proof of our faith being more precious than gold which is perishable. We are tested by fire that our trials might be counted to us in the result of praise, and glory, and honor at the coming of Jesus Christ. Furthermore, we have not seen Him, but we love Him, and though there is no evidence, we believe in Him, we greatly rejoice with joy, which is indescribable, and full of glory, having our faith made perfect and complete, even the salvation of our souls. Amen

The Church of Pergamos *313–538 AD*

The third letter to the church of Pergamos, which means: exalted city. Sometime around third century *BC*, Pergamos, became the center of cultural and intellectual Greek life. The city had one of the largest library collections of over two–thousand scrolls competing with Alexandria's library. And later became the Capital of the Roman province of Asia for two centuries. Pergamos distinguished itself by becoming the first site for worship of the Roman emperor, Caesar Augustus as early as *29 BC*.

There are approximately *(300,000)* churches in America, with the exception of three having worship on Saturday: The Asheville Seventh Day Baptist, Seventh Day Church of God, and Seventh Day Adventist. However, the Seventh Day Adventist is the largest of the three, and is estimated at about *19.1* million members worldwide. The Seventh Day Adventist Church is located in every state, and has missionaries in over *(2,000)* countries around the world. They are also considered as the only other worldwide denomination apart from the Roman Catholic Church, which derived directly from the Sabbath keeping church of Pergamos in the year *307 AD*, when the Edict of Milan Constantine the great declared himself as a Christian.

Spiritual State of the Church

Personally, I am neither Jew nor Gentile, but I am in Christ Who died for me. Can the church or denomination save? **John chapter 3:5** tells us that except a man is born of water and of the Spirit: he cannot enter into the Kingdom of God. **James chapter 1:23,24** tells us that if any be a hearer of the Word, and not a doer, he is like a man looking at himself in a mirror without recognizing his own face, which brings us to the sharp sword with two–edges. **Ephesians chapter 6:17, Hebrews chapter 4:12** tells us that the sword of the Spirit is the Word of God.

Revelation chapter 2:12,13 Christ makes His introduction as in previous letters. Unto the angel, or messenger of the church in Pergamos write these things says He which have the sharp sword with two edges; I know your works, and where you dwell, even where <u>Satan's seat is!</u> This refers to changes, which derived from Catholicism, after Rome began to make their transition into Papal Rome. After Constantine became emperor in *306 AD*, he embraced Christianity in *307 AD*, whereby putting an end to Christian persecution; and legalizing Christianity: making the church into a sacramental caste endowed with priestly position of undisputed popularity and power. From thereon the city of Pergamos was looked at as a leader in both religious and political power in Western Europe. As the religious capital of Asia Minor, it accommodated temples for many oriental religions such as Aesculapius, god of healing the serpent wrap around the cross, which can be seen on hospital buildings and other medical associations. Just like today, many craving for domination over people of all type of beliefs, the church of Pergamos was willing to compromise their love for God, and convert to many pagan doctrines and rites. However, all their compromises resulted in paganism.

- *307 AD*, baptism by sprinkling replaces immersion under water.
- *321 AD*, the day of rest was changed from the Seventh Day to Sunday, the day of the Sun.
- *325 AD*, the council of Nicaea concluded that Jesus was fully God.
- *375 AD*, worshiping of the saints began.
- *381 AD*, the council of Constantinople concluded that, in addition to being God, Jesus was also fully human.
- *400 AD*, worshiping of the dead was instituted.
- *416 AD*, the church began to baptize babies.
- *431 AD*, the council of Ephesus concluded that, Jesus was both divine, and fully human.

- *432 AD*, the worshiping of the Virgin Mary began.
- *451 AD*, the council of Chalcedonia concluded that the divine nature and human nature of Jesus, though combined in a single person, are nevertheless distinct one from the other.
- *496 AD*, King Clovis of the Franks got baptized on the *25th* of December, Christ-mass, and the birthday of Tammuz, the Sun god, during which time the first bishop of Rome was ordained.
- *508 AD*, the daily sacrifice was taken away, and the abomination that brings the desolation is setup. **Daniel chapter 9:27**
- *538 AD*, Rome became Papal Rome.

Praise and Acknowledgment

Revelation chapter 2:13 tells us that many Christians died at the hands of Constantine even though he had legalized Christianity. And you have (holdfast) My name, and have not denied My faith even in those days wherein you stood up against the antichrist and became a faithful martyr, whereby many were slain amongst you by Satan. Today, true Christians, and Christian faith lax, whereby many find ease in conformity as they did in Pergamos by giving Satan access to their lives.

Correction, Counsel and Restoration

Revelation chapter 2:13-16 tells us that Satan had his seat in Pergamos by way of compromising the doctrine and belief of the people. I have a few things against you, says the Lord Jesus Christ, because you have those that hold the doctrine of Balaam, who taught Balak to cast a stumbling block before the children of Israel, to eat things sacrificed unto idols, and to commit fornication. And you also have them that hold the doctrine of the Nicolaitanes, which I hate. Repent or else I will come unto you immediately, and fight against them with the sword of My mouth.

Numbers chapter 22:4-6 tells us that Balaam had a reputation just like many famous television ministers today who make false promises. And Balak the son of Zippor was king of the Moabites, and he sent messengers to find Balaam the son of Beor, saying, there is a multitude of people that came out of Egypt and they cover the face of the earth, and they are living next to me. Come and curse these people for they are mighty that I may prevail over them, and kill them, that I may drive them out of the land. For those that you have bless, they are blessed, and whom you curse, are cursed. What are we compromising today to have social honor?

Promise and Encouragement to Persevere

Revelation chapter 2:17 tells us that Christ is reminding us to have hope in Him: he that have an ear, let him hear what the Spirit says unto the churches; to him that overcome (holdfast) will I give to eat of the hidden manna, and will give him a white stone, and in the stone a new name written, which no man knows except he that receives it. The hidden manna is Christ Himself, and the white stone is the glory of God that everyone shall receive in Christ Jesus. Amen

The Church of Thyatira *538–1517 AD*

The fourth letter to the church of Thyatira, which means: savor of labor. Thyatira was a small city, renowned for its production of purple dye, the color of royalty. The city was also dedicated to the worship of Tyrimnos, Apollo god of the Sun, which was soon replaced by the worship of the Roman Emperor.

Correction, Counsel and Restoration

The church of Thyatira accomplished a lot of good works by building hospitals, orphanages, schools and missions. **Revelation chapter 2:18-24** tells us unto the angel, or messenger of the church in Thyatira write these things says the Son of God Who have His eyes like unto a flame of fire, and His feet are like fine brass. I know your works, and charity, and service, and faith, and patience, and works, and the last to be more than the first.

Christ made an evaluation of their works, and had a few things against them, because they allowed the teachings of Jezebel, who calls herself a prophetess, to be a part of the church: to teach and seduce His servants to commit fornication, and to eat things sacrificed unto idols. And He gave her time to repent of her fornication, and she repented not. Behold, I will cast her into a bed, and them that commit adultery with her into great tribulation, except they repent of their deeds. And I will kill her children with death; and all the churches shall know that I Am He, Who searches the reins and hearts: (conscience of the hearts) and I will give unto everyone of you according to your works. Furthermore, unto you I say, and unto the rest in Thyatira, as many as I have not found with this doctrine, and which have not known the depths of Satan, as they speak. I will put upon you no other burden.

Thyatira and Pergamos share some similarity in false doctrine. However, Balaam who wanted to infiltrate the Israelites camp and was unable to do so, had to cast a stumbling block in front of the children of Israel to get the men to marry with unbelievers; whereas we see Jezebel who is the product of Balaam's deception working from within the church of Thyatira. **1 Kings chapter 16:31** tells us that after a period of time it seemed pleasant for Ahab to walk in the sins of Jeroboam the son of Nebat, and Ahab took to wife Jezebel the daughter of Ethbaal King of the Zidonians, and went and served Baal, and worshipped him.

- *607 AD*, the bishop of Rome, became the first Pope.
- *709 AD*, the church adopts the rite of kissing the feet of the Pope.
- *787 AD*, the church institutes the worship of images and statues.
- *993 AD*, the church adopts the process of canonization of the saints.
- *1000 AD*, the church begins to impose celibacy on the priests.
- *1049 AD*, the church begins to celebrate masses for the dead.
- *1090 AD*, the rosary appears in the church.
- *1199 AD*, the church gives itself the power to forgive sins by creating the system of indulgences.
- *1215 AD*, the church institutes hearing of confession, becoming a mediator between God and men for the forgiveness of sins.
- *1216 AD*, the church adopts the philosophy, according to which bread and wine became the real body and blood of Jesus.
- *1343 AD*, the church institutes the additional works, which is added to the sacrifice of Jesus for salvation.
- *1439 AD*, the church adopts the notion of purgatory, a place where the righteous souls make amends for their sins before going to heaven.
- *1443 AD*, the church institutes the rite of conformation, making up for the problem of the baptism of babies, who are unaware of their choice.
- *1513 AD*, the church introduces the system of the indulgences sold to the people, so as to shorten the stay of the souls in purgatory.

Promise and Encouragement to Persevere

Revelation chapter 2:25-29 reminds us of the hope that we have in Christ Jesus: But that which you have already, (holdfast) till I come. And he that overcome, and keep My works (faith) unto the end, to him will I give power over the nations. And Christ shall rule them with the rod of iron; as the vessels of a potter shall they be broken to pieces: even as I received of My Father. And I will give him the morning star. He that has an ear let him hear what the Spirit says unto the churches. Amen

The Church of Sardis *1517–1755 AD*

The fifth letter to the church of Sardis, which means: that which remains. Sardis was aware of the danger of not being watchful. The city was considered to be safe from its enemies, because of its location on a high plateau at a height of about one thousand feet, and protected by very steep slopes. However, the city was invaded by surprise twice: once by the Persian King Cyrus in *547 BC*, during the reign of the rich and legendary King Croesus; and also in *218 BC*, by King Antiochus the Great. The city was the former capital of the Kingdom of Lydia, which was devastated by earthquake in *17 AD*, and lost its prestige.

Revelation chapter 3:1 Christ reveals the fullness of His seven-fold ministry of the Holy Spirit, whereby the investigative judgment is carried out under His direct supervision. Unto the angel, or messenger of the church in Sardis write these things says He that have the Seven Spirits of God and the Seven Stars. I know your works (faith), that you have a name that you are alive, but you are dead! **Isaiah chapter 11:1,2** tells us that they're seven spirits of the Lord.

1. The Spirit of the Lord
2. The Spirit of Wisdom
3. The Spirit of Understanding
4. The Spirit of Counsel
5. The Spirit of Might
6. The Spirit of Knowledge
7. The Spirit of the fear of the Lord.

Spiritual State of the Church

The first years of the reformation, a movement initiated by Martin Luther in *1517 AD*, brought about the rediscovery of the Bible and its message of salvation by the grace of Jesus Christ. However, the spiritual awakening didn't last. Protestantism soon became a national religion, whereby making the same errors as the church it had left. Theologians became more preoccupied with defining the gospel than living it in their hearts. Piety was transformed into a cold formalism, without any spiritual meaning or divine power.

Correction, Counsel and Restoration

Revelation chapter 3:2,3 tells us to be watchful and strengthen the things, which remain and are ready to die: because I have not found your works (faith) perfect before God. Remember what you have received and heard; and be patient and repent. Be watchful or else I will come as a thief, and you will not know the hour I will come to you. Christ certainly had a lot to say to the church of Sardis. Be alert, and be devoted to the truth, persevere in hope. Christ is calling for a revival of the churches.

Praise and Acknowledgment

Revelation chapter 3:4 tells us that they were a few people in Sardis, which had not defiled their garments. And they shall walk with Christ in white: for they are worthy. In every dead church you'll find believers who have not defiled their garments: the tears in this particular church was the majority, but Christ had a few believers there in Sardis, and He wanted to remind them to wake up, and strengthen the things, which remain, that are ready to die. **1 kings chapter 19:18** tells us that Christ had left for Himself seven thousand in Israel, all the knees which have not bowed unto Baal, and every mouth which have not kissed him.

Christ spoke of individuals like Martin Luther who was excommunicated during the reformation time period of the church of Sardis, for strengthening the Christian faith. **Daniel chapter 7:25** tells us that he will speak great words against God Who is the Most High, and shall kill many true Christians, which are the saints of the Most High God, and think to himself that he is able to change the unchangeable prophecy of God by changing times and laws.

The Gregorian calendar is widely used in many Countries around the world. The Gregorian calendar is a repetitive cycle of days, months, and years without any significant meaning, or conviction of the Sabbath days; meanwhile God's Calendar is inspired by the Holy Spirit to make us aware of the necessity of sanctification of the believer before Christ return. However, the true Sabbath days are gone. After the Jewish Calendar was abolished in *1582 AD*, the timeline for Jesus's return would become unknown according to Daniel chapter seven verse twenty-five. **Genesis chapter 2:2,3** tells us that thus the <u>heavens</u> and the <u>earth</u> were <u>finished</u>, and <u>all</u> the <u>host</u> of <u>them</u>. <u>And on the Seventh Day God ended His work</u>, which He had made; and <u>He rested on the Seventh Day from all His work</u>, which He had made. <u>And God blessed the Seventh Day</u>, and sanctified it, because that in it <u>He had rested from all His work</u>, which He created and made. The Seventh Day would become discernable to those that are true believer's in Christ, but as for the rest of the world they would not have the discernment of the Holy Spirit that the end is near.

Promise and Encouragement to Persevere

Revelation chapter 3:5,6 tells us that Christ gave us hope: he that overcome (holdfast) the same shall be clothed in white raiment; and I will not remove his name out of the book of life, but I will confess his name before My Father, and before His angels: he that has an ear let him hear what the Spirit says unto the churches. The white raiment is our righteousness that we have with the Father through Jesus Christ. Amen

The Church of Philadelphia *1755–1844 AD*

The sixth letter to the church of Philadelphia, which means: Philia Love (brotherly love). King Attalus II, after whom the city was named, built the city, which was inspired by the love he had for his brother Eumenes II. The city suffered a massive earthquake in *17 AD*, and had to be rebuilt. However, it was smaller than the previous city.

Revelation chapter 3:7 tells us that Christ being fully vested as Holy and True, having complete authority over all judgment. Unto the angel, or messenger of the church in Philadelphia write these things says He that is Holy, He that is True, He that has the key of David, He that opens and no man shuts; and what He shuts no man opens.

Praise and Acknowledgment

Revelation chapter 3:8 tells us that Christ found this little church of Philadelphia to be <u>Faithful</u>, <u>Holy</u>, and <u>True</u> in all their works. I know your works. Behold, I have set before you an open door, and no man can shut it. **Acts chapter 14:27** tells us that Christ opens a door of <u>faith</u> unto the Gentiles. **1 Corinthians chapter 16:9** tells us that a great door of effectual service was opened unto Paul, and there were many adversaries. Christ tells us that the church of Philadelphia had little strength and have kept His Word and have not denied His name. **Revelation chapter 14:12** tells us that here are the patience of the saints: here are they that keep the commandments of God, and the <u>faith</u> of Jesus.

Revelation chapter 3:9 tells us Christ will make them of the synagogue of Satan, which say they are Jews, and are not, but do lie; behold, I will make them to come and worship before your feet, and to know that I have loved you. **Isaiah chapter 60:14** tells us that the sons of them that afflicted you shall come bending unto you; and all they that despised you shall bow themselves down at the soles of your feet; and they shall call you, "The City of the Lord, The Zion of the Holy One of Israel."

Promise and Encouragement to Persevere

Revelation chapter 3:10 tells us that because you have kept the Word of My patience (holdfast) I also will keep you from the hour of temptation which shall come upon the world, to try them that dwell upon the earth. **2 Thessalonians chapter 3:5** tells us that Jesus will direct our hearts into the love of His Father, and into the patience of waiting for Him. **Revelation chapter 3:11-13** Christ reminds us to hold on: behold, I come quickly: holdfast to that which you have, that no man take your crown. He that overcome (holdfast) will I make a Pillar in the Temple of My God, and he shall not depart from it, and I will write upon him the name of My God, and the name of the City of My God, which is New Jerusalem, which is coming down out of heaven from My God: and I will write upon him My new name. He that has an ear let him hear what the Spirit says unto the churches.

Today, many churches are prophesying Christ as their Lord and Savior while holding onto the contemporary life of the world. Christ Remnant Church bears the fruit of the Holy Spirit, which is the Agape love of God, and Philia love toward one another. The Church of Philadelphia is the only church that met Christ requirements of being qualified to enter into His millennial Sabbath when He returns. Amen

The Church of Laodicea *1844–1928 AD*

The seventh letter to the church of Laodicea, which means: lukewarm. Antiochus II founded the city of Laodicea in third century *BC;* he named it after his wife Laodice. **Revelation chapter 3:14** Christ introduce Himself as the Amen, the Faithful and True Witness, the Beginning of the Creation of God. Unto the angel, or messenger of the church of Laodicea write these things says the Amen, the Faithful and True Witness, the Beginning of the Creation of God. **2 Corinthians chapter 1:20** tells us that Christ Who has made promises that are unchangeable, the Faithful and True Witness, the Beginning of the Creation of God. **John chapter 14:6** tells us that I Am the way, the truth, and the life: no one comes to the Father, but by Me.

Spiritual State of the Church

Christ knows our works, which is our faith in Him. **Revelation chapter 3:15,16** tells us I know your works that you are neither cold nor hot, I would rather you were cold or hot. So, because you are lukewarm, and neither cold nor hot, I will spit you out of My mouth. **Romans chapter 2:5-10** tells us that Jesus knows the deeds of everyone: righteous and unrighteous. Because of your unwillingness, and unrepentant heart, you have maximized evil against yourself for the day of condemnation, and revelation of the righteous judgment of God, Who will give to each person according to the deeds of his works. To those that persevere in doing good, seek for glory, and honor, and immortality, and eternal life. Condemnation will come upon the Jews first, and also upon the Gentiles, those who are self–seeking, and self–willed, and disobedient to the truth, and practice wickedness, there will be punishment, and vengeance, tribulation and extreme trials upon the soul of every man who practice doing evil. God is the one that rewards every man with glory, honor, and peace that do good, first the Jews, and also the Gentiles.

Correction, Counsel and Restoration

Revelation chapter 3:17-20 tells us that because you say, I am rich, and increased with goods and have no need of nothing; and know not that you are <u>wretched</u>, and <u>miserable</u>, and <u>poor</u>, and <u>blind</u>, and <u>naked</u>.

Even though the city of Laodicea water supply was tepid, they were at the apex of ease and laxity, because of their wealth in the black wool industry, and famous medical school for eye salve. Unlike the church of Sardis, Laodicea was completely defiled. Since, October of *2015*, the church began to recognize same sex marriage in many denominations. **Isaiah chapter 4:1** tells us that in the day of Judgment seven women, or seven churches will take hold of one man, which is our Lord and Savior Jesus Christ, saying, we will eat our own bread, which is to say, teach our own doctrine, and wear our own clothing, counterfeiting their own righteousness: only let us be called by Your name, to take away our shame. Today many churches, and church members are holding onto a form of godliness, although they have denied the true power of faith, which is Christ Jesus. **Revelation chapter 3:18-20** tells us that Christ counseled them to buy of Him gold tried in fire, that they may be rich, and white raiment that they may be clothed, whereby the shame of their nakedness is covered; and anoint their eyes with eye–salve that they may see. As many as I love, I rebuke and discipline. Therefore, be earnest, and repent. Hear I Am standing at the door knocking, if any man will hear My voice, and open the door, I will come in, and I will drink with him, and he with Me.

- True faith is gold tried in fire.
- Labor in love that you may be rich.
- Persevere in hope that you may be clothed in righteousness.
- Open your heart to the Holy Spirit and receive Christ's unconditional love.

Promise and Encouragement to Persevere

The final days are here: and Laodicea is the spiritual state of the churches. God's people are under the investigative judgment before Christ return: for we have a form of godliness, so that we may use Christ name to cover our sins. Furthermore, the churches are corrupt in doctrine, and righteousness. **Revelation chapter 18:1-4** tells us that John saw Christ coming down from heaven, having great power; and the earth was lightened with His glory. And He cried mightily with a strong voice, saying <u>Babylon the great is fallen, is fallen</u>, and has become the habitation of devils, and the jail for every evil spirit, and a prison for every unclean, and hateful bird. For all the nations drank of the wine of the wrath of her fornication, and the kings of the earth have committed fornication with her, and the merchants of the earth got rich through the abundance of her delicacies. And I heard another voice from heaven, saying, come out of her my people, and be not partakers of her plagues. **Revelation chapter 3:21,22** Christ reminds us to hold on: to him that overcome (holdfast) Christ will give the opportunity to sit with Him in His throne, even as Christ Himself also overcame, and sat down with His Father in His throne. He that has an ear let him hear what the Spirit says unto the churches. **John chapter 8:31,32** tells us that if we continue in His Word, we are His disciples indeed; and we shall know the truth, and the truth shall make us free. Today we are witnessing the end of grace, and the final hour of judgment of the world. My beloved brothers and sisters, I appeal to you one last time on the behalf of My Lord Jesus Christ that the end is near and the time for repentance is now; will you not heed to the last call for soul salvation? Behold, Christ come quickly. Amen

The First Resurrection, the Saved

Revelation chapter 12:7-12 tells us that there was war in heaven: and Michael, namely, Jesus Christ and His angels defended the throne of God against Lucifer, who became the dragon; namely Satan. And the dragon and his angels brought forth false accusations against God's divine Character, and prevailed not; neither was there place found for them anymore in heaven. And the great dragon was cast out, that old serpent, called the Devil, and Satan, which deceived the whole world: he was cast down to the earth and a third of the angels were cast out with him. And I heard a loud voice saying in heaven, "Now is salvation come, and strength, and the Kingdom of our God, and the power of Christ to rule: for the accuser of our brethren is cast down, which accused them before our God day and night. And they overcame him by the blood of the Lamb, and by the word of their testimony; and they feared not for their lives, but held onto their hope even unto death. Therefore let the angels of heavens rejoice, but woe to the inhabiters of the earth and of the sea! Because the devil has come down unto us, with rage and anger, knowing that he has but a short time.

Revelation chapter 12:13-17 tells us that during the dark ages Satan's agenda was to destroy the apostolic church. And when the dragon saw that he was cast onto the earth, he persecuted the woman, which is the remnant church that had given birth to the male child. And the woman was given two wings like a great eagle, so that she could fly into the wilderness: to a place were she would be nurtured for *1,260* years, away from the face of the serpent. And the serpent sent out a search party, which was like a flood to search for the woman and her offspring, but the earth opened her mouth, and swallowed up the people that the dragon sent to kill the woman and her child. The dragon is still angry with the woman for giving birth to the remnant church, which is Christ Himself, and he wants to destroy those who keep the commandments of God, and have the testimony of Jesus Christ.

The Remnant Church of Philadelphia started in *1755—1844*, where Christ Himself was perfected on the third day. **Luke chapter 13:32** tells us that Jesus said unto them, Go and tell Satan, behold, I cast out devils, and I do cures today, and tomorrow, and the third day I shall be perfected. Philadelphia received the sixth letter from Christ Himself, being Faithful, Holy, and True, in all their works. The Church of Philadelphia reached its perfection in *1844* as Jesus had prophesied.

Now that the evidence has been revealed against Satan that he is the deceiver, and a liar, all bets are off. The destruction of the devil is certain; God's Word cannot return void. The serpent has prepared himself for destruction, to be burnt to ashes. Are you prepared to join him in his defeat? I hope not, Jesus made it possible for you and I to escape damnation, and the fiery pits of hell. Accepting Christ invitation is by choice; He will not force us to accept His invitation. However, the alternative is scorching, blistering, blazing, red–hot. The lava pit at the center of the earth has been boiling for about *5,990* years, and soon it will be ready to receive those who have accepted Satan as their lord and executioner. **Revelation chapter 20:1-3** tells us that Christ Who holds the key to all things came down from heaven, having the key of the bottomless pit, and a great chain in His hand. And He laid hold on the dragon, that old serpent, which is the devil, and Satan, and bound him for a thousand years. Furthermore, he is cast into the bottomless pit, and Christ shut him up, and set a seal upon him, so that he could not deceive the nations no more, and after the thousand years is fulfilled: the devil must be loosed for a season.

The one thousand years, which is the millennial Sabbath is spent with Christ in heaven going over the books of the names of the unrighteous. **Revelation chapter 20:4-7** tells us that John saw thrones, and they that sat upon them God gave the authority to judge. And I saw the souls of them that were beheaded for the witness of Jesus, and for the Word of God, and which had not worshipped the beast, neither his image, nor received his mark upon their foreheads, or in their hands; and they lived and reigned with Christ a thousand years, this is the first resurrection. Blessed and Holy is he that has part in the first resurrection: on such the second death have no power, but they shall be priests of God and of Christ, and shall reign with Him a thousand years. However, the wicked will remain in their graves for a thousand years. And after the thousand years expires, Satan shall be loosed out of his prison; and he shall go out to deceive. The question here is? Who is Satan deceiving at this point? Remember; blessed and Holy is he that has part in the first resurrection? Amen

The Second Resurrection, the Condemned

Revelation chapter 20:8-10 tells us that Satan shall go out to deceive the nations which are in the four quarters of the earth, to gather them for the battle of Gog and Magog, the number of whom is as the sand of the seashore. And they marched across the broad plain of the earth and surrounded the camp of God's people, and the beloved City. And fire came down from God out of heaven, and devoured them. And the devil that deceived them was cast into the lake of fire and brimstone, where the beast and the false prophet were; and they will be tormented day and night, forever and ever. **Revelation chapter 20:11-15** tells us about the judgment of the dead: those that are lost, this is <u>the second resurrection</u>. And I saw a great white throne, and Him that sat on it, from whose face the earth and sky fled away; and there was found no place for them. And I saw the dead, small and great, stand before God. And the <u>books</u> were opened: and another book was opened as well, which is the <u>book of life</u>. And the <u>dead</u> were judged out of those things, which were written in the books, according to their works. And the <u>sea</u> gave up the <u>dead</u>, who were in it; and <u>death</u> and <u>hell</u> delivered up the <u>dead</u>, who were in them: and they were judged everyone according to their works. And <u>death</u> and <u>hell</u> were cast into the lake of fire. This is the <u>second death</u>. And whosoever was not found written in the <u>book of life</u> was cast into the lake of fire.

The lake of fire was designed to destroy sin. God had no intention of destroying any of His creation, not even Lucifer. However, if God allow sin to reign forever, He wouldn't be a just God. The close of probation is the end of mercy and grace for those who decided to follow Satan. It was never God's will that any should perish, but rather to be saved. As we draw closer to the end, it's obvious that something is wrong, and the unbelievers are in turmoil. They have lost all hope, and look to place blame on Christ's remnant church of Philadelphia. **Revelation chapter 14:8** tells us that there followed another angel, saying, 'Babylon is fallen, is fallen, that great city, because she made all the nations drink of the wine of the wrath of her fornication. This indicates that Satan's empire has come to an end, and Christ will reign forever and ever. Amen

Imagine with me for a second that you are completely deceived by what you know! Who can you trust? What if everything that you know about life is false, because the information that was given unto you came from someone who was clueless about the truth? **2 Thessalonians chapter 2:4** tells us that the man of sin blasphemes the name of God, whereby revealing himself as the son of perdition: who opposes, and exalts himself above all that is called God, or that is worshipped; so that he pretending to be God sits in the temple of God, showing himself deceitfully that he is God. **Psalm chapter 2:1-12** tells us that while the urge for promiscuity and self-indulgence heightens, the people imagine a vain thing, and the leaders of the earth take counsel together against the Lord, and against His anointed, saying, Let us break their commandments, and laws, and do away with their teachings. But God Who sits in the heavens will laugh. For the Lord shall have them in distress, and then He will speak unto them in His wrath, and vex them in His sore displeasure. For there is only one ruler, and I have set Him upon My Holy Mount Zion. And I will declare My law, says the Lord. For the Lord your God said unto Me, You are My Son, and this day have I declared You a ruler; ask of Me, and I will give unto You the people of the earth for Your inheritance, and the uttermost parts of the hills, and valleys for Your possession. You may beat them with the rod of iron, and break them in pieces like a potter's vessel. To the leaders, and rulers of the earth, I give you counsel: observe the commandments of your God, and fulfill His laws. Hear My instructions, serve the Lord with humility, and rejoice with praise. Give tribute to the Son, for He is the way of salvation, for the wrath of God is justice, and blessed are all they that put their trust in Him. Amen

The Lord's Prophecy Concerning Nineveh

Nahum chapter 1:2-9 tells us that God is jealous, and His anger burns with fury. The Lord will take vengeance on His adversaries. His wrath is reserved for His enemies. The Lord is slow to anger, and mighty in power, and He will not set the wicked free. The Lord has control over the winds, and storms, and the clouds are the dust of His feet. He rebukes the sea, and dries it up; He also dries up all the rivers. Bashan, and Carmel wither, and the flower of Lebanon fade. The mountains quake before Him, the hills melt, and the earth trembles at His presence, even the world, and all who dwell in it. Who can stand before His indignation? Who can endure His fierce anger? Therefore as the Lord's fury is poured out like fire, and the rocks melt like butter. Remember that the Lord is good, and we have refuge in the day of trouble; and He knows those who trust in Him. But with an overflowing flood, He will make an utter end of His enemies, and darkness will pursue them. What do you conspire against the Lord? He will make an utter end of it. Affliction will not rise up a second time. Hallelujah! Hallelujah! Hallelujah! Hallelujah! Hallelujah! Hallelujah! Hallelujah! Praise God! Amen

Revelation chapter 22:18-21 tells us that Jesus Christ testify unto every man that hear the words of the prophecy of this book, if any man shall add unto these things, God shall add unto him the plagues that are written in this book: and if any man shall take away from the words of the book of this prophecy, God shall take away his part out of the book of life, and out of the Holy City, and from the things which are written in this book, He Who testifies these things, says, surely I come quickly. Amen. So even I, come, the Lord Jesus. The grace of our Lord Jesus Christ is with you all. Amen

The Decalogue of the Written Law

The written law reveals the common state of the human heart. Over six hundred plus rules were given unto Moses for the Jewish nation to live by. If we were to keep the law today, the population would be down to zero. For it would be impossible for us to keep the law without the indwelling of the Holy Spirit. Was the law done away with? God forbid! The only thing that was done away with is the method of how we keep the law. When the law was first appointed unto mankind, it was placed upon his heart to do the Lord's will. However, after he disobeyed the separation between him and His Creator destroyed the moral law, which was written upon his heart. The Character and disposition of Jesus Christ is what we hope for! Furthermore, our present condition is sinful; and our personality is lacking self-control.

Character perfection is achieved through prayer, whereby we pray without ceasing: giving God thanks, and study His Word. Surrendering to the Holy Spirit moment-by-moment is the biggest challenge for any believer. Our personalities are opposing to the law of faith, and will only manifest the pride of life, if not nurtured and perfected by the Holy Spirit. He that lacks the fruit of the Spirit also falls short when it comes to having the disposition of Jesus Christ.

Most unbelievers who are presumed to be in love *(Eros)* they are completely deceived by the devil. Have you ever been around people who enjoy drinking alcoholic beverages, took drugs and smoke, but yet their relationship seems to be fine otherwise? Well don't be persuaded by the appearance of their colorful attitude that they are happy. The devil has many sedated under his influence to the point were it is impossible for them to tell the difference between good and evil. **1 Corinthians chapter 7:1-16** tells us that if you find peace in Jesus Christ and you do get married, most likely you will have trouble in your relationship, because the devil sees it as a threat and will use every means necessary to oppress you and your spouse.

The complexity of sin goes beyond human comprehension. Sin is a supernatural force of evil working against righteousness to fulfill unrighteousness. The world is divided into two categories: believers and unbelievers both groups working simultaneously to accomplish their master's will. Jesus refers to them as tares and wheat. The tares are very similar to the wheat with the exception of the fruit being produced. **Matthew chapter 7:16** tells us that you shall know them by their fruits.

However, the agenda of the wheat is to glorify God in everything that is done under the sun. As Jesus Christ preached repentance and made disciples of men and women, it is the same commission today as it was when He walked the earth almost two thousand years ago. The church of Christ seeks no reward, but hope for an eternal life, meanwhile the false church agenda is here and now!

The mark of the beast is viewed as principalities, and powers of darkness, and evil in high places fulfilling the unrighteousness of Satan's political agenda. World leaders have united themselves with the Prince of darkness to further their own selfish desires. History has revealed unto us that in the past Babylon was the first of ten kingdoms that ruled the earth for a period of time. And Rome would become the final earthly kingdom. After Constantine became Emperor, he legalized Christianity, whereby the reign of Papal Rome began in the year *538–1798 AD*, where Napoleon defeated Pope Pius and His troops. **Daniel chapter 7:23-27** tells us that Christians suffered for twelve hundred and sixty years during the dark ages. Papal Rome means: Papa or father, the words of a child to his biological father. **Matthew chapter 23:9** tells us call no man your father upon the earth: for one is your Father, which is in Heaven. Who should we believe, Christ or mankind?

The tower of Babel became the symbol of the Babylonians, whereby the infrastructure of the pyramid and its greatness became the movement of the people and the worshiping of the beast and it's image. The image of the great pyramid can be seen on the back of the American dollar bill as it stood for greatness centuries ago. **Genesis chapter 11:2-4** tells us that as they journeyed from the east, they found a plain in the land of Shinar, also called Mesopotamia; and they dwell there. And they said one to another, let us make brick, and burn them thoroughly. And they had brick for stone, and slime for cement. And they said, Come now and let us build a city and a tower, whose top may reach unto the heaven; and let us make a name for ourselves, less we will be scattered abroad upon the face of the whole entire earth. **Revelation chapter 14:9-11** tells us that a third angel followed them, saying with a loud voice, "If any man worship the beast and his image, and receive his mark in his forehead, or in his hand, the same shall drink of the wine of the wrath of God, which is poured out without mixture into the cup of His indignation; and those that have accepted the mark of the beast shall be tormented with fire and brimstone in the presence of the Lamb: and the smoke of their torment ascends up forever and ever, and they have no rest day or night, who worship the beast and his image, and whosoever receives the mark of his name.

Since the great controversy was about dominion of the earth, after Adam sinned, the devil took control of the earth, whereby he has placed his principalities upon the human heart. **Revelation chapter 13:1,2** tells us that John saw a multitude of people in his vision, which were like the sand of the sea. And also a country rising up, having seven political leaders serving in the seat of the dragon, and they have great influence over ten countries, and they all committed blasphemy. And the countries which he saw one had great speed like a leopard, and another the strength of a bear, and the third the roar of a lion: and the dragon gave them his power, and his seat, and great authority.

The leopard, the bear, and the lion are three different countries with one agenda for globalism. The merger of all religions and countries is the on going work of the beast to achieve supremacy over the entire world. Science and technology has become the vehicle for exhibiting growth and stability; meanwhile promoting a false sense of comfort to those that find pleasure in the world. **Revelation chapter 13:11-14** tells us that John saw another country rising up out of a diversity of people; and it had two horns like a baby lamb, but he spoke like a dragon, and he exercised all the power of the first beast that was before him, and he influenced all the people that dwell on the earth to worship the first beast, whose deadly wound was healed. And he preformed great wonders by making fire to come down from the sky on the earth in the sight of men. And deceive them that dwell on the earth by the means of those celebrations, which he had the power to do in the sight of the first beast, saying to them that dwell on the earth that they should make an image to the first beast, which had the wound by a sword, and did live.

The celebration of independence–day is a worldwide affair in the sense of globalism and socialism, they all have the same political agendum. Ideology began with Lucifer who was self–seeking and wanted to create his own kingdom. Since the fall of mankind ideology has enslaved one group of people, meanwhile the other group lives a life of luxury. The traditions of man has replaced the laws and commandments of God by means of which they have changed the day of worship, and cause all, both small and great, rich and poor, free and bond to receive the mark of the beast by putting their trust in theories that are far from the truth. After Constantine the great was put into office, he legalized Sunday as the official day of rest, whereby Catholicism became the image of Rome on March *7, 321 AD.*

133

Today, Catholicism is one of the largest multicultural religions around the world. **Revelation chapter 13:18** tells us that here is wisdom, let him that have understanding count the number of the beast: for it is the number of a man; and his number is six hundred and sixty-six. King James authorized the printing of the Bible, whereby fulfilling the prophecy of Revelation. He was born during the sixth month, in the year fifteen sixty-six. He made the Bible into a sacramental instrument: The Holy Bible. Today, many believers have placed the Bible above faith; and not realizing that God gave man the benefit of freedom, and free-will, and judgment in all things to worship Him that sat upon the throne of David. And at some point both man, and beast (Satan) will have to give an account to their Creator when they meet face to face.

Christianity is the seal of our righteousness in Him that was raised from the dead. True faith is the work of the Holy Spirit, the redemption of Jesus Christ Who gives us hope in knowledge, and wisdom, and peace, and salvation to come. And even though we can't predict the future, if we choose to have a relationship with Him, our salvation is sure. The Character and disposition of Jesus Christ is the reward of everyone who believes in Him; whereby the believer becomes more and more like his Creator, meanwhile the mark of the beast is the seal of unrighteousness, which will plunge the unbeliever into eternal darkness by becoming as one with the devil.

The pyramid movement involves the merger of people, countries, and religions under the rule of the false church, whereby church and state becomes one. The tower of Babel was the landmark of Satan's pyramid reign of terror and destruction. Our victory over sin came at such a high price that our dear Lord and Savior Jesus Christ had to come down from heaven to pay the penalty for our sins with His own life. Now that the merger is complete, and the stage is set for the devil's plan; we can look forward to the rise of a new campaign against God, but this time it would bring a false sense of security to many whose probation has long been closed.

The Left Behind Series, Once Saved Always Saved, and the Secret Rapture are just a few of many false doctrines that are opposing to where Christ calls the church to witness to the world on His behalf. Living life apart from Christ is common and salvation has become somewhat of a myth: making it much easier for the beast to captivate the focus of the people by lowering the standards of Christianity and the Sabbath to Sunday sacredness. Sun worshiping was the pitch point of paganism, namely Satan's church; whereby people who are closed-minded are led to believe a false sense of comfort and security about what's behind the scenes of the United Nations.

Globalism will only benefit those that are considered to be rich. Slavery is consistent throughout the reign of mankind. The laborer has no financial wealth of his own, but exist only to serve those who have no intent of rewarding him with a piece of the pie. Slavery was designed to keep the unsuspecting believer and unbeliever consumed with the cares of the world. Most people don't realize that faith is above material gain; for without faith no one can please God. **Isaiah chapter 1:13** tells us bring no more vain oblations; incense is an abomination unto Me; the new moons and Sabbaths, the calling of assemblies, I take no pleasure in them; it is sin, even the solemn meeting.

Even though one religion differs from another; religion apart from Christ has neither purpose nor value. Religions, cultures and denominations are alike; they separate people into groups, and label them as benefactors of racism and prejudicial opinions, which provides no spiritual growth. Religions have become one of the most seductive and manipulative ideas since the deception of Eve in the Garden of Eden. False religion is the vehicle for transporting lies, and promoting false doctrines as truth. Hypocrisy is the on going work of the unclean spirits, which came out of the mouths of the false prophets; whereby the false church is persistently pretending to hold unbelief as prophecy. Jesus Christ is the true Church, and He is the author of faith, and belief, and love, and hope in His eternal salvation to come.

Multicultural religions are detrimental to the spiritual growth of Christian, especially since they don't share the same doctrinal truth about soul salvation. As faith is the pathway to righteousness in Christ: according to God's will, mercy, and grace. The traditions of man are the avenues of death by the lawlessness of sin. **Proverbs chapter 14:12, 16:25** tells us that there is a way that seems right unto a man; but the end thereof is the ways of death.

Religion states that there are many paths unto god by means of which deceiving the unsuspecting believer into thinking that the law of the Sabbath was changed from the Seventh Day. The worshiping of the sun god was established through Nimrod the mighty hunter, whereby sexual immorality was the theme of Sodom and Gomorrah. Nimrod was influenced by the devil out of the act of rebellion. Satan purposely substituted the Seventh Day of worship, which God had commanded. **Genesis chapter 1:5-9** tells us that the days of the week are numbered vertically from evening to evening. **Genesis chapter 2:3** tells us that God blessed the Seventh Day, and sanctified it. **Acts chapter 20:6,7** Paul wrote, after the days of unleavened bread we left Philippi and after five days we arrive in Troas, we stayed the total of seven days. And upon the first day of the week, the disciples came together to break bread, Paul preached unto them, until it was time to depart the following day; he continued his speech until midnight. The breaking of bread was customary and had nothing to do with the changing of the Sabbath. Nowhere in these verses was a command given to change the Sabbath. Further more Paul did not have the power to change the law of the Sabbath, or else he would have made the spiritual gift of God's rest void. What does this mean for those who participate in this deceitful act? If your religion doesn't provide any evidence of faith, mercy and judgment, it is worthless! Why then make long–term commitments to something that doesn't work? **James chapter 5:16** tells us that we should confess our faults one to another, and pray one for another, that we may be healed. The intercession of a benevolent prayer of a righteous man has tremendous power.

Religion wasn't designed for the glory of man, but instead unto his destruction. Religion was formulated to rebel against the true form of worship by promoting spiritualism within the hip–hop community as a guarantee for success. Many believe that they have earned the right to go to heaven. **1 Peter chapter 5:8** tells us that Satan has reached his plateau, and we have to be sober and vigilant, because our adversary is as a roaring lion, roaming about, seeking whom he may devour. The dragon knowing that he has but a short period of time, before the fulfillment of the Lord's prophecy; he is now using every means necessary as a tool of deception to merge churches and states to supremacy: whereas the natural law replaces the moral law, and salvation becomes pro–choice, instead of pro–life.

Faith and salvation is the work of the Holy Spirit, whereby our hope and moral values are centered on God, but on the contrary the pilgrimage of the church has swept the faith of our Lord and Savior Jesus Christ beneath the welcoming mats to make way for the new hip–hop version of Sodom and Gomorrah. Evidently it's only a matter of time before we are face to face with the dark ages that once was in the medieval centuries. The merger of churches and states will enable Satan to have authority over the doctrine being preached, whereby the true protestant will have no legal rights apart from the church and state; it's where legalism replaces liberty, and bondage becomes pro–choice.

The Sinner is without Excuse

The shedding of Christ's blood was for the forgiveness of our sin, which brought forth peace and righteousness unto all who accepts Him as their Lord and Savior. However, with the present condition of the church, how does one go about finding pure religion? The Holy Spirit came from God the Father to revive the individual, and not the physical church, which has become the home of moneychangers and those that sold doves. The revival of the church needs not faith, but obedience unto the Word that was preached at the beginning. The evidence of true faith is living by faith, whereby the whole church body becomes one, even as Christ and the Father are one. Amen

The Holy Spirit rain on the just, and the unjust alike. You don't have to believe me; lets take a closer look at those who are excommunicated from God, but yet prosper in material abundance. **Psalm chapter 73:1-28** tells us that God did great things in Israel, especially to those that are righteous in heart, but as for me, I stumbled, and my feet slipped. I became envious of the foolish when I saw the prosperity of the wicked; their burdens are few and their strength is firm. They are not in trouble like other men, neither are they plagued like other men. Therefore pride surrounds the wicked like a chain, and violence cover them like a garment; their eyes bulge out with lust. And even though they have more than anyone's heart could desire, they speak wickedly against God, and with their mouths they lay claim to the earth and seek to oppress the poor, they are corrupt. Therefore God's people are forced out into the cold, for the wicked have consumed more than their fair share; and out of guilt they will say, how does God know? Is there knowledge in the Most High? The ungodly people prosper in the world, and increase in riches continually.

I tried to purge my heart of vanity, but it was impossible for me to overcome on my own. I face the same satanic snares daily; and even though I am convicted of my faults, I dare not speak openly, because people would judge me as a sinner. And when I tried to understand it on my own, it was too complex for me. It wasn't until I went into the house of God; then I understood the end of the wicked. Surely God did set them up for a fall, they're destroyed by their own evil imaginations due to the lack of discernment. The unbelievers are brought into desolation within a moment, and in the end they're completely consumed by fire. O Lord how You have despised their foolish ways. And now my heart is grieved with sorrow, because I was foolish and ignorant: my understanding was that of an infant. Nevertheless, You kept me upright by holding my right hand; You guided me with Your counsel, and afterward receive me into Your glory. Whom do I have to thank, but You O Lord. And there is none upon the earth that I desire beside You. My own strength and knowledge fell short, but God is the strength of my heart and my salvation forever. For indeed those who are far from You shall perish. You have destroyed all those who have deserted You for material gain, but it is good for me to draw near unto You. I have put my trust in the Lord God, that I may declare all Your works. Amen

Hollywood has exhausted every possibility of pleasure and desire known to this world. However, many will tell you that they are simply not satisfied. Now that self–worth has been diminished to hopelessness. Many have come to the conclusion that a marriage between a man and woman is monotonous; meanwhile hooking up for a one–nightstand is more romantic than long–term commitments, whereby family planning is simplified by latex–condoms, morning pills, or worst yet an abortion. We now view life from a balcony with despair, as pride becomes the price of death by sin.

How does one overcome oppression, and stop pride from consuming our inner peace and joy? It's very simple, we have to want to acknowledge Jesus Christ as the Creator of creation, and build a positive relationship with Him that is pure and genuine from the heart. Life isn't a burden for those who exercise faith in Christ. **Matthew chapter 11:28** tells us that Christ is calling us, saying, Come unto Me, all who labor and are heavily burden, and I will give you rest.

Spiritual oppression will overcome those who have allowed their hope and moral values to be capsized like a sinking ship. The rejection of the Holy Spirit becomes hopelessness, and from thereon the practicing of sin leads to the close of probation. Soul salvation is from faith to faith, and from glory to glory for those whom God foreknew from the foundation of the earth; He also predestinated them to be transformed into the Image of His only begotten Son. The gospel is a worldwide ministry that is being preached unto the entire world for repentance. However, many believers find it difficult to stay vigilant in these last days. **Matthew chapter 25:1-13** tells us that the Kingdom of heaven is viewed as ten virgins that went out with their lamps to meet the bridegroom. And five were wise, and five were foolish. They that were foolish took their lamps, and took no oil with them: but the wise took oil in their vessels with their lamps. However, while the bridegroom tarry all the virgins got drowsy and slept.

But while they slept, the Son of man came calling at midnight, and then they all arose and trimmed their lamps and went out to meet Him. Then the foolish said unto the wise, give us some of your oil, for our lamps are gone out. But the wise answered, no, there will not be enough for you and us, but rather go and buy from them that sell for yourselves. And while they went to buy, the bridegroom came; and they that were ready went in with Him to the marriage: and the door was shut. Afterward came also the other virgins, saying, Lord, Lord, open unto us. But, He answered and said, I tell you the truth, I know you not. Watch therefore, for you know neither the day nor the hour wherein the Son of man will come.

Romans chapter 3:19-21 tells us that whatsoever things are mentioned in the Bible, it only applies to those who are without a clean conscience, so that every mouth would be silent, and the entire world is held accountable in front of God. Therefore by the observing of the written law, no one will be justified in the sight of the Lord: for by the knowledge of the written law sin was made known. However, the righteousness of God is manifested through faith, which Moses and His prophets bear witness. **1Timothy chapter 1:8-10** tells us that the written law is good, if a man uses it lawfully, and also knowing that the law was not made for the righteous man: but for the lawless, and disobedient, for the ungodly, and for sinners, for the unholy, and profane, for murderers of fathers, and murderers of mothers, for manslayers, for whoremongers, for those which defile themselves with mankind, for kidnappers, for liars, for perjured persons, and if there be any other thing that is opposing to the Agape love of God.

Romans chapter 1:16-32, 2:1 tells us that the apostle Paul is not ashamed of the gospel of Jesus Christ: for it is the power of God unto salvation to everyone that believes. God made Himself known unto the Jewish nation first, then also unto the rest of the world. The righteousness of God is revealed from faith to faith: as it is written, the righteous shall live by faith. The righteousness of God's judgment is revealed from heaven against all ungodly men, who suppress the truth with unrighteousness. God revealed Himself unto mankind and gave them a conscience; whereby even the invisible things are clearly understood by the creation of the world, even God the Father, Jesus Christ the Son and the power of His Holy Spirit: so that we are without excuse. Simply, because when mankind knew God face to face they glorified Him not as God, neither were they thankful; but became vain in their imaginations and their foolish hearts were darkened, pretending to be wise, they became fools and changed the glory of the incorruptible God into an image made in the likeness of a corruptible man, and to birds, and four footed animals, and creeping insects. Therefore God also gave them over to uncleanness, and with the lusts of their own hearts, they dishonor their own bodies between themselves: who changed the truth of God into a lie, and worshipped and served the creature more than the Creator, Who is blessed forever. Amen

Therefore, God allowed them to pursue their own desires, and eventually their women did change their natural features into that which is against nature, and also the men leaving the natural purpose of the woman, burning with lust one toward another; men having sex with men doing that which is inappropriate and receiving unto themselves the penalty of death which was due. Even up until today humanity has made a choice to turn away from the truth of their own conscience not wanting to retain God in their hearts.

Therefore, God gave them over to a degenerate mind to do those things which are not acceptable; being filled with all unrighteousness: fornication, wickedness, covetousness, maliciousness, envy, murder, debate, deceit, violence, gossip, slanderers, haters of God, despiteful, proud, boasters, inventors of evil things, disobedient to parents, without understanding, covenant breakers, without natural affection, impossible to appease, unmerciful. Who knowing that the judgment of God is against those who commit such unlawful things are worthy of death, not only do the same, but have pleasure in those who participate in the same acts as well. Therefore you are inexcusable, O man, whosoever you are that is pointing the finger at another: for wherein you have judged another, you have condemn yourself, because while you are accusing someone else, you are guilty of doing the same things also.

2 Timothy chapter 3:1-5 tells us that the last days will become perilous. For men will become lovers of their own selves: covetous, boasters, proud, haters of the true living God, disobedient to parents, unthankful, unholy, without natural affection, money lovers, trucebreakers, accusers, sexual immorality, fierce, despisers of those that do good, traitors, high minded, lovers of pleasure more than lovers of God; having a form of godliness on the outward appearance, but denying the power of the Holy Spirit from within: from such a person withdraw yourself. Amen

The Seventh Day slogan isn't as mindboggling as many people would find hard to believe. The proclamation of the Seventh Day Advent of Jesus Christ is the teachings of the Bible. Many professing to be of Christ: In whom the Character and Image of God was not found. William Miller, a local Baptist minister who started the Millerites movement in the year *1782-1849 AD*. And after his proclamation of the coming of Christ did not happen in *1843*, according to the *1,335* days prophecy in the book of Daniel. This would mark and remain as the great disappointment. However, Ellen G. White and former student of William Miller has done more work spreading the gospel than her former teacher. Ellen G. White is the founder of the Seventh Day Adventist church, and she was inspired by the Holy Spirit to share many testimonial beliefs of faith, which I do support one hundred percent, as it is proven by the Bible to be Christ infallible truth.

However, somewhat differs from Protestant churches in many aspects. Unfortunately, even though Seventh Day Adventism focuses on the life, and journey of Christ to the cross were He became the sacrificial Lamb: the blueprint of faith, love, and hope; many church members have their faith centered on Saturday as the Seventh Day Sabbath, instead of Christ Himself Who is the true Sabbath, and will return during the millennial Sabbath. **Genesis chapter 2:1-3** tells us that the Sabbath was given unto the entire human race. Therefore, the heavens and the earth were finished, and all the host of them. And on the Seventh Day God ended His work, which He had made; and He rested on the Seventh Day from all His work, which He made. And God blessed the Seventh Day, and sanctified it: because that in it He had rested from all His work, which God created and made. This points to the future, simply because the Holy Spirit is working, and God is not resting.

The true Adventist faith, and belief is centered on Christ Who is Lord of the Seventh Day Sabbath, which is Christ righteousness by faith. The Holy Spirit plays a pivotal role in the preparation of the church, and the return of our Lord and Savior Jesus Christ according to the Word of God. The one–day, one thousand year prophecy is the fulfillment of the entire Bible, and also the movement of true Seventh Day Adventism to further personify the faith of the believer who wants to know more about Christ and His retroactive work, which is the fullness of the ministerial work of His Holy Spirit upon the human soul.

Many will abandon their cross at the end; leaving the Adventist faith in pursuit of another, whereby finding themselves facing hardship, because of their unwillingness to surrender to the Holy Spirit by means of which, cherishing pride, and lacking the spiritual discernment of the church's true identity and purpose of the gospel, which Christ Himself will reward everyone when He comes in His glory according to His Word concerning discipleship and witnessing to the world. They that have renounce their faith and made themselves dis–fellowship or excommunicated from the Adventist faith will become Christ greatest adversaries at the end, doing that which is opposing to the gospel of truth, whereby becoming accusers like the devil, sowing discord among the brethren from such withdraw yourselves! Fellowship, and discipleship goes hand–in–hand. Church members should build relationships through Christ Agape love, so that we may bring the fruit of the Spirit unto God by loving our neighbors as ourselves. This is true Sabbath keeping, which Christ Himself manifested at the cross for everyone that believes. Amen

Jesus Protested against Legalism

Matthew chapter 11:28-30 tells us that Jesus spoke these words, so that in Him, the captive might be set free. Come unto Me, all who labor and are heavily burden, and I will give you rest. Take up My work and learn of Me, for I Am gentle and kind in heart: and you will have peace of mind. My requirements are easy, so that your load may be lightened. Sometime during the Sabbath day, Jesus and His disciples were hungry, so they went through the cornfield and began to pluck the ears of corn to eat, but when the Pharisees saw it, they said unto Him, behold, Your disciples do that which is not lawful to do on the Sabbath day.

The Pharisees had no righteousness apart from Christ, and besides plucking and eating corn on the Sabbath wasn't a sin. As long as the Holy Spirit is leading us, we are justified. Sin only occurs when the Holy Spirit is rejected, which leads to blasphemy. Legalism doesn't make us righteous, and no one has the right to rebuke except the Holy Spirit. However, instructions that are given unto a brother out of unconditional love, is an acceptable way of teaching those who are in need of reproof. Righteousness by faith is the indwelling of the Holy Spirit. Those that presume to be righteous apart from Christ falls into legalism, and should be seen as closed-minded and the truth of His unfailing love isn't in their hearts. No one has the power neither to condemn, nor to forgive sinners of their sins except the Father in heaven. The false church is viewed as a sacramental instrument that has a caste endowed with priestly power to grant pardon to the sinner upon request; meanwhile the state will issue a license for same sex marriages to justify those who have accepted the mark of the beast. The only person that is above the church is Christ; His unconditional love can be seen in those that have the indwelling of the Holy Spirit. Faith and hope is transpired through the Agape love of God, which is poured out upon all who believes.

The fulfillment of marriage between a man and a woman, need not the consent of the church or state. Martin Luther who started the Protestant Reformation saw the danger of being subservient to the church. Today's social ministry has the same dramatic influence on the people, as did the godfathers of music, who started rock n' roll in the late forties, but didn't hit peak until the late seventies; whereby the clergy's job is to make promises that he himself can't fulfill. However, regardless of how sincere it may sound when preached from the podium, if the Holy Spirit isn't given access, the divine nature of God's Image and Character will not be reproduced in the hearts of new believers.

Spiritualism has crossover to a more seductive social media, and has become one of the most effective gateways to hell. I quote: the ushering of the Baptism Eucharist Ministry document unto all churches, which indicates a convergence in a sacramental and clerical direction, which is opposite to the direction in which the gospel calls the church as a witness to the world. And that this ecumenical document centers the faith, communion and Christian witness not on God and the gospel, but rather on the church as a sacred structure that has and gives guarantees of the spirit's actives through a caste endowed with priestly power, mediatorial and representing the divine.

The purpose of the Baptist Eucharist Ministry document is to change the church worship format, and merge all churches together as one: Christian and non-Christian alike. The 1982 Lima Peru agreement, and merger of churches, and religions involves: Eastern Orthodox, Oriental Orthodox, Roman Catholic, Old Catholic, Lutheran, Anglican, Reformed Methodist, United Disciples, Baptist, Adventist, and Pentecostal. To find out more details: see world council of churches.org

Now that the integration of the world is completed, the expression, go along to get along comes to mind. By choosing to observe the traditions of man over Christianity we have made the commandments of God void, whereby putting ourselves at risk of not finding inner peace and joy. Faith and salvation is centered on Christ, and not of our own observation. Now these three: politics, science, and religion bears witness to the world and the son of perdition. The world justifies sin; meanwhile the Word reproves the sinner. Today the rise of abortions, diseases, suicides, terrorism, and natural disasters are at the equivalence of Sodom and Gomorrah. More than two thirds of the population believes in the world, instead of the Word. Imagine 7.1 billion people living their lives apart from Christ. Some of the most self–righteous people that I know don't believe in God. And you might say, so what, aren't they entitled to their own opinions? However, the recommendation for the rapist and the murderers isn't as clear when it comes to justifying sin. For if the ungodly is justified in his own ways, then sin is natural and it should go unpunished. **Proverbs chapter 8:36** tells us that he who sins against Christ condemns his own soul: all who hate Me loves death.

The plan of salvation is presented to the rich and poor alike, God has no respect unto persons. He only wants to save His creation from sin. God has done everything that is possible to save us from destruction; all we have to do is accept Christ as our Lord and Savior. As the scriptures of the Bible are changed to usher the new world order: the dragon fails to see his error; whereby it is the Word of God over the church, the believer standing on his own two spiritual feet. For it is the power of God, which fulfills the plan of salvation unto His Majestic glory.

Many false churches are willfully supporting the Babylonian system, and after knowing the fact that the kingdom of grace was first given unto the Jews, and then also unto the Gentiles. **John chapter 4:21-24** tells us that Jesus said to her, Woman, believe Me, the hour is coming when you neither worship the Father in this mountain, nor in Jerusalem. You worship, but you don't understand Whom you worship: but we know Whom we worship: for salvation was commissioned unto the Jews. The hour is coming, and it is already here, when the true worshipers will worship the Father in spirit and in truth: for the Father seek such to worship Him. God is a Spirit: and they that worship Him must worship Him in spirit and in truth.

By the time Christianity got to us, the deviations were night and day and had centuries of paganism written all over it. So we took the pieces that we like and throughout the Pentecostal rest of the Lord's Sabbath, and called it religion. **Matthew chapter 5:18-20** tells us that until heaven and earth is destroyed, not one jot of the pen or one drop of ink, will by any means change the law until all is fulfilled. Whosoever break the smallest commandment and teach others to do the same, he will be called the least in the kingdom of heaven: but whosoever will teach the commandments of God, he will be called great in the kingdom of heaven. For I say unto you, unless your righteousness exceeds the righteousness of the scribes and Pharisees, you will not enter into the kingdom of heaven.

Matthew chapter 23:15 tells us that we should beware of false teachers that are like the scribes and Pharisees, for they are hypocrites, they will travel land and sea to convert one person, but after that person is converted, he's twice the child of the devil, even more so, than the teacher himself. The devil has advocates everywhere doing his will, even until the very end. **Revelation chapter 17:8** tells us that the beast which John saw was chained for one thousand years, but after a thousand years he was set free for a moment, and he ascends out of the earth just before the end, and they that are a part of the second resurrection the ones who's names are not written in the book of life from the foundation of the world, they are the ones who will wonder after him, even at the very end.

The State of the Dead

The tragedies of life can be a heavy burden to bear: and without the acknowledgment of God, the mind can become overwhelmed with the cares of the world. Faith, hope, and love are the basic necessities that are needed in order for us to overcome the world. Jesus is the light of the world, and in every situation God is still in control. **Proverbs 25:2** tells us that it is the glory of God to conceal a thing, but the honor of kings is to search out the matter.

State of the dead is a life apart from Christ, meanwhile born–again is the indwelling of His Holy Spirit by means of which faith transforms the heart of the believer into a child of God. Everyone is born separated from God, and have a need for restoration. **Genesis chapter 4:7-9** tells us that Cain knew the will of God, but he did it not, and therefore God rejected his offering. Cain later became angry and envious of his brother Abel who pleased God, whereby his rebellion led him to murdering his brother, but soon after he had to face God.

The unconditional love of God can be seen in those that are of a pure heart, and of a good conscience. **1Timothy chapter 1:5-7** tells us that genuine empathy is the work of the Holy Spirit, which many have deviated from the truth to vain speculations. Many desiring to be teachers of the law, but understand not what they say, nor having anything to confirm the Spirit of the law.

The unbeliever conscience is seared: therefore he will never come to the conclusion that he needs to accept Christ before he dies, but instead the devil gives him a false sense of security in the world. **Isaiah chapter 57:1** tells us that the righteous dies, and no man understand the reason why, for even the merciful shall be taken away, but none consider that the righteous is taken away from the greater evil to come. Most people consider their love ones to be in heaven with Christ after they die, but the Bible indicates otherwise. **John chapter 3:13** tells us that no man has ascended up to heaven, but He that came down from heaven, even the Son of man, which is in heaven.

Acts chapter 2:34-35 tells us that David is not ascended into the heavens, but he said unto himself, the Lord said unto my Lord, sit here on my right hand until I make your enemies into your footstool. **Acts chapter 13:36** tells us that after David had served his own generation by the will of God, fell a sleep, and was laid with his forefathers, and his bones are still here with us until this very day. **Hebrews chapter 11:13** tells us that these all died in faith, not having received the promises, but having seen them from a distance, and were persuaded of them, and embraced them, and confessed that they were strangers and pilgrims on the earth. **Ecclesiastes chapter 9:5** tells us that the living knows that they will die, but the dead know not anything, neither have they any more reward, for the memory of them is forgotten.

Matthew chapter 22:23-32 tells us that the Sadducees believe not in the resurrection: therefore they went to Jesus, and asked Him, saying, Master, Moses said, if a man dies and he had no children with his wife, his brother should have her, so that the family name could be established through the child of his brother. Now there were seven brothers: and the first married a wife, and after he died having no children, he left his wife unto his brother, but likewise the second, and also the third, unto the seventh died. And finally the woman died also. Therefore in the resurrection whose wife shall she be of the seven? For they all had her. Jesus answered and said unto them, you do err, not knowing the scriptures, or the power of God. For in the resurrection they neither marry, nor are given in marriage, but are as angels of God in heaven, but as far as the resurrection of the dead is concern, have you not read in the scriptures that which was spoken unto you by God, saying, I Am the God of Abraham, and the God of Isaac, and the God of Jacob? God is not the God of the dead, but of the living. Amen

Once Saved Always Saved

The first person to loose their disposition was Lucifer, followed by Adam, who unlike Lucifer he repented. If once saved always saved, then why repent? God appointed the first King of Israel, but after he rebelled against God, he was rejected and his soul was lost, because he repented not. **1 Samuel chapter 15:22,23** tells us about obedience by faith, and how God rejected Saul from being King. And Samuel said, unto Saul the King of Israel, the Lord has no delight in burnt offerings and sacrifices; obeying the voice of the Lord is better than sacrifice, and obedience is better than the gifts of animals. Rebellion is the same as witchcraft, and unwillingness is like iniquity and having another god, and because you have rejected the Word of God, He also has rejected you from being King. **Hebrews chapter 6:4-6** tells us that it is impossible for those who were once enlightened, and have tasted the heavenly gift and are made partakers of the Holy Spirit, whereby having tasted the good Word of God, and the powers of the world to come, if they should fall away from righteousness, they would not be renewed again unto repentance; since they took it upon themselves to crucify the Son of God afresh, and put Him to an open shame. **2 Peter chapter 2:20-22** tells us that many will escape the addictions of sin, and the pollutions of the world through the knowledge of our Lord and Savior Jesus Christ. However, if they are again entangled with sin, and overcome by the seductions of the world, the final condition is worse than the beginning. For it had been better for them not to have known the way of righteousness, than after they have known it, to turn from the Holy Commandment delivered unto them. But it has happened unto many according to the true proverb, the dog has returned to his own vomit again; and the pig that was washed to her wallowing in the mud.

Matthew chapter 12:43-45 tells us that whenever a person overcomes an addiction he must give God the praise, and stay focus on Christ or else the addiction will return seven times greater than before. People who overcame sickness have to remember to stay away from the things, which made them sick in the first place. For when the unclean spirit is cast out of a man, he walks around on the earth seeking someone else to torment, and when his search becomes tiresome, he remembers the man, which he came out of, and return to find him unoccupied, so he take with him seven other evil spirits besides himself and they all enter into the man: and the last state of the man is worse than the first.

God wants us to stay focus on Him by staying in the Word moment–by–moment, praying without ceasing, and being watchful for the day of Jesus's return. Amen

The Secret Rapture

Is there a Secret Rapture? The Latin word Rapio means: snatch away or carried off. There are many different views on the Secret Rapture. However, its' not supported by the Bible. The Secret Rapture is presented to Christians and unbelievers as a safety net, whereas it protects the church from trials and tribulations at the end. **Deuteronomy chapter 29:29** tells us that the secret things belong unto the Lord our God: but those things, which are revealed, belong unto us and to our children forever, that we may do all the words of this law. The Bible doesn't support the theory of the Secret Rapture in the sense that the church will not face trials and tribulations. **Acts chapter 14:22** tells us that the Apostles preached the gospel unto many saying, that they should continue in the faith, and that we will face many tribulations before entering the kingdom of God. **Romans chapter 5:1-5** tells us that we are justified by faith, and we have peace with God through our Lord Jesus Christ: by Whom also we have access by faith into His grace wherein we stand, and rejoice in hope of the glory of God. And not only so, but we glory in tribulations also: knowing that God uses our tribulation to work patience; and patience experience; and experience hope: and hope covers our nakedness by removing our shame; whereby the Agape love of God is poured out into our hearts by the Holy Spirit. Amen

The Fear of the World

When I was a young boy nothing was more thrilling than to hear my grandfather telling stories about the traveling Gypsies, how they would show up unannounced in the middle of the night and disappear by dawn with everything that they could get their hands on. This brought fear unto the people that were living in the village. My grandfather at the time didn't have the full understanding of the tree of knowledge of good and evil.

In today's urban development where evil has reached its peak, and the suicidal death rate has been maximized to the equivalence of abortion. Random shootings amongst teens has become an epidemic and the highlight of the media and local newspapers around the globe. When one student was asked the question, why did he shoot his fellow classmates? He simply replied, the voices in my head told me to do it. The plea of insanity has been around since the beginning of sin. **Genesis chapter 4:6,7** tells us that the Lord spoke unto Cain, saying, why are you upset? And why the sad face? If you had done well, I would have accepted your sacrifice. But instead you disobeyed, and now sin is knocking at your door. And his desire is unto you, but you shall rule over him.

Personally, I am not the kind of person to admit in public that I can hear voices. A padded room and a straight jacket, meanwhile spending time in a loony–bin is not my idea of being comfortable. There are three inner voices that we can hear audible: the first voice is the retroactive conscience working from within, which is the work of the Holy Spirit to cultivate faith into a proactive mind, whereby our senses are subdued under the influence of the Holy Spirit. The second voice is self and rebellion, which quenches faith, and destroys the hope that we have in Christ Jesus. And the third voice is demonic agents working from within the shadows to merge and possess our deepest thoughts under the control of devils.

Modern technology has long replaced the ancient ways of communicating with the dead; whereas the diversity of mediums has become the seduction of evil: television, smart–phones, laptops, computers and other electronic devices are just a few ways for evil to manipulate the unsuspecting believer into satanic snares. Technology never ceases to amaze me, especially now that wireless devices are made abundant for our everyday convenience. Cellular phones are a thing of the past, now that the iPhone has made it easier to text while driving.

What does the iPhone represent? The eye of Horus is an ancient Egyptian symbol of the pyramid of protection, royal power and good health; also known as Wad–jet meaning: green or the green one, which dates back to Nimrod the mighty hunter who worshiped the evergreen tree known as the Christmas tree. Globalism has become the mainstream for the media, and going green is the message being preached unto those who have accepted the media as their source of information. The difference between information and knowledge is simply the source that it's coming from. God ordained knowledge unto salvation, whereas the media publicize information to generate fear and oppression. When was the last time that the media had anything good to report? As one reporter briefly stated in his broadcast, "It's the government's job to fabricate the news, and its mine to report it to the public." I can only assume that we have mastered the skill of communication since the Garden of Eden. **Genesis chapter 3:1** tells us that the serpent was more deceiving than any other beast of the field, which the Lord God had made. The serpent was more or less a messenger or agent of the devil, which was used as a medium to deceive Eve.

The word medium is ancient, whereas telecommunication is the outsource of the world; whereby television, telephones and smart devices are just a few ways in which Satan is using mainstream networks to further hasten the downfall of mankind. **Genesis chapter 3:1-3** tells us that the serpent said unto the woman, you know that God said; you shouldn't eat of every tree in the Garden. And the woman said unto the serpent, we may eat of the fruit of the trees of the Garden: but the fruit of the tree which is in the middle of the Garden, God said, we should not eat of it, neither should we touch it, lest we die. Have you ever noticed that the media never disclose the source of their information? The serpent needed leverage in order to tell a more convincing story to Eve, who was deceived.

The disobedience of our forefathers has become the sins of the third, and fourth generation. Furthermore, moral values are a thing of the past. Hip–hop has become the new trend amongst rebellious teens that are more concerned about fashion and accessories than self–control. Satan has influenced many into becoming prom queens, and movie stars. Humanity has lost their touch with reality by means of which success is centered on how low their pants sags below the crack of their butt cheeks. The urge for promiscuity and the appetite for self–indulgence has become a one–way street for those who have rejected the Word of God. The more conceited you are, the more fame and gratification you will receive from the world. The lack of self–control have consumed the lives of more men and women in the last decade than the combination of world war one and two. **2 Corinthians chapter 11:3** tells us that the serpent will use any means that he can find to deceive you as he did unto Eve through the seductions of your mind, whereby you would be led astray from your sincere devotion unto Christ.

Mediums are everywhere creating a mental and psychological breaking point, whereas the mind is held captive by means of which the senses are nurtured into rebellion. However, mediums don't necessarily have to be devices, but mediums can also be human agents working to fulfill the devils plan. **Matthew chapter 10:35,36** tells us that Christ came to reveal the truth unto us, that apart from Him our love for each other is fake: a man against his father, and the daughter against her mother, and the daughter-in-law against her mother-in-law. And a man's enemy will be those of his own family. **Luke chapter 22:31,32** tells us that Jesus said, Simon, Simon, Satan desire to have you, that he may sift you like wheat, but I have prayed for you that your faith fail not: and when you are converted, strengthen your brethren. **Isaiah chapter 1:2-4** tells us that the Lord has spoken, I have nourished and brought up children, and they have rebelled against Me. The ox knows his owner and the ass his master's crib: but Israel does not know, and My people do not consider. A sinful nation, a people tormented by iniquity, a generation of evildoers, children that are corrupt: they have forgotten the Lord, they have provoked the Holy One of Israel unto anger, they are gone away backward.

A medium is by design from Satan to generate fear by planting the seed of hopelessness into the mind. Even though mankind fell into sin, the serpent was unable to destroy the Agape love of God for His people. **Revelation chapter 13:7,8** tells us that it was given unto Satan to make war with the saints, and to overcome them: and power was given unto him over all humanity, and language, and countries. And all that dwell upon the earth shall worship him, whose names are not written in the book of life of the Lamb slain from the foundation of the world.

Revelation chapter 14:9-11 tells us that a third angel followed them, saying with a loud voice, if any man worship the beast and his image, and receive his mark in his forehead, or in his hand, the same shall drink of the wine of the wrath of God, which is poured out without mixture into the cup of His indignation; and the unbeliever shall be tormented with fire and brimstone in the presence of the Lamb: and the smoke of their torment ascends up forever and ever: and they have no rest day or night, who worship the beast and his image, and whosoever receives the mark of his name. **Isaiah chapter 8:20** tells us that if they speak not according to the Word of God, it is because there is no light in them. **Matthew chapter 15:19,20** tells us that out of the heart proceed evil thoughts, murder, adulteries, fornications, thefts, false witness, and blasphemies. These are the things, which defiles a man.

Jesus wanted to make us aware of the snares of trusting family members beyond trusting Him. The analogy of pride is described as having another god. **Matthew chapter 23:23** tells us that Christ said, "Woe unto you, scribes and Pharisees, hypocrites! For you pay a tenth of your tithe in mint and dill from the abundance of your storehouse and leave off the weightier matters of the law: judgment and mercy: these things you should have done also. The love of Christ is the indwelling of His Holy Spirit and the perfection of our character in His righteousness. Amen

The Empty Promises of the World

Now that we have substituted the Word for the world by becoming the benefactors of guilt: and slaves unto a lifestyle that has very little to offer when it comes to spiritual growth. We have made every effort, however, motivation isn't the key to success and covering up the problem isn't the solution. The only approach that is recommended is Jesus Christ. I came to the conclusion that sin is still sin, even with the most indirect approach. Furthermore, it doesn't matter how well you wrap the package: its what's inside that really matters. **Psalm chapter 146:5-7** tells us that happy is he who has the God of Jacob for his help, whose hope is in the Lord our God, which made heaven, and earth, the sea, and all that therein: Who keeps the truth forever, and execute judgment for the oppressed and give food to the hungry. God set prisoners free. Therefore, no matter how good an idea may seem without the conviction of the Holy Spirit it is fruitless, and has neither purpose nor value to the individual or God the Father in heaven.

For example: the atheistic unbelief surrenders all authority unto the devil by saying, there isn't a God. If God doesn't exist then how do we explain creation? Lets say for argument sake there is no God, and chaos is random, why hope for anything that is good? However, you'll find that an atheist has more hope in the world than in the Word; and even though he knows the truth about soul salvation he will not exercise faith when it comes to trusting and obeying the Word of God. He only seeks after material gain that has no benefits or value when it comes to saving his own soul. Lets take a closer look at the big–bang theory. The big–bang theory supports evolution and the natural law. Furthermore, if every man is right in his own eyes, then terrorism is justified. However, if we believe that God is love and we of ourselves has the ability to create relationships out of brotherly love: what then can we hope to gain from excluding God from our lives? God is able to grant us peace by means of which joy will harmonize our lives with each other.

Evolution is some sort of fairytale from a children's book, which neither has purpose nor value to bring anything to perfection; meanwhile science is the research and development of theories by means of which ideologist leaders of the world invoke politics and technology as leverage to create a religious smoke screen to seduce, manipulate, and deceive those that are in the world. **Revelation chapter 16:13,14** tells us that John saw three unclean spirits like frogs, which came out of the mouth of the dragon, and out of the mouths of the leaders of the nations, and out of the mouths of the false prophets; for they are the spirits of devils, working miracles, which go out unto the kings of the earth and the whole world, to gather them to the battle of that great day of God Almighty.

The tree of knowledge of good and evil bears the fruit of unrighteousness by means of which the devil promotes the world over the Word. God gave His Word unto the church that we might find peace in Him, and have a place of refuge from the world. The traditions of man will never produce faith in him that is out of the way. Without God's love, who is able to have compassion on the ignorant? The Holy Spirit renews our mind, whereby faith gives us the discernment of God's will: wisdom, knowledge, and understanding by means of which we have hope in Christ Jesus. Furthermore, our hope is centered on Christ, whereby temperance, longsuffering, patience, and self–control is exercised daily to His glory. Now that we have made the Word of God void by putting the traditions of man above His commandments, evolution has blossomed into chaotic events amongst atheistic groups around the world. **Revelation chapter 17:13,14** tells us that these have one mind, and they will give their power and authority unto the devil. These will make war with the Lamb, and the Lamb will overcome them, for He is the Lord of lords, and the King of kings; and those who are with Him are called, chosen, and faithful.

In all things God is from everlasting to everlasting: from beginning without end. The traditions of men were never meant to supersede His commandments. Technology has evolved beyond the boundaries of everyday domestic appliances, whereas artificial intelligence is being recognized as a break through in modern science and technological warfare. However, technology has no value, and serves very little purpose to the average Joe; and is more likely a benefit to the profit margin of some big corporation. The last time I took an account of the universe, God was still in charge, and the plan of salvation was still His priority.

The influx of the media frenzy has become the number one box office hit of the twenty first century. The media has generated more than two-thirds of the population's income, whereby the expectation of happiness involves some-sort of social media, and other viewing products geared toward socialism. The plan of salvation is viewed by the world as a myth, and old wives tales. The craftsmanship of the devil can be seen through the political race for globalism. But who is this modern god that we seek to worship?

In GOD we trust: a slogan for guns, oil, and drugs! Entertainment is the mission statement of Satan's unfulfilling mirage, whereby it has altered the course of the human race by downsizing our faith and love for our Creator to a third of the population. The moral standards of the world are less likely to produce successful children, as they're being brain washed into believing that there isn't a God. Children are taught to depend on their own strength. The world sets the standards for which we live by. People are being led away from having a sincere conscience toward the Creator of the heavens and the earth. One of the most common deceptions is relying on self. **Jeremiah chapter 17:5** tells us that cursed is the man that puts his trust in man, and relies on his own hands, and whose heart has departed from God.

Now that we have made the Word of God obsolete, science and technology has become the final approach to every matter by means of which evolution has manipulated the unbeliever into believing that he isn't anything more than an animal. The wrath of God can be seen throughout the Bible as Him being vindictive, but on the contrary the wages of sin is death, and the devil is unjust. God has perfect foreknowledge and His sovereign judgment is absolute. For even while we were yet sinners living our lives apart from Christ, the plan of salvation was put in place to save us from the foundation of the world. The mark of the beast is the veil of deception placed over the mind of those that are in the world. Common sense isn't as common as one would like to believe, but true knowledge descends from above. I give God thanks and praise to the glory of His name. Furthermore, He is my provider, and protector. Amen

Idol Worshiping

Now concerning the worshiping of animals: cows and elephants etc. Religion is something that people believe in, and its something they practice on a daily basis. My personal affection for animals is based upon my love for Jesus Christ Who created all things. I am not telling you not to worship a creature. However, I choose to worship the Creator. It wasn't meant for us to worship things or animals which neither have wisdom nor understanding when it comes to making moral judgments. It only goes to show that people will conform to unbelief by putting their faith and hope into their own personal religion. **Isaiah chapter 44:6-20** tells us that the Lord is the King of Israel and their Redeemer. I Am the Lord of hosts: I Am the First and the Last; apart from Me there is no other God. Is there another that can reveal the things of the future as I do? If there is another God, let him declare it and lay it out before Me. For I was the One Who established the ancient prophecy of the future, and things yet to come to pass. All these things I will make known unto you by My people. Do not fear, nor be afraid for I have declared it unto you from the beginning of time.

You are My witnesses. Is there another God apart from Me? Indeed there is no other Rock but Me; I don't know of any. All the images that you have made are all useless, and your precious items will profit you nothing; you have made a witness unto yourself. An idol has neither wisdom nor understanding. People who worship idols will be sadly disappointed. Why form a god or mold an image that profits nothing? Surely anyone who partakes in idol worshiping will be disappointed. For an idol is made by mere men. Let them group all their idols together and make a stand. In the end fear will come upon those who worship idols, and their pride will bring them disappointment. The blacksmith with the strength of his arms uses the forceps to heat the iron in the furnace and then fashions it with a hammer into an idol.

Even while his strength fails and he becomes faint, he doesn't stop to eat or drink water. The sculptor stretches out his measuring tape, he marks it out with chalk; he fashions it with a chisel, so that it would have the likeness of a man. Then he takes it and stands it up inside of his home. A man will purposely plant four types of trees: cedar, cypress, pine, and oak. He secures it for himself amongst the trees of the forest, and the rain nourishes it while it grows, and after it has reached its maturity, he will cut it down for a double purpose. He burns half of it in the fire, so that he can make a meal, and says, "Ah, I have seen the fire and I am warm." And after he is satisfied, he uses the other portion to make a carved image into a god, and falls down before it and worship it. He will pray to it and say, "Deliver me, for you are my god." People who worship idols are blinded by Satan, they don't know the truth, for the devil has shut their eyes, so that they cannot see; and closed their minds, so that they cannot understand. And no one considers in his heart, neither is there knowledge nor understanding to say, "I have burned half of it in the fire, and I have also baked bread on its coals, I have roasted meat and eaten it." And now am I to make the rest of it an abomination? Why fall down before a block of wood and worship it? Worshiping an idol is the same as feeding on ashes. Idol worshiping leads to a deceived heart; whereby the unbeliever cannot deliver his own soul, or say, "Is this not a lie in my right hand?"

Anyone of us could be considered guilty of Idolatry. Many believers and unbelievers main focus in life is on their careers. The light bulb is one of the most widely used inventions of today, and plays a great role in everyday purposes. Thomas Edison who was never known to be a Christian or even having any kind of religious background was given the gift of wisdom, knowledge and understanding to invent the light bulb. **Exodus chapter 35:30-33** tells us that Moses spoke unto the children of Israel, saying, see, the Lord has called by name Bezalel the son of Uri, the son of Hur, from the tribe of Judah; and the Lord has filled him with the Spirit of wisdom and understanding, in knowledge and all manner of workmanship, to design artistic works, to work in gold and silver and bronze, in carving wood, and to work in all manner of artistic workmanship.

God established faith from the foundation of the earth, so that we might have hope in His salvation to come. God gave man hope in Christ: Who is love; whereby He sent us His only begotten Son, so that through Him, we might know the Father Who sent Him. Ideology is common amongst believers and unbelievers alike: due to the lack of self–awareness and discernment of God's will for our lives. The human race can be seen as self–centered and vague, whereby the sounds of echoes can be heard from a distance. We all have a general need for money. However, greed and self–indulgence has become our primary pursuit by means of which our love for Jesus Christ has become secondary. Why climb to the top of a mountain and then say, this isn't what I had hoped for. And afterward with disappointments and regrets you have to climb back down to reality. Why hope for something that is corruptible when God should be the center of our focus?

Career and money are both temporal, and all temporal things have an expiration date, but spiritual things are forever. Therefore to have hope in things that are temporal is to have dead hope. It is expedient that our characters are nurtured by the Word; and not to place focus on the world, whereby hindering the Holy Spirit from reproducing the Agape love of God in us, that we may bear fruit in Christ before the end of grace and the close of probation. By giving all diligence according to God's will and grace stewardship out of obedience is better than sacrifice. Our faith should be accompanied by our hope in Jesus Christ: holding fast to the things that are true. **Matthew chapter 6:20** tells us that wherever our treasure is, there will our hearts be also. Amen

The Love of Money is the Root of All Evil

1Timothy chapter 6:5-12 tells us that perverse disputing of men with corrupt minds, and destitute of the truth, supposing that material gain is godliness: from such persons withdraw yourself. True godliness is content; this is great gain in the eye of God the Father, for we brought nothing into this world and it is certain that we can't carry anything out. Money is necessary for food, clothing, shelter, and transportation: therefore let us be content with what money can buy. Christians shouldn't focus on being rich, whereby many have fallen into temptation, and finding themselves facing hardship, and many sorrows of oppression. For the love of money is the root of all evil: whereby greed becomes the error of coveting others for material things, and many have left the faith of Jesus Christ, and now finding themselves being pierced with many sorrows. I say to you my brothers and sisters, flee these things and seek after righteousness, godliness, faith, love, patience, and meekness. Fight the good fight of faith, lay hold on eternal life, where unto we are called to profess a good profession before many witnesses.

1Timothy chapter 5:8 tells us that if anyone comes to you and say that they have faith, but provides not for his own household, they have denied the faith of being a true servant, and has become unfruitful.

The contrast between having faith in God's sovereignty and having love for money boils down to trust. The rich young ruler had enough wealth, but not enough faith in God to show Philia love unto his fellow man by feeding the poor, whereby he being sorrowful after denying himself of true wealth and treasure to come by not trusting and obeying the commandment, which came from Christ. The love of money will not produce faith, which is the unconditional love of God. Faith and faith alone will produce the unconditional love of Jesus Christ in us. **Philippians chapter 2:5-8** tells us that we should have the same mind, which was also in Christ Jesus: Who being equal to God, but found no displeasure in being a servant, and while He was yet a man, He humbled Himself, and became obedient unto death, even the death of the cross.

God gave faith unto those who will honor Him by being a servant to the poor. The abundance of His Agape love is to the glory of His name, whereby we labor in love holding unto the hope that we have in Christ Jesus.

In that Day of Judgment when the former rain and the latter rain has past, and the earth becomes desolate as a barren womb, the sun will not give warmth nor light, at which point the seed that was planted and flourish not, will be plucked up by its roots, and the nakedness of the proud will be seen by everyone. **Colossians chapter 3:2** tells us that we should set our affection on the things above, and not on the things of the earth. **Matthew chapter 6:24-27** tells us that no man can serve two masters at the same time: for either he will hate God, and love the devil; or else he will hold unto God, and despise the devil. But on the contrary you cannot serve God, while your focus is on earthly wealth. "Therefore I say to you, take no thought for your life, by saying, what shall we eat, or what shall we drink: nor what shall we wear. The life of the body is much more than just food, and clothing. The birds of the air sow not, and reap not, nor gather foods into barns, but yet the heavenly Father feeds them. You are much more than the birds? Besides, which of you can use thought to add one inch to your height. **Matthew chapter 16:26** tells us what will it profit a man, if he gain the whole world, and lose his own soul, or what shall a man give in exchange for his soul? Whenever an idol becomes more important than the relationship that we share with God, apostasy becomes the final result. In today's fluctuating economy money has rendered itself against credit, whereas the borrower is a servant to the lender.

The word money is mentioned one hundred and forty times throughout the Bible from Old to New Testament. However, Philia love was established in the Kingdom of heaven, whereby the Agape love presented itself as a two-way street, namely God's unconditional love for humanity. Philia love *(brotherly love)* is the second greatest commandment of the law, namely love your neighbor as yourself. However, after sin Philia love was no longer the second law, but it became a rarity and rather slavery by sin became the alternative, whereas customer service presented itself as financial control over people by means of which money became the vehicle for greed. **Acts chapter 3:6** tells us that Peter said, "Silver and gold I have none; but such as I have I will give unto you: in the name of Jesus Christ of Nazareth rise up and walk." Amen

The Financial Meltdown

Genesis chapter 3:14 tells us that the Lord God said unto the serpent, "Because you have done this, you are cursed above all other animals, and above every beast of the field." Satan is the one behind the moneychangers and those that sold doves that Jesus drove from the temple. Today, we have a financial pyramid known as banks. From diplomas to PhDs a certified custodian is still a janitor, and middleclass is just another way of saying, from paycheck to paycheck. **Luke chapter 2:1** tells us that it came to pass in those days, that there went out a decree from Caesar Augustus, that the whole world should be taxed. **Matthew chapter 17:24-27** tells us that after Jesus and His disciples got to Capernaum, they that collected taxes came to Peter and said, does your Master pay taxes? He replied, yes. And after they got back home, Jesus said unto Peter, if I may ask you something, Simon Peter? Who do the kings of the earth collect custom taxes, from the citizen's or from foreigners? Peter said unto Him, from foreigners. Jesus replied I don't want to offend them. So I want you to go to the sea and cast in your hook, and take the first fish that comes up. And when you have opened its mouth, you will find a piece of money; take it and give it unto them.

Matthew chapter 22:15-21 tells us that the Pharisees went and conspire with Herod soldiers how they might trap Jesus with His own words. So they send their disciples with Herod soldiers unto Jesus, saying, Master, we know that you are true, and you teach the way of God in truth, and you show no impartiality in respect of persons. Tell us therefore, what do you think? Is it lawful to pay taxes unto Caesar, or not? But Jesus perceived their hidden agenda, and said, why tempt Me, you hypocrites? Show Me the money. And they brought unto Him a penny. And He said unto them, whose image and inscription is this? They say unto Him, Caesar's. Then He said unto them, let Caesar therefore have the things, which belong unto him; and let God have that which belong unto Him.

Satan's agenda is still the same today, as it was in the beginning. Financial wealth is determined by how much money you have or earn in a year. However, Jesus is my CEO and He bears witness that I testify that God is my provider. Furthermore, if you feel the need to borrow from a financial institution all you have to do is answer these questions. How much money do you need, and for what purpose? If you can answer those questions, most likely any financial institution on the planet will be more than happy to assist you with service for a fee. Philia love by faith doesn't require payment. **Matthew chapter 20:26-28** tells us that Jesus said, whosoever wants to be in charge, let him become a servant unto his brother, and whosoever wants to be a leader, let him become a servant unto all, even as I also came to be a servant unto you, and to give my life for a ransom for many. Amen

Money Versus Debt

Why do we need to work? **Genesis chapter 3:17-19** tells us that the Lord said, unto Adam, because you have allowed your wife to convince you to eat from the tree, which I have commanded you not to eat of: cursed is the ground for your sake, in sorrow you shall eat of the tree of knowledge of good and evil all the days of your life. Thorns and thistles shall it bring unto you, and you will eat the herb of the field; by the sweat of your labor you will eat bread up until you return unto the ground; for out of the ground you came, for dust you are, and unto the dust you will return.

God did not curse the ground to make our lives grievous, but instead to the fulfillment of His glory. Only through hardship can self be extinguish, so that the unbelieving soul may come to His righteousness, and omniscient peace, and unconditional love, which has a greater purpose and value than the hardship that we face on a daily basis. The primary focus of every believer is to find comfort in His loving arms, and strength to overcome trials, which is the testing of our faith, and tribulations, which is the perfecting of our character, and patience in the hope that we have in Him by means of which the believer's faith is centered on Jesus Christ moment–by–moment, whereby we say, the Lord is my helper giving God thanks always; meanwhile we labor in love toward each other as did Christ Jesus, Who is the Chief servant of mankind. However, man chose hardship out of rebellion by means of which he promoted financial greed by making money into an idol. In todays economical backdraft, where having debt is the norm, more than two–thirds of the population relies on some sought of credit, student loans, mortgages and other means of financial support. **Proverbs chapter 22:7** tells us that the borrower is a servant to the lender.

In the past, the banking system was in favor of the borrower. Money was generally considered to have the following four main functions: a medium of exchange for goods and services, a measurement of market value of goods and services, a standard of deferred payment to settle debt, and a retirement found is money saved.

However, today's private banking system has changed the borrowing rules by means of which a promissory note is a negotiable instrument or medium, wherein one party (the maker or issuer) makes an obligated promise in writing to pay a determinate sum of money to the other (the payee) either at a fixed or determinable future time or on demand of payee, under specific terms. The terms of a note usually include the principal amount, the interest rate if any, the parties, the date, the terms of repayment and maturity date. Sometimes, provisions are included concerning the payee's rights in the event of default, which may include foreclosure of the market's assets.

Promissory notes differ from IOUs in that they contain a specific promise to pay, rather than simply acknowledging that a debt exists. In other words, the terms, such as "loan," "loan agreement," and "loan contract" may be used interchangeably with a "promissory note" but each of these terms do not have the same legal meaning. Overall dollars and cents are FDIC approved up to at least $250,000 per deposit of any insured–banking institute. Whenever the minority controls the resources, the majority will always feel the pinch. Now that owning a home is but an illusion, and the price for transportation is comparable to having a mortgage, everyone can relate to the burden of having debt in one way or another, especially those of us who have dependents living at home. We burn through our paychecks like flash—paper at the supermarkets as the escalating food prices skyrockets to the moon, meanwhile our investments hit rock bottom. How did this happen overnight?

Debt is created for one particular purpose, to keep the population depending on the government and his bailout plan. Financial rescue has been around since Adam and Eve, It's the oldest trick in the book. Financial oppression is the greatest form of idolatry known to mankind; it's where the need to have money becomes greater than the relationship and love that we share with God and humanity. Money is used as a medium to evaluate commodities; whereby a monitory system was put in place to oppress individuals who have outstanding debt to income. Having money versus having debt is based on two things: the borrower, and the lender's agreement. Labor and resources will produce wealth if faith is exercise in God. However, disobedience to Christ leads to poverty, and borrowing becomes the substitute of having money, whereas debt becomes the downfall for the individual, and the economy on a global scale.

In order for us to improve our financial situation faith and hope have to be centered on the Agape love of God in order to bring purpose and value to our communities. Philia love is the only stimulation that the economy needs, whereby exercising faith in God and surrendering to the hope of Jesus Christ. The contrast between having money and debt is based on credit worthiness. People with FICO scores between 660—900 stand a better chance of getting better interest rates. God's solution is much simpler than trying to make money. Philia love should be the primary reason why we labor. Nine out of ten times debt is created out of covet, and frivolous spending on a new dress or your favorite team jersey. The economy is upside down for one particular reason, too much unnecessary spending. America is seen as the financial capital of the world, and she takes recommendation from no one. The fifteen trillion dollar deficit is overwhelming to many who believe that money have value, which I find mindboggling considering that we did not create this debt and it shouldn't have any financial bearing on the economy.

Why do we need to pay a debt that is owed to a chartered banking system that doesn't work nor contribute to the economy on any known infrastructure, when the fact of the matter is, we are the taxpayers and it's our money that runs the federal government? The banking system and the welfare system share one common goal, putting the squeeze on the laborer. **Matthew chapter 9:37,38** tells us that the Lord said, unto His disciples, "The harvest truly is plentiful, but the laborers are few; pray that the Lord of the harvest will send laborers into His harvest."

Personally, I support the needy, but if you are healthy enough to work; working is the best exercise for anyone who wants to contribute to his or her community. Getting everyone involved will make things easier on the economy. **1Timothy chapter 5:9,10** tells us that a widow shouldn't receive welfare if she is under the age of sixty, and make sure she is the wife of one man, with a good report of her charity toward her own children and neighbors. Someone who participates in communion: the washing of the saint's feet, and relieving the poor by following every good work. Amen

Vanity of Vanity, all is Vanity

I have not seen it rain silver or gold. However, I have seen the rich take their material possessions to heart. While a man lives, he will nurture his pride and not his soul. I have yet to see a U–haul transporting riches and wealth behind the decease in a hearse. **Psalm chapter 49:6-20** tells us that the afterlife is reserved for the soul of the righteous. I have seen the wicked and the ungodly prosper, and boast himself in the multitude of his riches. However, wealth and riches cannot redeem life from the grave, nor is there anyone that can give God a ransom for his soul. Life itself is precious, and when it is lost, it vanishes forever. The foolish man thinks that he will live forever and will not see death, but as wise men die, so shall the foolish and the brutish perish also.

The evidence shows that wealth and riches belong to the living; whereas the man that is vain in his thoughts, think to himself that he will continue forever, and his home will be past on from one generation to the next. A man will established a name for himself and leaves an inheritance for his children and grandchildren. But he that lacks wisdom is like an animal that dies without understanding. The life of the foolish is foolishness: he that put his trust in his wealth is dead in spirit, and death shall feed on his soul. But the faithful shall have dominion over death; meanwhile the grave will consume even the beauty of the foolish. For only God has the power to retrieve the soul from the grave. Covet not your neighbor because he is rich, for when he dies he will not be able to carry his wealth to the grave with him. Though while he lives in paradise and boast himself of his wealth, when he dies he will be laid to rest with his ancestors, and they will never see light again. A man that is rich and has no understanding is like an animal that dies without mercy.

Ecclesiastes chapter 12:1-8 tells us that we should remember to have reverence for the Creator while we are young. Before the days of evil draws near, and the years when we become old and say, I find no pleasure in them. While the sun, and the moon, and the stars gives light, and the clouds depart after the rain. The days are coming when men and women will tremble with fear, and the strong men will fall to their knees, and you will barely hear the mill as it grinds out the wheat, for the laborers are few. Before People had their doors wide-open, but now they peek from behind their window curtains. Now that the sound of the mill is low, he will rise up to the songs of birds in the morning, instead of hearing the music of young girls. Furthermore, violence will be at its maximum level, while terror lurks in the dark. Everyone knows that when the Almond tree flourish, the grasshopper becomes a burden. When a man dies his friends mourn at his funeral, but soon after they go about their business. Remember your Creator before the silver cord is loosed. Before the golden bowl is broken, or your favorite cup is shattered at the sink, or the wheel is broken at the well. Man came from the dust of the earth and he will return to the earth as it was, and the spirit will return to God Who gave it. Vanity of vanities, says the preacher, all is vanity.

Now that the world has become a bottomless pit, and life has become difficult for some more than others, we realize that no matter how sincere we are about being happy or otherwise, apart from Christ we can do nothing. For only God has the power to make a difference. I speak as a man, because, I was once convinced by the prince of this world that I am not worthy of being saved. But now I live through Christ Jesus; and I have nothing to fear from the devil. For Jesus Christ became our Lord and Savior, whereby the unconditional love of Christ makes a difference in me. Amen

177

The Kingdom of Grace

Brotherly love is rare among atheistic groups as well as people who called themselves Christians, but on the contrary without the Agape love of God no one can be saved. Since we have stopped praying and forgotten our moral values, many believe that a spiritual submission unto Jesus Christ is no longer a requirement to be saved. You have those who have rejected the power of His Holy Spirit and left the church in pursuit of Eros *(Romance)*. An atheist refuses to believe in anything than the norm; he doesn't believe that there is a God.

However, the danger of living a self-sufficient religious lifestyle is simply how one might perceive good things. The tree of knowledge of good and evil is the menu of the world, and death is the dessert. Addictive behaviors are not only costly, but at what price are you willing to die for your unbelief? Rebellion plays a major factor in spiritual oppression. Imagine with me for a moment that God has no addictions, and those that serve Him has no bad habits. How does a person identify the truth about their spiritual condition? In other words how does one become a servant of Jesus Christ? The selflessness of Christ's Character can be seen in those that are born–again, which are the attributes of a servant wanting to please his Master.

The Christian faith begins when we lay hold on His righteousness by confessing Christ as our Lord and Savior. True faith involves trusting and obeying the Word of God. Everyone that believes in God have free–will. Christians have freedom of choice to exercise faith in God by showing love toward one another. God's love is genuine empathy, which comes from the Holy Spirit that dwells within the believer who has surrendered self unto Christ. A good deed is from a pure heart and a clear conscience, whereby we preform to the best of our ability without expecting or wanting to receive any gratification in regards to the deed that was done. However, the people of the world seek their own reward by laying claim to the kingdom of grace by their own works. Fear manifest hate, and without having anything to hope for death follows.

178

The kingdom of grace cannot be discerned or explained to the natural man who has not surrendered self unto Christ. **John chapter 20:24,25** tells us that Thomas who was one of the twelve disciples called Didymus was not with them when Jesus came, therefore the other disciples said unto him, we have seen the Lord, but he said, unless I see His hands, which the nails have pierced and put my hand on His wound in His side, I will not believe. The spirit of man is the Son of man: our Lord and Savior Jesus Christ. God Who wanted sons and daughters created man in His Own Image and Likeness. **Titus chapter 1:15,16** tells us that unto the pure all things are pure, but unto the them that are defiled and unbelieving is nothing pure; but their mind and conscience is defiled, they profess God by mouth, and deny Him in their hearts, being abominable, and disobedient, and motived by pride to destroy the glory of every good work (faith).

Have you ever met someone who had more sensual knowledge than heart knowledge, and the one was contrary to the other? Most animals can be trained by a repetitive motion or routine, but unfortunately it's not the same when it comes to the human race. After God wrote the Ten Commandments and gave them unto the people at Mount Sinai, they all agreed to exercise faith in doing the Lord's will, but soon after they went back to doing things their own way. **Matthew chapter 4:4** tells us that when Jesus was tempted by the devil, He replied, man shall not live by bread alone, but by every Word that proceeds out of the mouth of God. The Commandments of God gives clarification and reproof to the sinner who wants forgiveness, and repentance of his sin, so that we are justified to enter into His kingdom of grace freely without any merits of our own, whereby Christianity and a Christ–like Character begins with the fullness of His ministerial work upon the human soul. However, the Holy Spirit finds no room in the hearts of the proud.

Many have yet to taste the good works of faith, and even though they are within the boundaries of the promises that were made at Mount Sinai, they are not at Mount Calvary embracing the power of His Agape love that was given unto all humanity. **2 Corinthians chapter 1:12** tells us that our rejoicing is the testimony of our conscience in simplicity and godly sincerity, and not according to worldly standards, but by the grace of God we exhort those that are in the world by the Word of God.

We have the responsibility as head of household, and much more especially toward our own brethren, for if the shepherd tend not to his own flock, how then can he reach the world not having done all that he can to save his own as did Christ our Lord and Savior. Since Christianity is the primary focus, and Jesus Christ is the Lord of the Sabbath that was made for man, theoretically speaking, if the doctor isn't in the house how can the patient receive his diagnosis? The primary function of the church wasn't to win souls, but rather to walk in the steps of Christ as men and women of faith, the Word of God over the church, whereby making the conscience supreme over the mind and senses. **James chapter 3:13-18** tells us that if anyone seems to be wise and have the gift of knowledge, let him show out of a good conversation his motive with meekness and wisdom. But if you have bitterness and anger in your heart, glory not, and lie not against the truth. This wisdom descended not from above, but is earthly, sensual, and devilish. For wherever you find envy and strife, there is confusion and every evil work. The wisdom that is from above is first pure, then peaceable, gentle, easily understood, full of mercy and humility, without partiality, and without hypocrisy. And they that make peace sow the fruit of righteousness in peace.

Romans chapter 10:1-4 tells us that Paul prayed to God, saying, brethren, my heart's desire and prayer to God for Israel is that they might be saved. I testify that they have a form of love for God, but not according to the knowledge of Jesus Christ. For they being ignorant of God's righteousness, and wanting to establish their own righteousness, and therefore they have not surrendered themselves unto the righteousness of God. For Jesus Christ put an end to the natural law, by giving us the moral law: righteousness by faith to everyone that believes. Amen

"Jesus is Lord of the Sabbath"

Chapter 7

The Seventh Day Sabbath

God is not only majestic, but He is also divine in all His work. There are no secret interpretations of the Bible, and the Seventh Day advent of Jesus Christ. The conflict of the ages came through the deception of the serpent; whereby Eve was deceived. **Genesis chapter 2:1,2** tells us that the plan of salvation is centered on the Seventh Day. Therefore, the heavens and the earth were finished, and all the things, which God made. And on the Seventh Day God ended His work, which He had made; and He rested on the Seventh Day.

This was foretold that God created the earth in <u>six literal days</u>, and He rested on the Seventh Day. **2 Peter chapter 3:8** tells us not to be ignorant of this one thing, that one day is with the Lord as a thousand years, and a thousand years as one day. **Proverbs chapter 25:3** tells us that the heaven is for height, and the earth is for depth. **Matthew chapter 5:17** tells us that Christ did not come to destroy the: (law) and (prophets) but to fulfill all unto the glory of His Father Who sent Him. **Matthew chapter 17:1-3** tells us that the transfiguration of the Son of man was made visible unto the disciples after <u>six days</u>: whereby His face did shine as the sun, and His clothing was white as light. And, behold, there appeared unto them Moses who represented the law, and Elias who represented the prophets, talking with Christ. God revealed His great plan of salvation unto Adam and Eve at the moment when they needed Him the most. Today, it is the same for you and I. The plan of salvation should be viewed, and studied, so that we can understand, and acknowledge God's great plan for saving humanity. God revealed unto us the plan of redemption by His Son Jesus Christ Who is blessed forever and ever. Amen

This chapter is not to convince you, but rather a dedication to my family, and friends. To my dear wife, Marva and our four beautiful children: Everton, Phillip, Stephenie and Stephen. I Stephen Howard Sergeant, hereby testify of my own free-will, and clear conscience that God created the heavens and the earth in six days, and rested on the Seventh Day. As human beings we were created as individuals, but to share one common belief of faith, love and hope in our Lord and Savior Jesus Christ. The plan of salvation was centered on Christ at the cross in many pivotal aspects, whereby His love for His Father and His people became visible, and the single greatest triumph in the history of mankind.

Colossians chapter 1:12-20 tells us that we should give thanks unto God the Father Who gave us the opportunity to become heirs to the inheritance of the saints in the kingdom of light. Furthermore, God delivered us from the domain of darkness, and translated us into the kingdom of grace of His beloved Son: In Whom we have redemption through His blood, even forgiveness of sins. Christ is the Image of the invisible God, the First born of every creature. For by Him were all things created that are in heaven, and earth, visible and invisible, whether they be thrones, or dominions, or principalities, or powers. All things were created by Him, and for Him. Christ existed before all things, and He put all things together. He is the head of the body, which is the church. Jesus Christ is the Beginning: the Firstborn from the dead, that in all things He might have the preeminence, whereby it pleased the Father to put Him in charge of everything to make it complete. Jesus made peace through the shedding of His blood on the cross, whereby reconciling all things unto Himself. Amen

The Ten Commandments

Exodus chapter 20:1-17 tells us that I Am the Lord your God, which have brought you out of the land of Egypt, out of the house of bondage.

- You must not have any other gods before Me. Do not make unto yourself any false gods, or any likeness of any thing that is in heaven above, or that is in the water under the earth.
- Do not bow down yourself unto them, nor serve them. For I the Lord your God, I Am a jealous God; visiting the iniquity of the fathers upon the children unto the third and fourth generation of them that hate Me; and showing mercy unto thousands of them that love Me, and keep My commandments.
- Do not take the name of the Lord your God in vain; for the Lord will not hold him guiltless that take His name in vain.
- Remember the Sabbath Day, to keep it Holy, six days you shall labor, but the Seventh Day is the Sabbath of the Lord your God: in it you shall do no work, you, nor your son, nor your daughter, neither your maidservant, nor your manservant, nor your cattle, nor the stranger that is within your home: for in six days the Lord made heaven and earth, the sea, and all that is in them, and He rested on the Seventh Day: therefore the Lord blessed the Sabbath day, and sanctified it.
- Honor your Father and Mother: that your days may be long upon the land, which the Lord God gave unto you. Furthermore, God gave us the edenic diet for longevity. *See page 262.*
- Do not murder.
- Do not separate yourself from the Lord God by committing adultery.
- Do not steal.
- Do not tell lies on your neighbor.
- Do not covet your neighbor's house, or his wife or his servants, or anything that belongs to him.

Honoring God by keeping His Sabbaths

Genesis chapter 2:1-3 tells us that after the heavens (plural) and the earth were finished, and all the host of them. And on the Seventh Day God ended His work, which He had made; and He rested on the Seventh Day from all His work, which He had made. And God blessed the Seventh Day, and sanctified it; because that in it He rested from all His work, which God created and made.

From the beginning of the creation of the heavens and earth mankind's weary soul have not found rest up until now. The Seventh Day is an acknowledgment of God's divinity and omnipotence. For He is an omniscient God, and apart from Him there is no other Rock. The birth of Christ was during the fourth millennium, as God had predicted on the fourth day of creation. The three days event of His death and resurrection is linked to the fourth, and fifth, and sixth millennium; whereby the restoration of humanity was placed upon His shoulder by means of which the church would be perfected at the time of His second coming. **Luke chapter 13:32** tells us that Jesus said unto them, Go and tell Satan I cast out devils, and do cures today and tomorrow, and the third day I shall be perfected. **Exodus chapter 19:10,11** tells us that the Lord said unto Moses, Go unto the people, and sanctify them today and tomorrow, and let them wash their clothes, and be ready on the third day: for the third day I will come down in the sight of all the people upon Mount Sinai. The days of the week are numbered vertically, one through six, whereby putting the Seventh Day at the top as a reminder of the true millennial Sabbath that is yet to come, whereby Christ Himself will come down as He did at Mount Sinai to gather His people.

- 7th —day—the Sabbath, the return of Christ ————————7000
- 6th —day—Glorification of the church————the third day——6000
- 5th —day—Sanctification of the church ———tomorrow——5000
- 4th —day—Justification of mankind————today————4000
- 3rd —day—Moses and the crossing of the Red Sea ————3000
- 2nd —day—Noah and the Ark, the great flood————————2000
- 1st —day— Mankind sinned, the plan of salvation————1000

186

The Seventh Day Sabbath is the commandment of God by faith, whereby if we believe in Christ, we will enter into His rest by surrendering our free–will unto His will. **Hebrews chapter 4:2-11** tells us that God revealed unto us the plan of salvation, as well as unto them that heard it in the wilderness; but the Word preached did not convict them, not being mixed with faith it had no power over those that heard it. If we believe, we will enter into His rest. As He had said, I gave them My Word that they should enter into My rest, for the works are finished from the foundation of the world. Christ spoke in a certain place of the <u>Seventh Day</u> on this wise, and God did rest on the <u>Seventh Day</u> from all His works. Twice God gave the tablet of stone with the same commandment saying, again, if they will enter into My rest seeing therefore it remain that some must enter therein. And they to whom it was first preached entered not in because of unbelief. Again, Christ reserved a certain day, saying unto David, today, after so many years as it was said before, if you will hear My voice, harden not your hearts. If Jesus had given the Israelites a spiritual rest in the land of Canaan then He would have not mention another day. Therefore a spiritual rest still remains unto the people of God. In order for us to enter into His spiritual rest, we have to cease from our own works, as God did from the creation of the world. Let us prepare ourselves to enter into that spiritual rest, so that we do not fall after the same example of unbelief.

Should Christians observe the Sabbaths today, or is it an ancient law that was done away with? Many Christians will argue that the Sabbath was during the old Levitical priesthood. **Exodus chapter 31:12-15** tells us that the Lord said unto Moses, speak unto the children of Israel, saying, verily My Sabbaths you shall keep: for it is a sign between you and Me throughout your generations; that you may know that I Am the Lord that do Sanctify you. You shall keep the Sabbath therefore; for it is Holy unto you: everyone that defiles it shall surely be put to death: for whosoever does any work in it, that person shall be cut off from among his people. Six days may work be done; but on the seventh day, it is the Sabbath of rest and it is Holy unto the Lord. Whosoever does any work on the Sabbath day; he shall surely be put to death.

Isaiah chapter 56:1-7 tells us that the Lord said, keep My judgment, and do justice: for My salvation is near to come, and My righteousness to be revealed. Blessed is the man that does this, and the son of man that lay hold on it; that keep the Sabbath from polluting it, and keep his hands from doing any evil. Neither let the son of the stranger that has joined himself to the Lord, say, the Lord has utterly separated me from His people: neither let the unfruitful say, God has made me barren. For the Lord said, unto the impotent man that keep His Sabbaths, and choose the things that please Him, and take hold of His covenant; He will give a place, and a name which is better than the inheritance of sons and daughters. I will give them an everlasting name that will be remembered. Furthermore, to the sons of the stranger that has joined themselves to the Lord to serve Him, and to love the name of the Lord, they that keep the Sabbath from polluting it, and take hold of My covenant; even them will I bring to My Holy Mountain, and make them joyful in My house of prayer: their consecration and their praise will be accepted and be remembered; for mine house shall be called an house of prayer for all the people.

There are actually seven Sabbaths in a year, which represents a tenth of our time, and devotion unto the Lord God. The Sabbaths should be viewed, and studied as a part of our daily devotional life to Christ, whereby it will further hasten our sanctification. In the Ten Commandments the Seventh Day wasn't a weekly Sabbath, but instead a yearly memorial. Jesus reassures us that the Sabbath wasn't done away with. **Mark chapter 2:27,28** tells us that the Sabbath was made for man and not man for the Sabbath: therefore the Son of man is the Lord of the Sabbath.

Spring, New Moon

1. The Passover: *(Justification By Faith)*
2. The Feast of Unleavened Bread: *(Word of God, which is Christ Love)*
3. The First Fruits Harvest: *(Spiritual rebirth, born–again)*
4. Pentecost: *(Sanctification, hope in Christ)*

Fall, New Moon

5. The Blowing of Trumpets: *(Preparation of the Church)*
6. The Atonement of Sin: *(Cleansing of the heart)*
7. The Feast of Tabernacle: *(Glorification, Character perfection)*

During the Passover Jesus and His disciples spent time in the upper room, whereby they fasted, and entered into Holy convocation with God the Father. The Lord's Passover is for the justification of mankind. God created the human race in His Own Image and Likeness: therefore we were created as God's children. Jesus had the likeness of Adam who was the first man, but His Character was that of His heavenly Father. Since we are created to be like Christ, we also have the opportunity to receive the Image of God's Character through Him. The plan of salvation is centered on Christ Who is the Lord of the Sabbath, whereby the Sabbath is made for mankind. God wants to restore our spirit, and give us a clear conscience to rule over our mind and senses. The human race was given the ability to exercise free–will, but free–will apart from Christ is like a car rolling down a hill out of control. Free–will without temperance is the recipe for disaster. The Sabbath is the fourth Commandment, which is a clear indication of submission and surrendering onto the first three by means of which our hearts are renewed to keep His law of love; and having victory by overcoming every sin, at which point the heart of the believer enters the kingdom of grace. The Character of our heavenly Father is the foundation of our faith, and belief. **Malachi chapter 3:6** tells us that I Am the Lord, I change not. Amen

The Sabbath is made for Mankind

By the revelation of Jesus Christ all things are made known. The Son of man came to save that, which was lost. Jesus spoke of the universe in a parable, whereby the earth represented the lost sheep. **Matthew chapter 18:11-14** tells us that if a man have a hundred sheep, and one of them went astray, will he not leave the ninety-nine and go to the mountains to seek after the one that went astray? And if he should find it, assuredly, I say to you, he rejoices more over that one sheep than over the ninety-nine that did not go astray. Even, so it is not the will of your Father Who is in heaven that one of these little ones should perish.

Daniel chapter 10:2-7 tells us that in those days the Messiah Yeshua was standing by the great river Hiddekel. And I, Daniel, was fasting for twenty–one days. I ate no pleasant bread, neither came food nor drink in my mouth, neither did I bathe myself, till three whole weeks were fulfilled. And in the twenty–fourth day of the first month of April/Abib, while I was by the side of the great river Hiddekel; I lifted up mine eyes, and behold a certain man clothed in linen, whose waist was wrapped with a belt made from fine gold: His body glowed as if it were made from precious stones, the appearance of His face were as lightening, His eyes like a flaming fire, His arms and feet were as bronze in color, and the sound of His voice were as a multitude of people. And I, Daniel, alone saw the vision, for the men who were with me did not see the vision; but great terror fell upon them, so that they fled and hid themselves.

Let every believer purpose in their hearts to stand still during the Sabbath day, so that faith might fulfill its perfect work, whereby moving our spirit forward to labor in love toward one another, and holdfast to the patience of hope that we have in Christ Jesus Who is yet to come. **Matthew chapter 5:17,18** tells us that Christ did not come to change the law or prophecies: "I did not come to destroy, but to fulfill. For certain, I say unto you, until heaven and earth is destroyed, not one jot of the pen or one drop of ink shall in no wise change the law, until all is finish."

John chapter 2:23 tells us that while Jesus was in Jerusalem at the Passover, on the day of the feast, many believed in His name, after they saw the miracles, which He did. **John chapter 9:16** tells us that while Jesus was healing on the Sabbath day, the Pharisees said, this man is not from God, because He does not keep the Sabbath: others said, how could a man who is a sinner do such miraculous sign? And there was a division among them. **Matthew chapter 12:10,11** tells us behold, there was a man who had a shriveled hand, and the Pharisees saw it as an opportunity to asked Jesus, "Is it lawful to heal on the Sabbath days?" So that they might accuse Him of working on the Sabbath. Jesus replied, unto them, "What man shall there be among you, that shall have one sheep, and if it falls into a pit on the Sabbath day, will he not lay hold on it, and lift it out? **Luke chapter 13:10-13** tells us that Jesus was teaching in one of the synagogues on the Sabbath day, and He saw a woman who was sick for eighteen years with back pain, and she was unable to standup by herself. And when Jesus saw her, He called her, and laid His hands on her and said, woman, you are free from your sickness, and immediately she stood up straight, and glorified God. **John chapter 7:21-24** tells us that Jesus said unto the Pharisees, I work on the Sabbath to glorify God, and you are all upset. Moses therefore circumcises on the Sabbath day; not because it was his decision, but rather the commandment of God; and you therefore also circumcise a man on the Sabbath day. If a man receives circumcision on the Sabbath day, so that the commandment of Moses should not be broken: are you angry with Me, because I have healed a man on the Sabbath day? Judge not according to the appearance, but judge righteous judgment by the discernment of God's will. **John chapter 9:14** tells us that it was the Sabbath day when Jesus made the clay, and opened the eyes of the blind man. Amen

Which day is the Sabbath Day?

The main focus of the Sabbath day is the Agape love of God. However, the religious format of how we worship is the focus for many people. **John chapter 4:24** tells us that God is a Spirit, and they that worship Him, must worship Him in spirit and in truth. Jesus Christ, the Son of man and the Lord of the Sabbath made it clear to the Pharisees about God's mercy and justice unto all. The ministry of Jesus Christ has nothing to gain by us observing one day above another, if our relationship with the Father is not renewed to the glory of His name: Jehovah Jirah, Jehovah Nissi, and Jehovah Shalom, whereby we are called unto repentance by His Holy Spirit.

The Seventh Day Sabbath is the return of Christ Who is Lord of the Sabbath. The relationship that we share with the Father through Christ is most important. **Colossians chapter 2:16-18** tells us that no man should therefore judge in meat, or in drink, or in respect of an Holy day, or of the new moon, or of the Sabbath days: which are a shadow of things to come; but the entire body belongs to Christ. Let no man deceive you of your reward with a false sense of humility, and the worshiping of angels, seducing you with things, which he himself has not seen, foolishly speculating by his own imaginative mind.

Jesus Christ is calling us unto repentance through faith. **Revelation chapter 3:20** tells us that Christ is knocking at the entrance of our hearts: and anyone who hears His voice, and open their heart to Him, He will go in unto him, and they will both drink together. Let us therefore love one another, as Christ Himself is love. Whichever day you are convicted to worship on, the Holy Spirit is given unto humanity to discern both good and evil. Throughout the Bible churches debated the law, but never came to any conclusion that would give glory to God. I quote: Jesus Christ is the end of the law, and the beginning of free–will; whereby, we exercise faith in God the Father. If you have truly accepted Christ as Lord and Savior, then He is your eternal Sabbath now, and forever, because you have entered into rest with Him; thereby, if you have entered into rest with Christ, then you have cease from your own works of the human nature, and peace and joy fills your heart toward God and mankind. Amen

Jesus is the Lord of the Sabbath

Just as Jesus Christ was crucified on the cross at Calvary; even so, must our mortal bodies be crucified by spending time in the Word, persevering in prayer and fasting. The selfless life of Christ should be viewed by every believer, and knowing that His death paid the price for our sins. **Matthew chapter 26:1-4** tells us that Jesus said unto His disciples, "In two days the Son of man shall be betrayed, and crucified at the feast for the Passover." Then the chief priests, and the scribes, and the elders of the people, went unto the palace of the high priest, who was called Caiaphas, and consulted together how they might take Jesus by deception and kill Him. **John chapter 13:1-5** tells us that before the feast of the Passover, when Jesus knew that His hour was come that He should depart out of this world unto the Father, having loved His own, which were in the world: He loved them unto the end. And the supper being ended, the devil was now put into the heart of Judas Iscariot, Simon's son, to betray Him. Jesus knowing that the Father had given all things into His hands, and that He came from God, and it was the hour for Him to return to the Father Who sent Him; He got up from the table, and laid aside His clothing; and took a towel, and wrap it around Himself. After which He poured water into a basin, and began to wash the disciples' feet and wipe them with the towel that He had wrapped around His waist.

Today, we have communion with God through Jesus Christ Who is the Lord of the Sabbath. The washing of the saint's feet is a reminder that He Himself washes our entire body that He might present us to the Father without spot or wrinkle. The Sabbath is for true believers, the distinction between the call, and the chosen. **Matthew chapter 22:14** tells us that many are called, but few are chosen. **John chapter 17:12, 18:9** tells us that Jesus said, these that You have given unto Me Father I have lost none. By the Word of God, which is Christ, not one believer will be lost, but all shall be saved. Amen

The Plan of Salvation

God established the Sabbath as the great plan of salvation to save humanity. The study of the Sabbath is more or less a teaching tool to further personify our faith in God. The Sabbath was made for man, and not man for the Sabbath. Jesus Christ is the Lord of the Sabbath. The Lord's Sabbath began with the Passover after the fall of mankind; whereby the Lord revealed His plan of salvation unto Adam and Eve. **Genesis chapter 3:8-11** tells us that they heard the voice of the Lord God walking in the Garden in the cool of the day. In other words it was during spring that the Lord God visited them. And Adam and his wife hid themselves from the presence of the Lord God among the trees of the Garden. And the Lord God called unto Adam, and said unto him, "Where are you? And he said, I heard Your voice in the Garden, and I was afraid, because I was naked; and I hid myself. And the Lord God said, who told you that you were naked? Have you eaten from the tree, which I commanded you not to eat of?"

Adam's fall is the reflection of Christ's death on the cross at Calvary. After Adam sinned, the countdown began, whereby Christ came and died during the fourth millennium. However, while Christ was on earth time stood still, as it did in the Garden of Eden: for He did not sin, and sin has to do with time, and time with death. After Christ ascension, the countdown for His return began. From Christ death to present day is about 1,990 years with some variables due to the changes made to the Genesis Calendar in the year 1582, whereby 5 days added to each year. **Genesis chapter 1:1-31** tells us that in the beginning, God created the heaven and the earth, whereby He layout the history of creation unto us by letting us know that creation and mankind is based upon six literal days, and the close of probation of all creation would take place in six thousand years. Today, we acknowledge the Gregorian calendar as the Christian calendar, instead of the book of Genesis chapter one, which is the true Calendar from God Himself. There are only six days in a week according to the book of Genesis: the Seventh Day is the Sabbath when Christ Himself Who is the Lord of the Sabbath will return.

God's Calendar
- Six days: 1 week, 360 days: 1 year
- Adam Sinned: 33 BC
- The Great Flood: 2000 BC
- The Crossing of the Rea Sea: 3000 BC
- The Birth of Christ: 4000 BC—01 AD
- The Death of Christ: 33 AD
- The Resurrection of Christ: 33 AD
- From 01 AD—33 AD, time stood still for Christ did not sin.
- Christ ascended: 34 AD, the countdown began for His return.
- The adoption of the Gregorian calendar: 1582 AD

The Gregorian calendar
- Seven days: 1 week, 365 days: 1 year
- From 1582 AD, present day 2017 AD, 5 days added to each year.
- 2017–1582 equals to 435 years times 5 equals to 2,175 days, divided by 360 days equals to 6 years. 2017 plus 6 years equals to 2023 minus the 33 years of Christ life on earth; for He did not sin, which brings us to 1990 with some variables. No one knows the day or the hour when Christ will return, but we have hope in Him. The Gregorian calendar is a repetitious cycle of days, and months, and years; and differs from God's Calendar in the sense that one deals with time and death, and the other is the fulfillment of prophecies, and eternal life. The relationship that we have with Jesus is moment–by–moment. Furthermore, we have to stay focus on Him by surrendering our entire life to the indwelling of the Holy Spirit, whereby our lives are transformed and made ready to meet the Father in heaven. The true Sabbath is Jesus Christ Himself, whereby the Son of man is Lord of the millennial Sabbath. Amen

The Prophecy of the Great Flood 2000 BC

The worldwide flood occurred during the second millennium in the year *1,656 BC*. Before the flood, it had never rained on the earth. A mist watered the earth from the ground, but after the flood most of the water that was under the earth was now on top of it, forming oceans and seas. After the great flood, God had to separate the water from off the earth, whereby placing it above and beneath the earth. Before the flood the icebergs as we know them now didn't exist. The seven days of delay that occurred before the rain was the close of probation for those that refuse to enter into the ark. History will repeat itself seven days before the end of the 6th millennium. **Genesis chapter 1:6-8** tells us that God said, let there be a firmament between the land and the sky to separate the water that was on the earth from the water that was beneath the earth. And God made the atmosphere with an open sky. And God made the elevation above the earth and called it heaven. And the evening and the morning were the second day. **Genesis chapter 7:1** tells us that the Lord said unto Noah, come now, you and your household into the ark, because I have seen the righteousness of your generation before Me. **Genesis chapter 7:4** tells us that God caused it to rain upon the earth forty days and forty nights; and every living creature that was made was destroyed from off the face of the earth. **Genesis chapter 8:13** tells us that it came to pass in the six hundred and first year, in the first month of April/Abib, that the water dried up from off the earth: and Noah removed the covering of the ark, and looked, and behold the face of the ground was dry. God saved, but eight people in the flood: even though He had the power to save all. Today many will die in the world, and tomorrow the close of probation will come upon all the earth. But, are you willing to surrender right now to the unconditional love of God through Jesus Christ. Amen

The Son of Promise

God made a promise unto Abraham and his son Isaac. God did not make the promise unto sons, but instead He made a promise that His only begotten Son Jesus Christ would come and fulfill the free gift of salvation through Abraham's seed. **Genesis chapter 12:1-3** tells us that the Lord said, unto Abram, leave this land and your relatives, and from your father's house, and I will show you a land where I will make you a great nation, and I will bless you and make your name great; and you shall be a blessing: and I will bless them that bless you, and curse him that curse you: and in you shall all the families of the earth be blessed. **Genesis chapter 15:1-7** tells us that after these things the Word of the Lord came unto Abram in a vision, saying, fear not, Abram: I Am your shield, and your provider. And Abram said, Lord God, what will You give unto me, seeing I go childless, and the steward of my house is this E-lie'-zer of Damascus? And Abram said, behold, You have not given me an heir: and now there is a child being born in my house, who will become mine heir. Then the Lord said, unto Abram, he will not be your heir; but you shall have a son born of Sarah, he will be your heir. And the Lord took him by the hand, and said, look toward heaven and behold the vast numbers of stars, so shall your descendants be. And he believed in the Lord, and the Lord blessed him with righteousness.

And the Lord said unto him, I Am the Lord that brought you out of Ur of the Chaldeans, to give you this land to inherit it. God gave us hope through Abraham the father of faith, because he believed in the Lord. **Galatians chapter 3:16-22** tells us that the covenant that was established between God and Abraham revealed that Christ would come as a promise, which was four hundred and thirty years before the written law was given unto the Jewish nation by the hand of Moses. Furthermore, the written law cannot void the promise of God. The inheritance that God had promise unto Abraham was not of a sensual nature, but by the promise of faith. The written law was only added because of our disobedience. Christ made it known by His messengers that He Himself would come and fulfill the requirements of the written law by dying on the cross at Calvary. Christ became our mediator, because of the separation between us, and the Father. Amen

From Egypt to the Promise Land 3000 BC

God is Omniscience, His providence was declared by the death of His Son Jesus Christ on the cross at Calvary, which brought forth spiritual deliverance: and the saving of mankind's weary soul.

Genesis chapter 15:13,14 tells us that the prophecy of the crossing of the Red Sea was declared unto Abraham by God four hundred and thirty years before He delivered Moses, and the Israelites from Pharaoh's army by parting the Red Sea, and making a way for them to cross on dry ground. This was foretold on the third day of creation.

Genesis chapter 1:9-13 tells us that God said, let the waters under the heaven be gathered together unto one place, and let the dry land appear: and it was so. And God called the dry land earth; and the gathering together of the waters He called Seas: and God saw that it was good. And God said, let the earth bring forth grass, the herb producing seed, and the fruit tree producing fruit after his kind whose seed is in itself upon the earth, and it was so. And the earth brought forth grass, and herb producing seed after his kind, and the tree producing fruit whose seed is in itself after his kind. And God saw that it was good. And the evening and the morning were the third day.

The retroactive work of His Holy Spirit can be seen from Moses the lawgiver unto Elijah and the prophets, but it was the Father Who sent them unto the children of Israel. The Godhead is three in one: Father, Son, and Holy Spirit. And if it weren't for sin there would have been no need of mediation. Is the written law against the promise of God? Certainly not! The law that was given unto Moses by God had not the power to give life; therefore righteousness came not from the written law, but it exposed sin unto us, whereby the scripture concluded that all have sinned, so that the promise would be established through faith in Jesus Christ unto them that believe! Amen

The Lord's Passover *(Pasch)*

Exodus chapter 16:23 tell us that Moses said unto the Israelites, this is what the Lord said: <u>tomorrow is the rest of the Holy Sabbath unto the Lord</u>. The Seventh Day is God's promise to His people: a time of peace and prosperity and fellowshipping with Christ for a thousand years in the New Jerusalem. After the new covenant was made between God and Abraham, the law was given unto Moses and the Israelites four hundred and thirty years later.

The Seven Sabbaths reminds us that Christ will return at the completion of the sixth millennium, and <u>we must be ready to enter into His rest</u>. The Sabbaths are the gateway to the third heaven where our Mediator is standing in the throne room with His hands stretch out waiting to intercede on our behalf. Mankind was given free-will to enter into rest with God, without free-will, love cannot be achieved. Pasch is the first Sabbath: the <u>covenant</u> between God and Abraham. God fulfilled His promise to Abraham four hundred and thirty years later, whereby He brought the Israelites out of Egypt. The feast of unleavened bread was celebrated as the eating of the body of Christ: <u>Manna</u>, which came down from heaven. Christ Who became the sacrificial <u>Lamb</u> for the <u>Atonement of sin</u>. **Exodus chapter 12:1-15** tells us that the Lord spoke unto Moses and Aaron in the land of Egypt, saying, <u>the first new moon in spring shall be unto you the beginning of months</u>: it shall be the first month of the year unto you. Speak unto all the congregation of Israel, saying, <u>in the tenth day of April/Abib</u> they shall take unto themselves every man a lamb, according to the members of his family. And if the household is too small for a lamb, let him share it with his neighbor that lives next door. Your lamb shouldn't have any defect, a male one year old: sheep or goat. And you shall keep it until <u>the fourteenth day of the same month</u>, and the whole congregation of Israel shall kill it in the evening. And they shall <u>take of the blood of the lamb and place it upon the two side frames of the door entrance of their homes, and also at the top of the door. And they shall eat the lamb in that night, roasted by fire with unleavened bread; and with bitter herbs they shall eat it.</u>

The lamb must be roasted by fire, and shouldn't be eaten raw or cooked in water; its head and legs must remain attach to it's body. Everything must be eaten; nothing should remain until the next day, but if any should remain it must be burned by fire. The lamb should be eaten in haste: with your belt around your waist, and your shoes on your feet, and your staff in your hand; it is the Lord's Passover. For I will pass through the land of Egypt this night, and I will kill all the firstborn who are not sanctified by blood, both man and animal; and against all the false gods of Egypt I will execute judgment: I Am the Lord. And the blood that's upon the doorway of your house shall be for your protection: and when I see the blood, I will pass over you, and the plague shall not be upon you when I smite the land of Egypt. And this day will be a memorial for you; and you shall keep it as a feast to the Lord throughout your generations; this feast is by commandment forever. Seven days you must eat unleavened bread.

The Passover was the fulfillment of the promise that was made unto Abraham by means of which God delivered the Israelites from bondage, and sin. **Exodus chapter 14:13,14** tells us that Moses said, unto the people, fear not, stand still, and see the salvation of the Lord God, which He will show to you this day, for the Egyptians whom you saw, you will see no more forever. The Lord will fight for you, and you will hold your peace.

The retroactive work of the Holy Spirit is the on–going ministry of soul Salvation moment–by–moment. The Holy Spirit is everywhere fulfilling the promise that God made unto Abraham many years ago. Today, we have hope in the promise that was made unto our forefather Abraham that Christ will return for you and I; therefore let us be ready to meet our Lord and Savior Jesus Christ. Amen

Feast of Unleavened Bread (Hag HaMatatzah)

During the Passover Hag HaMatatzah, or the feast of unleavened bread is celebrated by eating unfermented dough: symbolizing Manna, which came down from heaven. The purity of the gospel of Jesus Christ Who is the Word of God. Justification by faith is most likely the theme God wants us to acknowledge during the Passover season. **Exodus chapter 12:14-17** tells us that there is a memorial for God's people, who overcame spiritual oppression. From the first day of the month of April/Abib, all manner of leaven should be put out of our homes: whosoever use leaven from the first day until the seventh day, that individual shall be cutoff from spiritual Israel. The beginning of the new moon is a Sabbath, and in the first day there shall be a Holy conversation for seven days, and no manner of work shall be done in them, except for the food, which you shall eat, until seven days are fulfill. The feast of unleavened bread should be observed throughout your generations every year at this exact time in memory of the day I brought you out of Egypt. It is to be kept throughout your generations forever.

(Hag HaMatatzah) is a leap of faith, the substance of eternal salvation, and even those things, which we hope for in Christ, and evidently cannot be seen or explained by the carnal mind, but rather conscience over mind to rule over the senses. For without the justification of faith no one shall be saved. **Hebrews chapter 11:1-4** tells us that faith is the source of things hoped for without any evidence. Furthermore, the forefathers obtained a good report. Through faith we understand that Jesus Christ, the Son of the living God created the universe, so that the invisible things would become more precious than the things, which are seen. By faith Abel offered a more excellent sacrifice than his brother Cain. God also witness that he was righteous, whereby He testified of his gifts: and by it while his body was dead God heard him take his last breath.

The relationship that we share with Christ gives us freedom from bondage, and sin. God commanded the Israelites to keep His law while they were living in the wilderness, but instead they committed adultery and died after forty years. **Psalm chapter 78:1-72** tells us that the Lord spoke, unto the Israelites, saying, Pay attention to the commandments, which I have given unto you. I will make things simple for you, so that you can understand the things concerning the beginning of time, which were made known by the teachings of your forefathers. I will not keep the truth from you, but I will give wisdom unto you and your children concerning the praise of My name. I will tell you of My strength, and of My wonderful works, which I did in the land of Egypt.

I will established My salvation with Jacob, and appoint My law unto the Israelites, which I also commanded them to make known to their children and grandchildren; that the generation to come might know them also, and declare the decree of My law, and put their hope in Me, and be mindful of the miracles, which I did in the land of Egypt. And keep My commandments diligently, and be not disobedient like their forefathers: a stubborn and rebellious generation; a generation which set not their hearts to know Me, and whose spirit was not faithful unto Me. The children of Ephraim being armed with bows, flee in the day of battle; being fearful, instead of being faithful, they kept not the covenant, but refused to walk in My uprightness, an instead chose to ignore My magnificent signs, and wonders that I did in the sight of their forefathers, in the land of Egypt, in the valley of Zo-an. God divided the Red Sea, so that the Israelites could pass through it. In the daytime He also led them with a cloud, and through the night with a light by fire. He opened the rock in the wilderness and gave them water to drink. Furthermore, He made streams flow out of the rock like a river, but needless to say, they sinned yet against Him by provoking the Lord, and they tempted God in their hearts by asking for meat to satisfy their desire.

Presumptuously they murmured against the Lord; and said, can God furnish a table in the wilderness? Can He give bread also? Can He provide food for His people? They chose to ignore their conscience, and forgot how He had split the rock open and made the water to rush out like a river. Therefore, God heard the murmurings of the people, and it displeased Him; for He had commanded the clouds from above to open the doors of heaven, and made it rain <u>Manna</u> upon them. God gave them corn from heaven, and man did eat angels' food. He also sent them meat to the full, but their appetites were not satisfied with what God had given them, for they had a taste for fish, cucumbers, melons, leeks, garlic, and onions. So then God caused an east wind to blow in the heaven, and with His power He brought in the south wind; and He rained quails upon them like the dust of the air; whereby the quails were as plentiful as the sand of the sea: and He let them fall in the middle of their camp.

So they did eat, and were filled with the meat of their desire. And even though God fulfilled their desire by satisfying their appetites, they murmured just the same. But while the food was yet in their mouths, the wrath of God came upon the chosen men and women of Israel, and He slew the strongest of them. For His judgment was pronounce upon the Israelites, and His justice was carried out. The Lord's righteous indignation burnt like a fire among the people, and it consumed them. The people had rebelled from under His hand, and His judgment was pass against the house of Judah, and the close of probation came upon Israel, because they believed not in God, and they trusted not in His salvation. Even while they were being punished they sinned continually, and believed not in His power. Furthermore, their days were consumed in vanity, and their years in trouble. But soon after their sins became unbearable, they cried unto the Lord, and they beg Him for forgiveness. And they remembered that God was their Rock, and the Most High was their Redeemer. Nevertheless they did flatter Him with their lips, and they lied unto Him with their tongues, for their hearts weren't genuine toward Him, neither were they in agreement with His covenant. But, He being compassionate and merciful, He forgave their iniquities, and destroyed them not.

However, continually they sinned, and God delayed His judgment by showing them mercy, and extending His grace. For He remembered that mankind was like a wind that passes away and come not again. They committed adultery, and provoke Him in the wilderness, and grieved Him in the desert. They rebelled continually by tempting Him, and limiting the Holy One of Israel. The people remembered not His mercy, nor the day when He delivered them from their enemies. And how He had shown His signs and wonders in Egypt, and also in the field of Zo-an: when their rivers were turn into blood, and diverse swarms of flies, and frogs devoured their enemies. God also gave their harvests unto the caterpillar, and their labor unto the locust. He destroyed their vineyards, and cattle with hail, and their flocks with hot thunderbolts. He also destroyed their sycamore trees with frost.

And cast upon them the fierceness of His anger by allowing evil angels to dwell among them. And death walked through the land, and He spared not their souls, but their lives were cut short by plagues; which devoured all the first born children of Egypt; even the strongest descendants of Ham. However, God protected His people and led them forward like a sheep safely through the Red Sea, but as for the enemy the floods of the deep overwhelmed them. And He brought them to the border of His sanctuary, even to this mountain, which His right hand purchased. He also cast out the unbelievers that lived in the land, and divided the land among the Israelites, which He had made to live in tents. But again they tempted, and provoked the Most High God, and kept not His commandments; but turned back, and dealt unfaithfully with Him as did their forefathers: they were turned aside like a faulty bow. For they provoked, and grieved the Most Holy One with their high places, and moved Him to jealousy with their graven images, and their idols.

The people made the Lord angry by committing adultery. They had return to a life of sin, rejecting the tabernacle of Shiloh; the tent that He had placed among men; and His people was delivered into captivity, and His glory into the hand of the enemy. He allowed the sword to destroy His people, while He was longsuffering with His inheritance. Their young men were killed, and their virgins were not given to marriage, meanwhile the husbands were put to death by the sword, and their wives did not mourn. Then the Lord gave a shout like a mighty man awoken out of a deep sleep, and destroyed the enemy and put him to an everlasting shame. God rejected the house of Joseph, which is the tribe of E-phra-im: and chose the tribe of Judah, and He established the throne of David, which became His beloved Mount Zion. The Lord also built a sanctuary above and beyond the valley; it was a magnificent palace, whereby He put David in charge of His people. David who was a humble shepherd, diligent and tender hearted toward his sheep; the Lord appointed him to lead the tribe of Judah, and the house of Israel. David led them according to the integrity of his heart; and guided them by the skillfulness of his hands.

Exodus chapter 33:17-23 tells us that the Lord said, unto Moses, I will do this thing also that you have ask of Me: for you have found grace in My sight, and I know you by name. And Moses said, I beg you O Lord, show me Your glory. And the Lord said, I will make My goodness pass before you, and I will proclaim My name before you. For I will be gracious to whom, I will be gracious, and I will be merciful to whom, I will show mercy. And the Lord said unto Moses, My face shall not be seen. For no man shall see Me, and live. And the Lord said, behold there is a place by Me, and you shall stand upon a rock, and I will make it so that My glory passes by, and I will cover you with My hand, while I pass by. And I will take away Mine hand, and you shall see My back parts: but My face shall not be seen.

Exodus chapter 34:8-10 tells us that Moses made haste, and bowed his head toward the earth, and worshipped Him. And he said, if now I have found grace in Your sight, O Lord, then let not my Lord be angry, for these people are very stubborn; but I beg You, to be with us; and to forgive us of our sins and let the Lord's glory be as promised. And the Lord said, <u>behold I make a covenant</u>: before all the people, and I will do marvelous things, which have not been done before in all the earth, nor in any other nation: and all the people will see the work of the Lord.

After Moses had seen the goodness of the Lord, there was no denying His sovereignty, but yet for forty years the Israelite's saw the goodness of the Lord, and repented not. Blessed is the man that takes hold of the Lord's goodness. For His goodness will endure forever. Now that we are sanctified by the blood of Christ should we continue to live life apart from Him? God forbid! Don't you know that eventually lawlessness leads to the close of probation! How should we live now that we have received the free gift of grace and the promise of eternal salvation? Since we all face different challenges moment–by–moment, and grace is the imputed gift of sanctification; its only logic that every decision should be presented unto God for justification. Sanctification can only be defined as the seal of His righteousness: whereas grace is the witnessing of the ministerial work of the Holy Spirit unto those that are made perfect in His Agape love. Amen

The First Fruits Harvest *(Yom HaBickkurim)*

The First fruits of Jesus' resurrection are those that ascended with Him to heaven. **Exodus chapter 13:1,2** tells us that the Lord spoke unto Moses, saying, sanctify unto Me all the firstborn that comes out of the womb among the children of Israel, both man and animal: they are Mine. **Exodus chapter 23:16** tells us that the First fruits harvest of our labors, which we have sown in the field, and the feast of ingathering, which is the end of the year also belong to the Lord.

The First fruits harvest is the memorial of the firstborn unto the Lord: even Christ Jesus Who was resurrected from the dead. Jesus Christ was the Son of God Who became the sacrificial Lamb for our sins. For He being the First fruits of every living creature, it was also of a necessity for Him to become the First fruits of the dead. **Revelation chapter 14:13** tells us that John heard a voice from heaven saying, write, blessed are the dead, which die in the Lord from hereafter: yes says the Spirit, that they may rest from their labors, and their works do follow them. **Matthew chapter 27:46-53** tells us that while Jesus was yet on the cross He cried with a loud voice, saying, E'-li, E'-li, la'-ma-sa-bach-tha-ni. My God, My God, why have You forsaken Me? But on the contrary Jesus did not cry to be saved, but instead He was letting His Father know that it was done according to His will. And after Jesus had cried again with a loud voice, He gave up His Spirit, and behold the curtain of the temple, which divided the Most Holy Place, and the bread of life, and the incense of prayer was separated from the top to the bottom; and the earth quaked, and the rocks fell. And the graves of the First fruits of the saints that slept were opened and many bodies arose, and came out of the graves after His resurrection, and went into the Holy City, and appeared unto many.

The saints that arose that day weren't numbered, but I believe that the twenty-four elders arose that very same day. There were twenty-four divisions of the earthly sanctuary according to the description that God gave unto Moses to make the replica of the heavenly sanctuary. After the resurrection, Jesus appeared unto Mary Magdalene, and afterward unto His disciples. Mary Magdalene who was of the First fruits of the living unto the Kingdom of grace, Jesus increases her faith in Him by revealing Himself, unto her. **John chapter 20:17-23** tells us that Jesus said unto her, touch Me not; for I Am not yet ascended to My Father: but go to My brethren, and say unto them, I ascend unto My Father, and your Father; and to My God, and your God. Mary Magdalene came and told the disciples that she had seen the Lord, and that He had spoken these things unto her. Then the same day at evening, being the first day of the week, after the disciples were assembled together, they shut the doors because they were afraid of the Jews, then came Jesus and stood in the middle of them, and said, "Peace be unto you." And then He showed them His hands and His side. Then the disciples were glad to see the Lord. Then Jesus said unto them, peace be unto you: as My Father has sent Me, even so I will send you. And after He said this, He breathed on them, and said, receive the Holy Spirit: whosoever sins you forgive, they are forgiven; and whosoever sins that are not forgiven, they will remain. **Acts chapter 1:8,9** tells us that Jesus spoke unto His disciples about receiving the Holy Spirit during Pentecost. And when He was finish speaking, He was taken up; and a cloud of angels received Him out of their sight.

Psalm chapter 24:7-10 tells us that when Jesus got to heaven with the First fruits harvest, He cried with joy from a distance that the gatekeeper should make the gates ready to receive glory, "lift up your heads and open the gates; raise up the everlasting doors; and the King of glory shall come in." The gatekeepers of the twelve gates of glory, then replied, who is the King of glory? Jesus shouted, the Lord strong and mighty, the Lord mighty in battle. Lift up your heads and open the gates; raise up the everlasting doors; and the King of glory shall come in. The gatekeepers replied again, who is this King of glory? And again Jesus proclaimed His Father's victory. The Lord of hosts, He is the King of glory. Selah

Revelation chapter 4:4 tells us that John saw twenty-four seats on which sat twenty-four elders dressed in white and wearing crowns of gold. The sacrifice of the lamb represents the work that Christ did on our behalf while He was here on earth. Jesus not only paid the price for our sins, but after His ascension, He became our Lord and Royal High Priest: being able to enter into the Most Holy place: knowing our thoughts, and the intent of our hearts. Christ being the First fruits of the living by means of which Enoch, Elijah and Moses were translated into the Kingdom of God, and did not see death for God took them. Jesus became the First fruits of the dead, whereby He was raised on the first day. **Genesis chapter 1:3** tells us that God said, let there be light. Jesus is the light of the world. **Genesis chapter 1:5** tells us that God called the light Day, and the darkness He called Night. And the evening and the morning were the first day.

No one dies without getting the opportunity of making a conscientious decision for soul salvation. Sensual knowledge doesn't give us the power to overcome sin. We all share the same weakness of rebellion, which leads to disobedience, but only those that are tried in fire purified seven times have the power to overcome sin. The First fruits harvest is the victory of Jesus Christ over Satan. The glory of God's sovereignty, and omniscient power to give life not only unto His firstborn, which is Christ, but also unto those who were resurrected at His ascension. Amen

The Day of Pentecost *(Shavuoth)*

Pentecost is forty–nine days after Jesus's resurrection, which is the total of fifty days. Pentecost occur in the month of Sivan (May/June) **Esther chapter 8:9** is the only place in the Bible where the month of Sivan is found. Pentecost is the outpouring of the Holy Spirit upon God's children. The resurrection of our Lord Jesus Christ marks the first day, whereby, He became the light of the world as God had prophesy on the first day in the book of Genesis, followed by forty–nine days that would complete the promise He made unto His disciples. The former rain, and latter rain is the outpouring of the Holy Spirit upon the true disciples of Jesus Christ to do the Fathers' will. **Leviticus chapter 23:15,16** tells us that you shall count the days after the Sabbath, from tomorrow, up to <u>fifty days</u> from the <u>First fruits harvest</u>, seven Sabbaths you shall number and you shall offer new meat offering unto the Lord.

Luke chapter 24:49 tells us that Jesus commanded His disciples to remain in Jerusalem after His departure for the outpouring of the Holy Spirit. **Acts chapter 1:2-10** tells us that after the <u>forty days</u> were ended Jesus was taken up into heaven; whereby He commanded His disciples to remain in Jerusalem for the outpouring of the Holy Spirit. **Acts chapter 2:1-6** tells us that when the day of Pentecost came; the disciples were all fasting and praying together for the outpouring of the Holy Spirit in the same house, and suddenly there came a sound from heaven like the rush of a mighty wind, and it filled the entire house where they were sitting. And there appeared unto them a burning flame, and it sat upon each of them. And they were all filled with the Holy Spirit, and they began to speak other languages, as the Holy Spirit empowered them. During the Passover, Jews and devout men: believers from every nation under the heaven came to Jerusalem for the worshiping of the Lord's Passover. Now when it was made known unto the public that the disciples were given the gift of discernment by the Holy Spirit, they came together and were astonished; because every man heard them speaking in their own native language. Amen

The Blowing of Trumpets *(Yom Teruah)*

(Yom Teruah) is the blowing of trumpets, the final call before the close of probation for the earth and it's inhabitance. The feast of Trumpets, the Atonement of sin, and the feast of Tabernacle occur in the <u>seventh</u> month of Ethanim (September/October). The blowing of trumpets is the final call for repentance, this happens seven days before the atonement for sin. (Yom Teruah) is the fifth Sabbath by means of which the church is made ready to be sanctified by the blood of Jesus Christ. Furthermore, our hearts are prepared to receive the atonement for sin.

During the days of Noah, he preached the message of repentance: as did Jesus Christ according to the law and prophets. Noah preached for a hundred and twenty years before the flood came, saying, repent repent: for the kingdom of God is at hand. The end came not without warning, and those that were cleansed from their unrighteousness went into the Ark. As it was in the days of Noah, so shall it be in the end. **Leviticus chapter 23:24-44** tells us that Moses spoke unto the children of Israel, saying, from the first day of the <u>seventh</u> month is the beginning of the Sabbath, a memorial of the blowing of trumpets, and a Holy conversation. You shall do no subservient work, but give an offering made by fire unto the Lord. Furthermore, God spoke unto Moses, saying, on the <u>tenth day</u> of the seventh month, it shall be a day of <u>atonement</u>: come before Me with a Holy conversation; and repent of your sins, and give an offering made by fire unto Me. And you shall do no subservient work in that same day: it is a <u>day of atonement,</u> to make atonement for you before Me. Anyone who repents not by surrendering his soul in that same day will be cut off from among his people. And whosoever does any subservient work in that same day, the same soul I will destroy from among his people. You shall do no manner of work: it shall be a law forever throughout your generations in all your dwellings. It shall be unto you a <u>Sabbath of rest,</u> and you shall repent and surrender your souls.

From the ninth-day of the month, at evening unto evening, you shall celebrate the beginning of the Sabbath. And the Lord God spoke unto Moses, saying, speak unto the children of Israel, saying, the fifteenth-day of the seventh month is the feast of tabernacles for seven days unto the Lord. The first day shall be a Holy conversation: you shall do no subservient work. Seven days you shall offer an offering made by fire unto Me. The eight-day shall be a Holy conversation unto you, and you shall offer an offering made by fire unto Me: it is a solemn assembly; and you shall do no subservient work. These are the feasts of the Lord, which you shall proclaim to be Holy conversations, to offer an offering made by fire unto the Lord: a burnt offering, and a meat offering, a sacrifice, and drink offerings, everything upon His day. Furthermore, pertaining to the Sabbaths of the Lord, your gifts, and all your vows, and all your free-will offerings, which you offer unto the Lord. Also on the fifteenth-day of the seventh month when you have gathered in the fruit of the land, you shall keep a feast unto the Lord seven days.

The first-day of the seventh month is a Sabbath, and the eight-day is a Sabbath. And you shall take with you on the first-day large branches of palm trees, and willows of the brook, and you shall rejoice before the Lord your God seven days. And you shall keep a feast unto the Lord seven days in the year. It shall be a law forever in your generations: you shall celebrate it in the seventh month. All those who are Israelite born shall live in tents seven days, that your generations may know that I made the children of Israel to live in tents, when I brought them out of the land of Egypt: I Am the Lord your God. And Moses declared unto the children of Israel the feasts of the Lord.

1 Kings chapter 8:2 tells us that all the men of Israel assembled themselves unto King Solomon at the feast in the month Ethanim, which is the <u>seventh</u> month. **Joel chapter 2:1,2** tells us, blow the trumpet in Zion; sound the alarm on My Holy hill. Let all who live in the land tremble, for the day of the Lord is coming. It is close at hand; a day of darkness and gloom, a day of dark clouds: whereby the Lord's angels will fill the sky, so much as over shadowing the sun; like sunrise spreading across the mountains, a large and mighty army comes, such as never was in ancient times, nor ever will be in ages to come. **Jude chapter 1:14,15** tells us that Enoch also the <u>seventh</u> son from Adam, prophesied of these things, saying, behold, the Lord comes with ten thousands of His saints to execute judgment upon all, and to convince all that are ungodly of all their ungodly deeds, which they have ungodly committed, and of all their ungodly speeches, which ungodly sinners have spoken against Him. **Revelation chapter 1:7** tells us behold, Jesus comes with clouds of angels; and every eye shall see Him, and they also, which killed Him: and all the inhabitance of the earth shall cry out because of Him. Amen

The Atonement for Sin *(Yom Kippur)*

The Atonement for sin was the sanctuary message that was given unto the Israelites in the wilderness as well as unto us, that in the year *1810–1844* Christ would make an Atonement for our sins, whereby the church of Philadelphia would be perfected by the year *1844*. **Exodus chapter 40:1-17** tells us that the Lord spoke unto Moses saying, on the <u>first day</u> of the <u>first month</u> of <u>April/Abib</u> you shall set up the tabernacle of man for the meeting. You shall make a room for the <u>Most Holy place</u>, and place the <u>Ark of the Covenant</u> in it, and divide the <u>Most Holy place</u> from the rest of the tabernacle with a curtain. And the second room shall be called the <u>Holy place</u>, and you shall put a table therein for the <u>Sacred–bread</u>, and place a <u>Lampstand</u> with <u>Seven–candlesticks</u> on top of the table next to the Sacred–bread. And you shall make an <u>Altar of gold</u> for the <u>Incense of prayer</u>, and place it before the Ark of the testimony, and put hanging doors at the entrance of the tabernacle.

And you shall make a second <u>Altar for the Burnt Offerings</u> in front of the doors of the tabernacle in the courtyard. And you shall make a <u>Basin with water</u> for the washing of hands and feet between the tabernacle and the <u>Altar of Burnt Offerings</u>. And you shall make two courtyards at the length of the tabernacle; the one on the right shall be for the court of priests, and the other for the court of the men of Israel, and you shall put curtains at every entrance of the tabernacle. And you shall take the <u>Anointing Oil</u>, and anoint the tabernacle, and all the vessels therein, and make them Holy unto the Lord. And you shall anoint the Altar of the Burnt Offering, and all the vessels, and sanctify the Altar: and it shall be an Altar Most Holy. And you shall anoint the Basin from top to bottom, and sanctify it.

Then you shall bring Aaron and his sons to the door of the tabernacle, and wash their hands and feet with water from the Basin. Then you shall put Holy garments on Aaron, and anoint him and consecrate him, that he may minster unto Me as priest. And you shall bring his sons and clothe them with coats, and anoint them also as you did their father that they may minister unto Me as priest.

215

And their anointing shall be an everlasting priesthood throughout their generations. And Moses did according to all that the Lord had commanded him. And it came to pass in the first month of the second year, on the first day of the month that the tabernacle was raised up.

Daniel chapter 8:13,14 tells us that Daniel heard one of the saints in heaven speaking one to another. And he said, unto that certain saint, which spoke. How long will the prophecy concerning the daily sacrifice for the atonement of sin be delayed before the heavenly sanctuary is cleansed? And he said unto me, two thousand and three hundred days; then shall the sanctuary be cleansed. **Ezekiel chapter 4:6** tells us that a day in prophecy is equivalent to a year. "I have appointed you each day for a year."

Daniel chapter 9:24-27 tells us that seventy weeks are given, which is equivalent to the sum of _490 years_ unto the Jewish people living in Jerusalem, to finalize transgression, and to make an end of sin, and to make reconciliation for iniquity, and to bring in the everlasting righteousness of Jesus Christ. Know therefore, and understand that from the going forth of the commandment to restore, and rebuild Jerusalem unto the coming of the Messiah the Prince, it shall be _483 years_; ending with Christ ministry, and the streets and wall shall be built again, even in perilous times. However, before this can happen, _434 years_ are given unto the Jewish nation, and at the end there will be blood shed, not by God's will, but the army of the prince of Persia shall come and destroy the city of Jerusalem, and the sanctuary; and the end thereof shall be like a flood, and at the end of the war the army is destroyed. Then Jesus will come and confirm a new covenant with many for seven years. And after three and a half years He shall do away with the old sacrifices and offerings, and He shall cause the Jewish nation to become desolate, even until the consummation and cut off point of all the unbelieving souls. The cutoff point is where Christ died on the cross at Calvary for our sins, and also the close of probation for the Jewish nation.

Four hundred and ninety years were given unto the Jewish nation to prepare them for the first coming of the Messiah. This was foretold in the Book of Genesis chapter one that on the sixth day the ministerial work of the Holy Spirit upon the human soul would be completed sometime during the sixth millennium. And the character of Christ would be perfected in believers before His second coming, whereby the Character of God would be found in human attributes.

The seven–fold ministry of Jesus Christ is the fullness of His Holy Spirit upon the human soul. In the Old Testament we see the high priest mediating between the sinner and God the Father. **Leviticus chapter 4:27-35** tells us that the sinner would bring a lamb as a burnt offering, and a goat as a sin offering, whereby transferring their confessed sins (or unpunished debt) to the goat to be set free in the wilderness for a period of time. The goat represents Satan who is set free to tempt humanity for six thousand years. The lamb represents the sacrifice of the Messiah Yeshua, by means of which the high priest would then transfer the blood of the lamb into the Holy Place, whereby the new covenant in the heavenly sanctuary is also by blood. **Hebrews chapter 9:19-28** tells us that after Moses had spoken every precept to all the people according to the law, he took the blood of calves, and goats with water, and scarlet wool, and hyssop, and sprinkled both the book, and the people, saying, "This is the blood of the testament which God have commanded unto you. Furthermore, he sprinkled the blood in the tabernacle, and all the vessels of the ministry; whereby all things pertaining to the law is purged with blood; for without the shedding of blood there are no forgiveness of sins. Therefore, it was necessary for God to outline the patterns of these things unto us, that heaven should be purified with a better sacrifice. For Christ entered into the Holy Place: in heaven to appear in the presence of God for us. However, Christ did not enter yearly, as the earthly high priest must often do with blood for others; but He entered once in the end of the world to put away sin by His own sacrifice. Just as we are appointed to die once and face judgment after, even so Christ was offered once to bear the sins of many, and unto them that look for Him, He will appear the second time without sin unto salvation. Amen

The death of Christ on the cross was the slaying of the Lamb of God that would take away all the confessed sins of mankind by transferring our sins to Himself. This was done here on the earth as a ransom for our sake. The cross is the altar where Christ the Lamb of God was slain representing the outer court of the heavenly sanctuary, and now He has entered into the presence of God once on our behalf. **Acts chapter 3:19** tells us to repent therefore, and be converted, that our sins may be blotted out when the times of refreshing shall come from the presence of the Lord.

God in His perfect-foreknowledge place it upon Christ His only begotten Son to bear our sins from the foundation of the world, so that His grace may abound. **Luke chapter 3:21,22** tells us that Jesus was thirty years of age when He began to pray and the heaven opened, and the Holy Spirit descended in a bodily shape like a dove upon Him, and a voice came from heaven, saying, "This is My beloved Son, in Whom I Am well pleased."

The ministry of Jesus Christ lasted for three and a half years on earth, and after His ascension the gospel was proclaimed by His disciples throughout the world winning souls on His behalf, and multiplying new believers unto the glory of the Father in heaven. After Jesus ascended to heaven, His ministry continued in the heavenly sanctuary. Christ was thirty-four years old when He ascended to heaven. Furthermore, as our High Priest He spent one thousand eight hundred and ten years transferring the sins of the people who accepted Him as their Lord and Savior into the first apartment of the heavenly sanctuary, which is the Holy place.

In the year *1844*, the sanctuary was cleansed, after which point Christ moved into the Most Holy place, whereby He intercedes on our behalf in front of God the Father. **Daniel chapter 7:9,10** tells us that Daniel saw thrones being setup, and God the Father took His seat Whose garment was white as snow, and the hair of His head like pure wool: His throne was like a chariot with wheels of fire, and a fiery flame and steam was sent out from before Him. The judgment was set, and the books were opened. **Leviticus chapter 23:26-32** gives us a summary of (Yom Kippur) which is the intercessory and mediation of Jesus Christ our Royal High Priest in the heavenly Sanctuary; whereby a confession is made by mouth with a broken spirit, and a contrite heart. And the Lord spoke unto Moses, saying, on the tenth day of the seventh month there shall be a Day of Atonement: it shall be an Holy conversation unto you; and you must surrender your soul, and offer an offering made by fire unto the Lord. And you shall do no work in that same day, because it is a Day of Atonement, to make Atonement for you before the Lord your God. Furthermore, any soul that doesn't surrender in that same day, he shall be cut off from among his people. And whatsoever person that does any work in that same day, he will be destroyed from among his people. You must not do any work: it shall be a decree forever throughout your generations in all your dwellings. This decree shall be a Sabbath of rest for you, and you must surrender your soul from the evening of the ninth day of the seventh month you hall celebrate your Sabbath. **Psalm chapter 51:1-19** tells of David's confession unto God, him asking for forgiveness of his transgression and sin. The circumcision of the heart made without hands is the work that our Lord and Savior Jesus Christ is doing on our behalf in the heavenly Sanctuary. Amen

The Feast of Tabernacle *(Sukkot)*

The Feast of Tabernacle is the seventh and final Sabbath before Christ returns. (Sukkot) is the feast of tabernacle: the wedding garment of the Lord's righteousness by means of which we have victory over sin and our characters are made perfect. **Leviticus chapter 23:33,34** tells us that the Lord spoke unto Moses, saying, speak unto the children of Israel, saying, the fifteenth-day of the seventh month shall be the feast of tabernacles for seven days unto the Lord. **John chapter 14:6** tells us that the preparation of the Sabbath is the relationship that we have with the Father through Christ. "I Am the way, the truth, and the life: no one comes to the Father, except by Me."

Even though Adam and Christ died, because of sin: they did not share the same disposition. Adam died spiritually after he ate from the tree of knowledge of good and evil; meanwhile Christ died a physical death on the cross at Calvary, and was resurrected in three days. The three days event of Christ life was to restore balance to the universe. The <u>fourth</u>, <u>fifth</u>, and <u>sixth</u> <u>millennium</u> was the completion of His retroactive work upon the human soul, whereby the Holy Spirit was sent to restore mankind's seared conscience to the perfection of Christ Character. **Genesis chapter 8:21,22** tells us that after the great flood, the Lord reason by Himself, saying, I will not curse the ground anymore for mankind sake; even though the imagination of man's heart is evil from his youth; nevertheless I will not smite anything living as I have done before. Night and day will continue while the Holy Spirit is working, and planting seed during the cold winter and the hot summer months, for the harvest is not yet ready. **Jeremiah chapter 8:20** tells us that Jeremiah mourned, because the harvest was past, and the summer had ended, and his people were not saved.

Today, I find myself mourning for the very same reason. Mankind has seen the Light, which is Jesus Christ, but the world hasn't change much since the fall of Adam. Many have made Darkness their home of refuge, instead of choosing the Light. And without Christ humanity doesn't stand a chance to be saved. **Matthew chapter 9:37,38** tells us that Jesus said, unto His disciples, the harvest is truly plentiful, but the laborers are few; pray that the Lord of the harvest send forth laborers into His harvest. **Matthew chapter 13:37-39** tells us that the disciples wanted to know the parable of the harvest. Then Jesus replied, "He that planted the good seed is the Son of man, and the field is the world; and the seed is the good children of the kingdom of God; and the tears are the children of the devil; the harvest is the end of the world; and the reapers are the angels." **1Timothy chapter 2:5** tells us that there is one God: and one mediator between God and men, the man Christ Jesus. **Daniel chapter 12:1,2** tells us that during the feast of tabernacle Michael shall stand up, the great prince which stands for the children of your people: and there shall be a time of trouble, such as never was since there was a nation even to that time: and at that time your people shall be delivered, everyone that shall be found written in the book of life. And many of them that sleep in the dust of the earth shall awake, some to everlasting life, and some to shame and everlasting contempt. Amen

Jesus the Light of the World

In the Garden of Eden we see the Lord sacrificing the first animal to clothe Adam and Eve, but it wasn't up until the death of Jesus Christ on the cross at Calvary that the debt was paid in full. The sin offerings were used as credit to put the payment on hold until Christ would come and pay the debt on our behalf. Those that lived before Christ came were given the free gift of grace, but after He came, it was no longer by grace, but by the sanctification of His own blood that we were justified by faith unto salvation. The sacrificial system has changed in the sense that we are no longer required to sacrifice animals. However, each time we conscientiously sin, we crucify Christ afresh, and there is no more sacrifice except a fearful judgment.

Jesus Christ is the most mentioned name throughout the universe, but how many people know Him as their personal Lord and Savior? **Psalm chapter 40:7,8** tells us that in the volume of the book it is written of Him, I delight to do Your will, O God: Your law is within My heart. **Genesis chapter 1:14-19** tells us that the coming of Jesus Christ and John the Baptist was foretold on the <u>fourth day</u>. "And God said, let there be lights in the heaven to divide the day from the night; and let them be for signs and seasons, and for days, and years: and for lights in the heaven and also upon the earth. And God also created (two great lights) the greater to rule the day, and the lesser to rule the night: and to divide the light from the darkness; and He made the stars also. And God saw that it was good. And the evening and the morning were the <u>fourth day</u>." **John chapter 1:8** tells us that during <u>the fourth millennium</u> John the Baptist who was the <u>lesser light</u> was preaching in the wilderness bearing witness unto Christ Who was the <u>greater light</u> by preparing the way for Him. Amen

From Adam to Christ

The name Adam means: mankind, the first male and female of their kind. Adam lived for thirty-three years without sin. However, after Adam disobeyed, the separation of the man and woman from the Father brought forth sin by means of which the woman was called Eve. The name Eve means: mother of all living. It is important for us to know that, it was after sin, that the woman was called Eve. **Genesis chapter 2:23** tells us that because she was taken out of man, she was called woman.

The lineage of Adam began with Cain. Personally, I don't know how old Adam was when he became the father of Cain and Abel. However, we know that he was *130* years old when he became the father of Seth, which means: Mankind is appointed. And Seth was *105* years old when he became the father of Enos, which means: mortality. And Enos was *90* years old when he became the father of Cainan, which means: a fixed dwelling place. And Cainan was *70* years old when he became the father of Mahalaleel, which means: God, Who is praised. And Mahalaleel was *65* years old when he became the father of Jared, which means: come down. And Jared was *162* years old when he became the father of Enoch, which means: to instruct. And Enoch was *65* years old when he became the father of Methuselah, which means: one who is sent forth like a sword. And Methuselah was *187* years old when he became the father of Lamech, which means: wounded. And Lamech was *182* years old when he became the father of Noah, which means: rest. And Noah was *500* years old when he became the father of Shem, which means: good news.

When we place the meaning of the names from Adam to Shem together, it reads: mankind is appointed to mortality, a fixed dwelling place. God Who is praised comes down to instruct, one sent forth like a sword, wounded for our sake, bringing comfort and rest to mankind weary soul, and good news.

Noah was born in the year *1056 BC*, and the flood came in the year *1656 BC*. Noah lived for *350* years after the flood, and died in the year *2006 BC*. Shem was *300* years old when he became the father of Arphaxad, which means: spread out or breech of language. And Arphaxad was *35* years old when he became the father of Salah, which means: sprout. And Salah was *30* years old when he became the father of Eber, which means: opposite side. And Eber was *34* years old when he became the father of Peleg, which means: division. And Peleg was *30* years old when he became the father of Reu, which means: companion. And Reu was *32* years old when he became the father of Serug, which means: to twine or mingle. And Serug was *30* years old when he became the father of Nahor, which means: to snore or short temper. And Nahor was *29* years old when he became the father of Terah. And Terah was *70* years old when he became the father of Abraham, which means: father of many nations.

Abraham was born in the year *2146 BC*, and he was *100* years old when he became the father of Isaac, which means: laughter. And Abraham lived for *75* years after the birth of Isaac and died in the year *2321 BC*. And Isaac was *60* years old when he became the father of Jacob. And Jacob's name was changed to Israel, which means: he strives against God. And Jacob became the father of Judah, which means: Yahweh is praise. And Judah was the father of Phares that was born of his daughter–in–law Tamar, which means: breech. And Phares was the father of Esrom, which means: courtyard. And Esrom was the father of A-ram, which means: highland. And A-ram was the father of Aminadab, which means: my people give freely. And Aminadab was the father of Na-as-son, which means: serpent.

And Na-as-son was the father of Salmon, which means: coat or clothing of righteousness. And Salmon and Ra-chab (the prostitute) were the parents of Bo-oz, which means: lively or spirit filled. And Bo-oz and Ruth were the parents of O-bed, which means: My servant. And O-bed was the father of Jesse, which means: strength. And Jesse was the father of David the second king of Israel, which means: My beloved. And David and Bath-sheba (the wife of U-ri-as) were the parents of Solomon, which means: Yahweh is peace. And Solomon was the father of Ro-bo-am, which means: Yahweh enlarges the people. And Ro-bo-am was the father of A-bi-a, which means: Yahweh is my Father. And A-bi-a was the father of A-sa, which means: Yahweh healed me. And A-sa was the father of Jos-a-phat, which means: Yahweh is a righteous judge. And Jos-a-phat was the father of Jo-ram, which means: Yahweh is exalted. And Jo-ram was the father of O-zi-as, which means: the strength of Jehovah. And O-zi-as was the father of Jo-a-tham, which means: Jehovah is perfect. And Jo-a-tham was the father of A-chaz, which means: possessor. And A-chaz was the father of Ez-e-ki-as, which means: Yahweh will strengthen. And Ez-e-ki-as was the father of Ma-nas-ses, which means: Yahweh has caused me to forget trouble.

And Ma-nas-ses was the father of Amon, which means: Yahweh is faithful. And Amon was the father of Jo-si-as, which means: Yahweh heals. And Jo-si-as was the father of Jech-o-ni-as, which means: Jah establish. And Jech-o-ni-as was the father of Sa-la-thi-el, which means: I have asked of God. And Sa-la-thi-el was the father of Zo-rob-a-bel, which means: descendant of Babylon. And Zo-rob-a-bel was the father of Abi-ud, which means: My Father is glorious. And Abi-ud was the father of E-li-a-kim, which means: Yahweh will rise up. And E-li-a-kim was the father of A-zor, which means: Yahweh is our help. And A-zor was the father of Sa-doc, which means: Yahweh is righteous. And Sa-doc was the father of A-chim, which means: Jehovah will rise.

And A-chim was the father of E-li-ud, which means: Jehovah is high and mighty. And E-li-ud was the father of E-le-a-zar, which means: Jehovah is our help. And E-le-a-zar was the father of Mat-than, which means: a gift from Jehovah. And Mat-than was the father of Jacob, which means: Israel. And Jacob was the father of Joseph, which means: let him add. And Joseph was the husband of Mary (the mother of Jesus Christ). And Mary, which means: defiant one. The genealogy of Christ started with Adam, the first male and female of their kind. But, after sin occupied the earth God made the lowest of people a part of His family tree, so that you and I might become heirs to His kingdom of grace. Amen

The Lion of Judah

Genesis chapter 1:14-19 tells us that on the fourth day God said, Let there be lights in the firmament of the heaven to divide the day from the night; and let them be for signs, seasons, and for days and years. And let them be for lights in the firmament of the heaven to give light upon the earth: and it was so. And God made two great lights; the greater light, which is the Sun represents Jesus Christ to rule the day, and the lesser light, which is the Moon represents John, the Baptist to rule the night: He made the Stars, which represents the children of God. And God set them in the firmament of the heaven to give light upon the earth, and to rule over the day and over the night, and to divide the light from the darkness. And God saw that it was good. And the evening and the morning were the fourth day.

This was foretold that during the <u>fourth millennium</u> Christ would come from the tribe of Judah, who was the <u>fourth</u> son from Jacob: he would be chosen from among his brethren to bare seed to the lineage of Jesus Christ. The evidence shows that Jesus sprang from the root of David out of the house of Judah. **Genesis chapter 49:8-10** tells us that the hand of God is seen through His divine intervention by means of which Judah was exalted above his brethren. His hand shall be around the neck of his enemies. Your father's children shall bow down before you. Judah is the lion's cub, from his prey he has gone up: he couched. And when he lies down as an old lion to rest, who would dare to disturb him? For out of Judah came the Scepter of righteousness, and it will not depart from Him, for He is the law and testimonies of Shiloh; and He will establish the people through His righteousness forever and ever. **Numbers chapter 24:17** tells us that I will see the Lord, but not now, I will see Him, but not soon, for there will come a Star out of Jacob, and a Scepter will rise out of Israel, and He will smash the corners of Moab, and destroy all the children of Lot.

Deuteronomy chapter 18:15-19 tells us that the Lord Himself will give you an appointed Prophet from among your brethren, and He will teach you according to all that you have desired of the Lord your God, in Ho—reb of Mount Sinai, where we stood before the Lord, and the people said, we would rather not to hear the voice of the Lord, neither do we wish to see His consuming fire anymore, because we shall surely die. And the Lord said unto Moses, "They have well spoken that which they have spoken. I will anoint a prophet from among their brethren, and I will put My words in His mouth, and He will speak unto them all that I will command Him. And I will take an account of anyone who will not regard My words that the prophet will speak in My name." **Isaiah chapter 7:14** tells us that the Lord Himself will give you a sign; "Behold, a virgin will conceive, and bare a Son, and His name shall be called Immanuel."

Isaiah chapter 9:6,7 tells us that a child is born, unto us a Son is given, and the government will be upon His shoulder, and His name will be called, "Wonderful, Counselor, the mighty God, the Prince of Peace and His government will increase in peace and righteousness. There will be no end to the throne of David, and His kingdom will not only proclaim it, but also establish it with judgment and with justice from now until, evermore. The zeal of the Lord of hosts will perform this. **Isaiah chapter 11:1,2** tells us that there will be a descendant from Jesse, David by name, and a branch will grow out of his roots. And He will have the Spirit of the Lord resting upon His shoulder: wisdom, knowledge, understanding, counsel, power and humility, whereby His obedience will be proclaimed unto the Lord. **Isaiah chapter 42:1-4** tells us behold My servant, Whom I uphold; Mine elect, in Whom My soul delight; I have put My Spirit upon Him. He will establish My judgment with the people. He will not cry, nor exalt Himself, nor cause His voice to be heard in the street. A bruised stem (twig) He will not break or cause a flickering flame to go out. In His faithfulness, He will bring forth justice and equality for all. He will not lose hope or courage, nor will He give up until He has established justice throughout the earth.

Isaiah chapter 53:2-12 tells us that He will grow up before the Lord as a tender plant, He will be like a root out of dry ground: He has neither outer beauty nor charm, face to face there is no beauty that we should desire Him. He is despised and rejected of men; a man of sorrows, and acquainted with grief, we will turn our faces away from Him. He was despised and we showed Him no pity. However, willingly He took on our griefs, and carried our sorrows. We believed that He had brought it on Himself, and was being punished, and afflicted by God. But, He was wounded for our transgression; He was bruised for our iniquities: for He was the solution for our sins, and the restoration of our peace was upon His shoulder; and by His stripes we are healed. We are all like sheep gone astray; we have turned to our own way; and the Father had laid our sins on Him.

He was oppressed, and He was afflicted, yet He opened not His mouth. He was led as a lamb to the slaughter, and as a quiet sheep before her shearers, so He opened not His mouth. He was judged without mercy. Who will declare this generation? For He was killed from the land of the living: for the sins of my people He was nailed to the cross. And He satisfied the penalty of sin, by making His grave with the wicked, so that in His death we might be made rich unto salvation. Neither violence nor deceit came from His mouth, yet it pleased the Father to bruise Him; He had put Him to grief: by making Him the sacrificial offering for sin. God bear witness to His Son, and prolonged His days with the fulfillment of the Lord's prophecy that it may prosper in His hand. God approved of the sacrifice that was made, and was satisfied. By the knowledge of Him, many will be justified, for He will bear their sins. Therefore, the Father will give Him a place among the great, and He will share His reward with those who are faithful. He sacrificed Himself unto death: and was numbered with the transgressors, and carried the sin of many, and made intercession on their behalf. Amen

The Angel Gabriel Sent unto Mary

Luke chapter 1:24-33 tells us that after Elizabeth the mother of John the Baptist became pregnant for her husband Zacharias, who was a Levite, she hid herself from the public for five months, saying, The Lord has blessed me and has removed my shame. And in the sixth month of Elul, sometime around late August to early September the angel Gabriel was sent from God unto the city of Galilee in Nazareth, to a virgin who was married to a man named Joseph, a descendant of king David, the son of Jesse. And the angel came in unto her and said, praised be the Lord God, for He has favored you among women. And after beholding him, she was afraid, because of the words, which he spoke unto her. Mary did not understand the manner of his salutation. And the angel said unto her, fear not, Mary: for the Lord God favors you, and you will conceive a Son in your womb, and His name shall be called Jesus. He shall be great, and He shall be called the Son of the Highest: and the Lord God shall give unto Him the throne of His father David. And He shall reign over the house of Jacob forever; and of His Kingdom there will be no end.

Jesus wasn't born on the 25th of December as many would hope to believe, but rather sometime during spring, according to the Hebrew lunar calendar. To the best of my knowledge and the discernment given unto me by the Holy Spirit, I believe that the first Adam was tempted for thirty-three and a half years before he fell: at which point the countdown began where Jesus Christ became the ransom four thousand years later. Jesus Christ was born sometime during the new moon in spring *4,000 BC,* and died in the year *33 AD.*

The Gregorian calendar, also known as the western calendar, or Christian calendar, is the internationally accepted civil calendar of the entire world today. Pope Gregory XIII first introduced it: after whom the calendar was named, by a decree signed on the *24th of February 1582;* the reformed calendar was adopted later that year by a handful of countries. **Daniel chapter 7:25** tells us that the beast shall speak great words against the Most High, and shall kill the saints of the Most High, and think to change times and law. The reason for changing times and law is to deceive as many as possible by making it seem as if Christ isn't coming soon. Jesus was the sacrificial Lamb, and He came at the appointed sacrificial time. Lets see if God will allow us to have the wisdom, knowledge, and understanding that we seek to the glory of His name. **Matthew chapter 2:1,2** tells us that when Jesus was born in Bethlehem of Judea in the days of Herod the king, behold, there came wise men from the east to Jerusalem, saying, "Where is He that is born King of the Jew? For we have seen His star in the east, and are come to worship Him." **Luke chapter 2:1-6** tells us that it came to pass in those days, that there went out a decree from Caesar Augustus, that the entire world should be taxed. And this taxing was first made when Cyrenius was governor of Syria. And all went out to be taxed, everyone in his own city. And Joseph also went up from Galilee, out of the city of Nazareth, into Judea, unto the city of David, which is called Bethlehem; because he was of the house and lineage of David: to be taxed with Mary his espoused wife, being great with child. And so it was, that, while they were there, the days were accomplished that she should be delivered.

Leviticus chapter 12:1-4 tells us that the Lord said unto Moses, speak unto the children of Israel, saying, If a woman have conceived seed, and born a man child: then she shall be unclean seven days; according to the days of the separation for her infirmity she shall be unclean. And in the eight day, the flesh of his foreskin shall be circumcised. And she shall then continue in the blood of her purifying thirty–three days; she shall touch nothing sacred, nor come into the sanctuary, until the days of her purifying be fulfilled. **Leviticus chapter 12:6** tells us that when the days of her purifying are fulfilled, for a son, or daughter, she shall bring a lamb of the first year for a burnt offering, and a young pigeon, or a turtledove, for a sin offering, unto the door of the tabernacle of the congregation, unto the priest. **Luke chapter 2:21-24** tells us that when eight days were accomplished for the circumcising of the child, His name was called Jesus, which was so named of the angel before He was conceived in the womb. And when the days of Mary purification according to the written Law of Moses were accomplished, her and her husband Joseph brought Jesus to Jerusalem, to present Him to the Lord. As it is written in the Law of the Lord: every male that open the womb shall be called Holy unto the Lord. And to offer a sacrifice according to that which is said in the Law of the Lord: a pair of turtledoves, or two young pigeons.

Joseph and Mary went up to Judea during tax season. As we all know tax season is from the first day of April up until the fifteenth day, which is the deadline. Coincident? How about all fools day? Is that another coincident also? I'll let you be the judge of that. Most people are preoccupied with their income tax return during tax season, and not realizing that it is the Lord's Passover and Holy conversation.

Even though Jesus died because of sin, He did not sin after the likeness of Adam. Three major things took place at the cross: God's Character was vindicated; the penalty for sin was paid in full, and the reconciliation of the relationship between us, and our Father in heaven. The vindication of God's Character became visible by the life and example that Christ lived leading up to His death on the cross. In other words what got started at Mount Sinai was completed at Mount Calvary. Those who rejected Him at Mount Sinai died before two or three witnesses, and those that He foreknew from the foundation of the earth were justified in front of God at Mount Calvary. It was declared unto the universe that He paid the price for our sins, and therefore God was justified to raise Him from the dead. **Isaiah chapter 53:5** tells us that by His stripes we are healed. **John chapter 14:8-10** tells us that Philip one of the twelve disciples said unto Jesus, Lord, show us the Father and we will be satisfied. Jesus replied, I have been with you all this time, and yet you say that you don't know Me, he that have seen Me, have seen the Father also. How can you then say, show us the Father, believe Me when I tell you, that I Am in the Father and the Father is in Me.

Jesus made it seems so easy, I Am in the Father and the Father is in Me. Every now and then, you'll see someone kissing a crucifix, what does it mean? Not a thing! The biblical principle behind true faith is, Christ, and Christ alone. **Galatians chapter 5:17** tells us that sensual–knowledge goes against faith, the one will contradict the other, so that we cannot do the things that please God. Therefore we're justified by faith, even as Christ trusted His Father to do His will. **Romans chapter 10:17** tells us that true faith comes by hearing, and hearing by the Word of God, which is Christ Jesus. The evidence showed that Abraham lied about his relationship with Sara his wife. Furthermore, he took Sara's handmaid for wife. However, Abraham's righteousness came not by his own works, but by Jesus Christ Who is the Chief builder of our faith, and obedience to do the will of the Father in heaven, whereby we justified by His righteousness.

Psalm chapter 8:4,5 tells us, "What is man that You are mindful of him, or even the Son of man that You would visit Him? Who was created a little lower than the angels, but yet He was crowned with glory and honor and was put in charge of the works of Your hands." As we see Jesus Christ Who was clothed in righteousness, but yet humbled Himself unto death at the cross, bearing the express Image of His Father, and the humility of a servant. Let God be praised, and His Son be magnified: for we are now justified in front of God, the Father by His only begotten Son as heirs: to be called sons and daughters of the true living God. Amen

The Ministry of Jesus Christ

In the Book of Genesis God foretold that on the fifth and sixth day Christ ministry would become a worldwide movement that would restore the relationship between us, and Him during the fifth and sixth millennium. **Genesis chapter 1:20-23** tells us that God said, let the waters bring forth abundantly the moving creature that have life, and birds that fly above the earth in the heaven. And God created great whales, and every living creature that move, which the waters brought forth abundantly, after their kind, and every bird that have wings after their kind: and God saw that it was good. And God blessed them, saying, be fruitful, and multiply in the earth. And the evening and the morning were the fifth day.

Genesis chapter 1:24-31 tells us that God said, let the earth bring forth the living creature after his kind: cattle, and creeping things, and beast of the earth after his kind: and it was so. And God made the beast of the earth after his kind, and cattle after their kind, and everything that creep upon the earth after his kind. And God saw that it was good. And God said, let us make man in Our Image, after Our Likeness: and let them have dominion over the fish of the sea, and over the fowl of the air, and over the cattle, and over all the earth, and over every creeping thing that crawl upon the earth. So God created man in His Own Image, in the Image of God, He created him: male and female, He created them.

And God blessed them, and God said unto them, be fruitful and multiply, and replenish the earth, and rule over it: and have dominion over the fish of the sea, and over the birds of the air, and over every living thing that move upon the earth. And God said, I have given you every herb bearing seed, which is upon all the face of the earth, and every fruit tree that has seed shall be for food. (Edenic diet) Furthermore, every beast of the earth, and every bird of the air, and every insect upon the earth, wherein there is life I have given you dominion. I have given every green herb for food. (Edenic diet) And God witness to everything that He had made, and saw that it was very good. And the evening and the morning were the sixth day.

Jesus was the second and last Adam, the true representative of humanity, Who died on the cross at Calvary, whereby He paid the penalty for sin; a debt He didn't owe. Jesus Christ our Lord and Savior, the Spiritual Rock that brought forth the brook of life. **John chapter 4:14** tells us that whosoever drinks of this water that I shall give unto him, shall never thirst again: for the water that I shall give him is a well of everlasting life.

Mankind's dead soul was given a second chance at the cross where our Lord Jesus Christ died for us at the beginning of the <u>fourth millennium</u>. The <u>fifth</u> and <u>sixth day</u> are the only two days in which <u>life</u> and <u>blessing</u> was given according to: **Genesis chapter 1:20-31.** Christ ministry was for three years at which point He died during the evening on the <u>fourth day</u> of the <u>fourth millennium</u>, and laid to rest during the <u>fifth day</u>, and was raised on the <u>sixth day</u>, which was a clear indication of being born again: a new and living way for you and I, which would mark the <u>first day</u> of the <u>First fruits harvest</u> of Jesus Christ unto the glory of the Father Who sent Him. **Luke chapter 13:32** tells us that Christ said, Go and tell that fox, meaning, Satan that I cast out demons, and cure sinners <u>today</u>, and <u>tomorrow,</u> which is the <u>fourth</u> and <u>fifth millennium</u>, and I shall be perfected on the <u>third day</u>, which is the <u>sixth millennium</u>.

The three days event of Jesus's death and resurrection was to give everlasting life to His beloved Church. Christ accomplished the investigative judgment and finalized sin, and made restoration to the Remnant Church of Philadelphia, which began in the year *1755–1844.* **Revelation chapter 1:8** tells us that I Am Alpha and Omega, the beginning and the ending, which is, was, and to come, the Almighty. **Revelation chapter 1:17** tells us that I Am the first and the last, which is the First fruits of God, and the true millennial Sabbath. Amen

The Foreknowledge of God

God having perfect foreknowledge, knowing the intent of our hearts: man and beast alike, whereby He predestinated the plan of soul salvation unto the glory of His name. By His grace we are sanctified to walk in the newness of life: according to the gospel that was preached unto them that heard it in the wilderness. As we all know by now that the human nature is sinful, and we cannot work to secure our own salvation. The sacrifice of animals in the Old Testament did not make anything perfect. However, God already knew that the people would rebel. God established His grace with a rebellious people, so that we could behold His mercy, which is far beyond human nature. Jesus was perfect from the beginning, and also at the end; therefore, God had no need of sacrifice. However, after Adam sinned, the Ten Commandments were instituted; and death came upon all humanity, whereby justification and sanctification by faith was granted unto us, so that all could be made righteous in Christ Jesus.

Think of character perfection as the combination of faith, love and hope by means of which trust and obedience becomes the final result of every believer who has surrendered self unto Him that was raised from the dead. **Luke chapter 13:32** tells us that Jesus casted out demons by faith, and cure sinners with His unconditional love during the fourth millennium, and His Holy Spirit continued His retroactive work throughout the fifth, and sixth millennium, which gave us hope in God. The retroactive work of Jesus Christ began from the foundation of the earth, whereby we are perfected in Him on the third day, which is the sixth millennium.

The plan of salvation was already in place before Adam and Eve sinned. The foreknowledge of Christ enabled Him to see the future of mankind's downfall; and thereby His retroactive work began before it was needed, and was finished at the cross of Calvary. Once Jesus died on the cross, the payment was made in full for all the righteous saints, who had lived and died before He came. Mankind was created as a conscientious being; and after the fall, we had a need to be restored. The death of Jesus on the cross vindicated His Father's name, and exposed Satan as Christ enemy, and also the world as being sinful unto death. Furthermore, the Father was justified to resurrect His only begotten Son, and renewed our relationship with Him through His redemptive work at the cross. **2 Timothy chapter 1:7** tells us that God did not give us the spirit of fear, but of power, and of love, and of a sound mind.

How should we live now that we are under His grace? For even though we wait patiently on the Lord to receive the promise of glorification unto eternal life, but while the bridegroom tarry, not wanting that any should perish. However, at the close of probation of the earth when the heavenly sanctuary is no longer open for intercession and mediation: Christ will put on His kingly apparels, and return to judge the world. So while there is time will you not hear the last call for repentance? **Jeremiah chapter 29:11** tells us that the thoughts of the Lord is thoughts of peace toward us, and not of evil, to give us an expected end.

Looking back at the Atonement of sin. Personally, I know how difficult an apology can be, especially when there is no godly grief or godly sorrow. It's always easier to justify self rather than to swallow our pride. However, self–denial must be exercised in order to overcome the lawlessness of sin. Don't be persuaded by an emotional life of guilt that you are not worthy of repentance. God grants us mercy and gave us grace: whereby we are inducted into His Kingdom of grace unto the glory of His name: Jehovah Jirah, Jehovah Nissi, and Jehovah Shalom. Amen

Our Imputed Righteousness in Him

Righteousness is imputed unto us by faith, and apart from Christ we have no reward. For without the free gift of grace sanctification is impossible, and the cleansing of our hearts would become void. The forty days, and forty nights of grace that was given unto the Israelites was the appropriate amount of time needed to fulfill the promise that God had made unto Abraham.

The former rain fell upon both the just, and the unjust alike for forty years, but in the end when the latter rain came only Joshua and Caleb found grace in the sight of the Lord, but all the rest died in the wilderness because of unbelief. No matter how difficult the situation may seem, let us be steadfast in prayer: praying without ceasing, so that grace may abound, which for some people grace might not be enough. But if you had a choice for longevity and perseverance, what would it be? Remember the thief on the cross, he was at the close of his probation, but mercy and grace was given nonetheless. The sinner has no need to think of the debt owed in the time of trouble. God gave us the free gift of grace from the foundation of the earth, and also paid the price for our sins at the cross. Jesus is willing and able to save lives within seconds. **John chapter 3:17** tells us that God did not send His Son into the world to condemn the world, but that the world through Him might be saved. **2 Thessalonians chapter 2:13** tells us that for this particular reason, we are obligated to give God thanks always, for we are loved by the Lord, and God chose us from the beginning for salvation through sanctification of the Spirit and belief of the truth. **Hebrews chapter 12:1,2** tells us that we are surrounded by clouds of witnesses, therefore let us lay aside every weight that comes with guilt, for it is the smallest things in life that creates the most distraction and takes us off the path of righteousness. Therefore, let us run with patience the race that is set before us, looking unto Jesus the author and finisher of our faith; Who for the purpose of salvation, willfully and joyfully fulfill the task that was set before Him and endured the cross, despising the shame, and He is now sitting down at the right hand of the throne of God.

God gave us free–will to choose life or death. Sanctification is not something that we speak of; but it's the life that we live that expresses the glory of God. **Romans chapter 4:3** tells us that Abraham believed God, and it was counted unto him for righteousness. **Romans chapter 4:17,18** tells us that when God spoke unto Abraham, he made a decision to believe. "As it is written, I have made you a father of many nations. God Who called Abraham, and he believed. Even God Who raise the dead, and prophesy those things, which are not as though they were. For where there was no hope, God gave hope unto him that was weak in faith, so that His Son might be made known through Abraham the father of many nations. God testified of Abraham's righteousness in Him, and gave him faith to overcome his unbelief by prophesying those things, which were not, as if they were, even while he was weak in faith. **Mark chapter 16:15,16** tells us that Christ said unto His disciples, go unto the entire world, and preach the gospel to every creature, and he that believes with his whole heart, and be baptized shall be saved; but he that believes not, will be condemned.

The evidence of God's sovereignty can be seen through His retroactive work, whereby we understand that faith and hope is the work of the Holy Spirit. Mercy and grace is Jesus Christ testifying of our righteousness in Him. **Mark chapter 16:17,18** tells us that these signs shall follow them that believe; in My name they will cast out devils; and they will speak a new language, and they will have the ability to take up serpents: and if they drink any deadly thing, it will not hurt them, they will lay hands on the sick and they will recover.

The Pharisees were known for their criticism, and the keeping of the Sabbath one would suppose, but on the contrary if they were keeping the Sabbath Christ would have been able to reach them. **Matthew chapter 15:1-6** tells us that the Pharisees and scribes which were living in Jerusalem came to Jesus, saying, why do your disciples transgress the tradition of the elders? For they wash not their hands when they eat bread. Jesus answered, and said unto them, why do you also transgress the commandment of God by your tradition? For God gave the commandment, saying, honor your father and mother, but according to your tradition, whosoever says, I have given my money unto the church is free from helping their parents, and why should parents profit from their children. By doing this you have made the commandment of God void by your tradition, whereby children don't have to honor their parents. Jesus made it clear, if love for God isn't the primary reason for our motive, He doesn't acknowledge our good deeds.

Matthew chapter 12:31,32 tells us that all sin including where we have curse God, will be forgiven, but the turning away from the Holy Spirit will not be forgiven. Why then holdfast to religious beliefs that are contrary unto faith? **Matthew chapter 7:22,23** tells us that many will say, Lord, Lord, have we not prophesied in Your name? Jesus replied, "I never knew you: depart from Me, workers of iniquity. **Philippians chapter 2:5-8** tells us that we should have this mind in us, which was also in Christ Jesus: Who having the powers of God, considered not Himself equal to God: but made Himself of no importance, and became a servant, and being found vulnerable as a man, He humbled Himself, and became obedient unto death, even the death of the cross. Amen

Confessing to Our High Priest

I speak the truth in Christ, I lie not, my conscience also bears me witness in the Holy Spirit that I am in subjection unto obedience according to the gospel that was preached unto them that heard it in the wilderness. However, they that heard it did not profit from it, because of unbelief. Conscience over mind by faith is the circumcision of the heart made without hands: the Holy Spirit bearing witness to our spirit, that we are the children of God. **Colossians chapter 2:11,12** tells us that in Whom also we are circumcised with the circumcision made without hands, overcoming the sensual nature of the body, and also the sins of the mind and senses by having the conscience of Christ: the mind and senses being inactive to sin; whereby we are buried with Him in baptism and also risen with Him through the faith of God.

The courtyard of repentance is godly grief, followed by godly sorrow, whereby we surrender all thoughts and desires in confession. The incense of prayer is the communication that we have with the Father through Jesus Christ our High Priest, Who is the intercessor and mediator of the mercy seat. The revelation of the Most Holy place is made known: the secret things of the heart. **1 John chapter 1:9** tells us that if we confess our sins, He is faithful and just to forgive us of our sins, and to cleanse us from all unrighteousness. **Psalm chapter 32:1** tells us blessed is he whose transgression is forgiven, whose sin is covered. **Romans chapter 10:9,10** tells us if we will confess with our mouth, the Lord Jesus Christ, that He is our Savior, and believe in our hearts that God has raised Him from the dead, we will be saved. For with the heart men believe unto righteousness; and with the mouth confession is made unto salvation.

Hebrews chapter 4:11-16 tells us to labor in love, so that we may enter into His rest, for less we fall after the same example of our ancestors, which were disobedient. For the Word of God is quick, and powerful, and sharper than any two-edged sword, being able to pierce and divide the soul and spirit, the joints and marrow, knowing the thoughts and intent of the heart. And there is no creature hidden from His sight, but all things are naked and open to the eyes of Him: to Whom we must give an account. Since we have a great High Priest Who was lifted up through the heavens, Jesus the Son of God, let us holdfast to our profession. For we have a High Priest that can relate to our discomfort and illnesses, and He was put through the same test as us, but yet He did not sin. Let us come boldly in front of the throne of grace that we may obtain mercy, and find grace to help in our time of need.

Hebrews chapter 5:1-14 tells us that every high priest that was taken from among men is ordained for man to make intercessions unto God, both in gifts and sacrifices for sin. But who is able to have compassion on the ignorant, and also on those that have gone astray? For the high priest that was ordained, he himself is flawed and also has a need to offer gifts and sacrifices for himself. Therefore, no man can take it upon himself to become a high priest, except the Lord calls him, as was Aaron. For Christ did not wish to become a High Priest, but it was the will of His Father Who said unto Him, You are My Son and for this reason I gave birth unto You. God also said it in another place; You are a High Priest forever after the order of Melchizedek, who while he was a High Priest in his days, offered up prayers and plea, for mercy with tears unto God Who was able to save him from death, and he was heard because of his faithfulness unto God.

Even though Jesus was God's Son, yet He had to learn obedience by the things, which He suffered; and being made perfect, He became, the author of eternal salvation unto all that obeyed Him. Jesus called by God a High Priest after the order of Melchizedek. There is a lot to be said, about the Royal Priesthood of Melchizedek, but words will not permit me to speak out, seeing that it may fall on deaf ears. By this time you should have been teachers, but instead you have a need for someone to teach you again. The first principles of faith are the discernment of the knowledge and understanding of God. However, you are an infant in need of milk. Everyone who drinks milk is an infant; and therefore, you are unskilled in the Word of righteousness. Strong doctrine belongs to them that have the discernment of the Holy Spirit. For without the knowledge and understanding of God we are ignorant about the truth, but those who exercise wisdom knows the difference between good and evil.

Hebrews chapter 7:11-16 tells us that perfection was not obtained by the Levitical priesthood, whereby the people received the written law. Furthermore, Jesus Christ would have no need to become a High Priest after the order of Melchizedek. As we all know that the priesthood was given unto the Levites, and Aaron was the high priest. However, Jesus Christ was not a High Priest after the priesthood of Aaron, but after the Royal Priesthood of Melchizedek. For the priesthood being changed, there was a necessity also for the written law to be changed. The new Priest came from another tribe, of which no man gave service to at the altar. For the evidence shows that Jesus sprang from the tribe of Judah, and Moses said nothing concerning Him being a Priest. The infallible proof shows that Jesus was after the order of Melchizedek. For Jesus was not ordained to become a High Priest by a written commandment, but with the power of an endless life.

Psalm chapter 110:4 tells us that God the Father has spoken, and will not change; You are a High Priest forever after the Royal Priesthood of Melchizedek. The first priesthood not being successful, it was discontinued, for the written law made nothing perfect, but when Jesus Christ became our Royal High Priest, we were given new hope in God. For Jesus Christ was made a Royal High Priest by God Himself, with endless power.

True faith comes from knowing Jesus Christ, as our own personal Lord and Savior. In order for a person to become a doctor, or a lawyer, he or she must complete the necessary course with distinction in order to achieve ones' goal. Christianity has similar steps to be followed in order to have salvation in Jesus Christ. **2 John chapter 1:9-11** tells us that if anyone breaks the law of God, and abide not in the principle of Christ, he doesn't know God, but he who abides in the teachings of Christ, he has both the Father and the Son. If there comes any unto you, and bring not this doctrine, receive him not into your home, neither encourage him to sin. Furthermore, whosoever says unto him, may God bless you; he is also a partaker of his evil deeds. Abiding in Christ is moment–by–moment, staying focus on God, and praying without ceasing. Amen

The Heart Covenant

Christianity is the product of the Holy Spirit, whereby our hearts are circumcised by the faith and obedience of Jesus Christ to do the will of our Father in heaven. The process of sanctification is the inward cleansing of the heart, whereby the individual becomes passive. **John chapter 15:5** tells us that Jesus is the vine, and we are the branches; he who abides in Me, and I in him, bears much fruit; for without Me you can do nothing. **Mark chapter 2:27,28** tells us that the Sabbath was made for man, and not man for the Sabbath: therefore the Son of man is Lord also of the Sabbath. Since Jesus Christ is the Lord of the Sabbath, whatever He did on the Sabbath days was to the glory of His Father in heaven. Each Sabbath is a closer step to Christ in faith. If you remember the story of Cain and Abel, then you will realize that God cannot be pleased without faith. Rebellion is unacceptable in the Kingdom of heaven; therefore it is unacceptable here on earth as well. **Matthew chapter 16:19, 18:18** tells us that whatsoever is bound on earth: is bound in heaven: and whatsoever is loose on earth: is loose in heaven.

The discipleship of Christ came not by works of a sensual nature, but by faith and power from God the Father. Jesus fasted forty days, and forty nights; whereby His Spirit was poured out upon the just, and the unjust alike. **Joel chapter 2:23** tells us to be happy for we are the children of God, rejoice in the Lord your God for He has given us the former rain moderately, and He will pour out His rain upon us, the former rain and the latter rain in the first month of April/Abib. In the Ten Commandments God said, Remember the SABBATH DAY. However, Sabbaths were given unto the Israelites as the former rain, which was the sacrifice of animal's blood. The old covenant seen in the earthly tabernacle was done in order to prepare the Israelites for the coming of the latter rain, which was the true sacrifice, the Lamb of God, Jesus Christ Who is the true Sabbath Day, and eternal rest. **Isaiah chapter 66:23** tells us that from spring to fall everyone shall come and worship before Me, says, the Lord.

In today's society, modern day Christians err to the unbelief of living life apart from Christ. The life of a Christian comes through the abundance of His faithfulness; whereby the conscience is washed in the blood of the Lamb, and the mind is sanctified to do the will of God. Salvation begins with the acceptance of the gospel of Jesus Christ, and doesn't come through the obligated works of the church. Let us therefore labor in love, whereby putting all hope in Christ Jesus. For it is the faith of Jesus Christ that justifies a man pertaining to his conscience over mind to rule over his senses. **Acts chapter 23:1** tells us that Paul, earnestly beholding the council, said, men and brethren, I have lived in all good conscience before God until this day. **Acts chapter 24:16** tells us that Paul also exercised himself, to have always a conscience void of offence toward God and men.

1 Corinthians 11:3-12 tells us that as a man accepts Christ as his Lord, and a woman accepts her husband as head of the family, even so Christ accepts the authority of His Father. Because of the culture we live in, certain things we do make a statement about our relationship to God. For instance, if a man keeps his hat on while he's praying or preaching, he's understood as showing disrespect for God. It's the opposite for a woman, if she prays or speaks without wearing something on her head, she's understood as showing disrespect for her husband and for God: as much as if she had shaved her head. If she doesn't cover her head, then as far as people are concerned, she might as well have shaved her head. It is considered to be undignified for a woman to shave her head as much as praying without covering her head while worshiping God. However, a man has no need to cover his head as some are starting to do, because he was created in the Image of God for glory. The woman, on the other hand, came from the man, and she is in subjection unto the man for his glory. God gave Eve unto Adam and not the other way around. Man was created first, indicating that the man should assume the role as head of the family. Woman was created as a companion for the man.

Even though the woman having power on her head like the angels; nevertheless, the man and the woman doesn't have any power apart from the Lord. It is clear that the woman belongs to her husband; and the husband belongs to the woman, and both belong to God.

Without the conviction of the Holy Spirit, no one would come to Christ. The Holy Spirit is the direct source of the heart covenant, which is only given unto true disciples' of Christ, who has completely surrendered their lives unto Him: as did the thief on the cross. Many will thirst for the gifts of God, but denying access to the Holy Spirit from within their hearts; and therefore, becoming as trees without roots, and branches without fruits, and finally the branches are broken off at the close of their probation. Furthermore, let us examining our walk with Christ, and abide in Him always. Amen

Walking by Faith

And I looked, but not by sight, for my eye (mind) was yet to be opened, but rather in a vision, I saw the church of the Most High God eating grass in the middle of a garden. And I also beheld a man dressed in a white robe standing over them. Then I said unto him, why are these eating grass like animals? He replied, you Stephen Sergeant are a beast: you have made the Word of God void in your heart by holding fast to the teachings of men. And these also have received the mark of the beast in their foreheads from the disobedience and iniquities of their forefathers, and have not yet received sanctification by the one that lives and cannot die. Therefore, now that you have received sight by faith, let your glory be unto God from now until forevermore. For the eye is not by sight, but by faith, whereby the conscience is washed and purified by the blood of the Lamb, namely Christ Jesus Who lives, and reigns forever. Amen

Character perfecting is something that everyone struggles with; even Jesus Christ our Lord and Savior Who during His life on earth, He offered up prayers and supplications with tears unto God, and He was heard, because of His sincere request. For even though He was loved as the only begotten Son, God allowed Him to learn obedience through the things, which He suffered. **Hebrews chapter 5:9** tells us that Jesus being made perfect He became the author of eternal salvation unto them that obey Him. **Isaiah chapter 1:18,19** tells us that the Lord said, come now, and let us reason together, though your sins are like blood red, they'll become as white as snow. Though they are as crimson, they shall be like wool. If you are willing and obedient, you shall eat the good of the land. **Romans chapter 14:11,12** tells us that the Lord said, every knee shall bow unto Me, and every tongue shall confess unto God. So then, every one of us shall give an account of himself unto God. **Joel chapter 2:28,29** tells us that God will pour out His Spirit on all people. Your sons and daughters will prophesy, your old men will dream dreams; your young men will see visions. Even on My servants, both men and women, I will pour out My Spirit in those days.

Acts chapter 2:17-20 tells us that it shall come to pass in the last days, says the Lord, I will pour out of My Spirit upon the entire human race, and your sons and your daughters shall prophesy, and your young men shall see visions, and your old men shall dream dreams. And on My servants, and on My handmaidens I will pour out in those days of My Spirit; and they shall prophesy. And I will show wonders in heaven above, and signs in the earth beneath: blood, and fire, and vapor of smoke. The sun shall be turned into darkness, and the moon into blood, before that great and notable day of the Lord's coming. **Hebrews chapter 8:10-12** tells us that God will make a new covenant with the house of Israel in the last days, and He will put His laws into their mind, and write them in their hearts: and He will be to them a God, and they shall be to Him a people. And no man will have to teach his brother or his neighbor, saying, know the Lord, for all shall know Him, from the smallest to the greatest. For He will be merciful to their unrighteousness, and their sins and their iniquities will He remember no more.

The life of Jesus Christ wasn't based upon religion or denomination, but instead His focus was on doing His Father's will no matter how undignified it appeared in the sight of men. For Jesus did that which was not acceptable on the Sabbath in the eyes of men who were highly esteem according to their own righteousness. Many have covered their sins with a form of religion. **Proverbs chapter 28:13** tells us that he that covers his sins shall not prosper: but whosoever confess and forsake them shall have mercy. **Isaiah chapter 45:22** tells us that the Lord said, turn unto Me and be saved; for I Am God, and there is no other. **Isaiah chapter 46:9** tells us to remember the former things, those of long ago; I Am God, and there is no other; I Am God, and there is none like Me. **Isaiah chapter 55:8,9** tells us that His thoughts are not our thoughts, neither are our ways His ways, says the Lord. For as the heavens are higher than the earth, so are My ways higher than your ways, and My thoughts than your thoughts.

Isaiah chapter 66:1 tells us that the Lord said, heaven is My throne, and the earth is My footstool. Where is the house that you have built for Me? Where will My resting place be?

Many new believers struggle with sin, but sin by itself has no power or effect on our lives. For where there are no posted laws, no rules can be broken. I have known people, who have smoked for many years, and alcoholics who have drank for more than a decade, but yet nothing has happened to them up until now. Wherever you find good, evil is present and sin becomes active; whereby self–seeking becomes our primary motive for rebellion against the Word of God.

Have you ever been told not to do something, and no matter how simple it was the temptation was still the same? God gave the commandment unto Adam not to eat of the tree of knowledge of good and evil that was in the middle of the Garden. If God had told him to eat of the tree of life that stood next to the tree of knowledge of good and evil, it would have been a more difficult task for him to accomplish. It is the hardest thing to do good, wouldn't you agree? Adam and Eve were of one mind, and needed to surrender self in order to become more like Christ. The evidence proved that the man and his wife did that, which was evil in the sight of the Lord. Self–seeking leads us away from God by means of which rebellion becomes the point of access for pride and disobedience, which will then manifest the desires of our human nature. **Matthew chapter 4:4** tells us that when Christ was tempted to turn stones into bread, He replied, Man shall not live by bread alone, but by every Word that proceeds out of the mouth of God. **Proverbs chapter 14:12, 16:23** tells us that in the beginning self–seeking may seem good unto a man, but in the end decisions that are made without the conviction of the Holy Spirit leads to death. **Isaiah chapter 26:3** tells us that God will keep us in perfect peace: those who keep their minds steadfast on Him, because they trust in Him. **Colossians chapter 3:14** tells us that love binds virtues together in perfect unity. **1 John chapter 4:18** tells us that there is no fear in love; but perfect love drives out fear, because fear has to do with punishment. The one who fears is not made perfect in love. **Matthew chapter 5:48** tells us to be perfect therefore, as our heavenly Father is perfect. Amen

Consecration and Sanctification

Jesus spent time on His knees praying to God the Father. Without a devotional life of consecrating self unto God, it is impossible to renew the mind. The Bible confirmed that Jesus fasted for forty days and forty nights during the Lord's Passover. **Luke chapter 4:1,2** tells us that after John baptized Jesus, Him being full of the Holy Spirit returned from Jordan, and was led by the Spirit into the wilderness, where He was tempted of the devil for forty days. And in those days He ate nothing.

Consecration is the ministerial work of the Holy Spirit upon the human soul by means of which the seed of hope gives life abundantly to the believer, who has completely surrendered unto Christ. The faith of Jesus Christ is given unto the entire human race. However, self–surrender is a challenge for every believer when comes to the reproduction of the fruit of the Spirit, which is the Agape love of God. We are the branches and Christ is the vine that will reproduce the fruit of the Spirit in us. Without faith hope is dead, and the branches will remain barren. Obedience is from faith to faith: the first step toward salvation; and trust is the final result of character perfection. Self–surrender is where the individual becomes passive, meanwhile the conscience moves the mind forward in faith to believe upon Him: in Whom we trust and obey. Consecration is the adhesive that makes us single–eye in the Lord; whereby the conscience and the mind becomes one to rule over the senses, even as God the Father and Christ the Son and the Holy Spirit are one.

The summary of our spiritual walk in Christ is: justification plus sanctification equals to glorification. **John chapter 8:31,32** tells us that if we continue in His Word, then we are His disciples indeed; and we will know the truth, and the truth will make us free. Consecration is the time spent with Christ, whereby our focus is on spiritual things. Spiritual growth comes after we surrender to Christ; only then can the work of the Holy Spirit be carried out in us. **Matthew chapter 19:24-26** tells us that Jesus explained, how the human race didn't have the power to do anything apart from Him, the disciples then replied, who then can be saved, Jesus answered, and said, with the knowledge and understanding of humanity it is impossible for them to save themselves, but with God all things are possible. Consecration is the gift of the Holy Spirit. **Proverbs chapter 20:9** tells us that who can say, I have made my heart clean, I am pure from my sin? **Proverbs chapter 28:13** tells us that he that hides his sins will not prosper, but he that confesses them and repent will have mercy.

The life of a Christian is the relationship that we share with the Father through Christ and the Holy Spirit. **James chapter 1:2-7** tells us that we should count it as joy when we fall into various trials, knowing that the testing of our faith produces patience. Furthermore, we must persevere in patience, being longsuffering, so that we are made perfect and complete, lacking or wanting nothing. If anyone falls short in wisdom, let him ask of God, and it will be given unto him. God gives unto all generously without criticism. But he that is in need, let him ask in faith, not doubting, for he who doubts is like the waves of the sea driven and tossed by the wind; don't think for a second that God will answer your prayer. A double minded person is unstable in all his ways.

James chapter 1:25-27 tells us that whosoever looks into the perfect law of God's Agape love: and continues in it, and forget not what he had heard, but exercise faith in it; he is blessed in whatsoever he does. If anyone thinks that they are religious, but cannot control his tongue, he deceives his own heart, and his religion is worthless. Pure religion and undefiled before God the Father is this: a Christ–like Character that will manifest the Agape love of God, whereby Philia love can be seen in the simplicity of charity unto others: to orphans and widows in their time of discomfort; and being able to live a life of purpose and value. Furthermore, abstaining from the pollutions of the world unto the glory of God. Christianity doesn't justify sin, but rather separates the sinner from sin.

Our righteousness in Christ enables us to do charity unto our brethren, but charity by itself doesn't make us righteous. Sanctification is moment–by–moment, just as sinning is moment by moment also. The implication of the rich young ruler not making it into the Kingdom of heaven wasn't because of his earthly wealth, but because of his disobedience unto Christ. There are some situations that you can't throw money at, and salvation is one of them. When was the last time that you saw a rich person doing a good deed by making his fellow man his equal? Rich people that do charity work for others; usually like to boast themselves unto the media. **Matthew chapter 6:1** tells us to be careful not to practice our charity in front of others to be seen by men. If we do, we already have our reward. Charity that comes from the Agape love of God is the only true charity.

The story of Adam and Eve is not as complex as one would think. God gave life unto Adam, and gave him a woman to love. Whenever we show love to each other; we are simply returning love to God. Sanctification and consecration goes hand–in–hand. **Psalm chapter 51:16,17** tells us that God desire not sacrifice or else David would have given it, He has no delight in burnt offering, but the consecration of God: are a broken spirit and a humble heart, O God, You will not despise.

In order for the heart to become circumcised, the individual must surrender his free–will unto Christ. Sanctification can only be administered to the believer who has surrendered his free–will unto God. Even though a broken spirit, and a contrite heart is the work of the Holy Spirit, we have to want to surrender to God. Salvation is not by force, and most believers don't spend enough time in the Word for a greater measure of discernment and healing. Unfortunately, many will end up being spiritually dwarf. Conscienteously, we have to make every effort to abide in Christ, so that we may overcome every sin. Amen

Abiding in Christ

2 Peter chapter 1:2-8 tells us Grace and Peace be multiplied unto you through the knowledge of God, and Jesus our Lord. God's divine power has given us everything we need to live life in godliness, through the knowledge of Jesus Christ Who called us unto glory and virtue by means of which precious promises are made; so that we may participate in His divine power to live life above the corruption and emotional desires of the world. Furthermore, add to your faith, goodness, and to goodness knowledge, and to knowledge temperance, and to temperance patience, and to patience godliness, and to godliness brotherly love, and to brotherly love the Agape love of Christ, that selfless love of God. For if these precious gifts are found in you; and remain, you will never become unfruitful in the knowledge of our Lord Jesus Christ.

Conscience over mind by faith to rule over the senses is the perfecting of our character; whereby trusting and obeying becomes the foundation of our faith in Christ. For when children obey their parents: it is counted as righteousness unto them in the eye of the Lord. However, even with the influence of the Holy Spirit no man has the desire to be perfect. Repentance only comes through godly grief, and godly sorrow. God allows us to go through trials and tribulations, so that the infirmities of our sinful nature will manifest themselves as obstacles and strongholds while we remain as sinners living life apart from Christ. **Exodus chapter 34:6,7** tells us that God reviews everyone. I Am the Lord your God Who is merciful and gracious, longsuffering, and abundant in goodness and truth, showing mercy unto thousands, forgiving iniquity and transgression and sin, and I will by no means clear the guilty; visiting the iniquity of the fathers upon the children, and upon the children's children, unto the third and to the fourth generation.

A broken spirit and a contrite heart will allow the Holy Spirit to remove the dross from our hearts. At which point a sincere confession is made by the individual in front of our Father Who then forgives the sinner, not because of the confessed sins, but because Christ the Lamb paid the penalty for our sins, and He is also our Mediator: this is where the blood of Christ covers the sinner. As we draw the line between the call and the chosen: it was God the Father Who gave the twelve disciples unto Christ, and even though Judas answered the call in the end he was not among the chosen: for he did not surrender himself unto the Agape love of Christ. God did not call the righteous, but sinners unto repentance. Most people that I meet are already righteous. Therefore, they have no need for repentance? **Romans chapter 10:15** tells us that no man has the power to please God, except he is called by faith. For how will they preach the gospel, except they are sent? The law revealed sin unto us: for all have sinned and come short of the glory of God. The earth is a prison for sinners, and we are its prisoners and Christ is our Advocate and Mediator. Abiding in Christ is moment–by–moment: this is where the believer carries his cross daily, and put into practice the faith that was delivered unto him by the Holy Spirit, so that we may overcome. Amen

The Mystery of the Lord's Salvation

Mark chapter 13:32 tells us that no one knows the day or the hour when Jesus will return, not even the angels in heaven, but the Father only. However, the faithfulness of the faithful is judged according to our righteousness in Christ before He returns. Lucifer was perfect and he lived in heaven, but because of his disobedience he was cast down to the earth, where he tricked Adam into disobeying the commandment of God. **Matthew chapter 24:4,5** tells us to take heed that no man deceives us. For many shall come in My name, saying, I Am Christ; and shall deceive many. **Revelation chapter 10:7** reminds us that in the days of the voice of the seventh angel, when he shall begin to sound, the mystery of God will be finished, as Jesus had declared it unto His servants the prophets.

The blowing of trumpets, the atonement of sin, and the feast of tabernacle is the completion of the ministerial work of the Holy Spirit upon the human soul, which will signify that the bridegroom is on His way to the marriage. And the First fruits of the living, which is the hundred and forty–four thousand righteous in Christ, will be standing on the earth like a bride waiting to receive her groom. And they sang a new song, as the resurrection of the dead in Christ shall rise. **Revelation chapter 7:4** tells us that John heard the number of them, which were sealed. And there were an hundred and forty–four thousand that came out of the twelve tribes of Israel, and out of the great tribulation at the end of the world. **Revelation chapter 14:4** tells us that these are they, which were not defiled with women, for they are spiritual virgins. These are the First fruits of the living unto God and to the Lamb; unlike the First fruits of the dead they shall not see death.

1 Corinthians chapter 15:51-57 tells us behold, I will show you a mystery; we shall not all sleep, but we shall all be changed in a moment, in the twinkling of an eye, at the last trump. For the trumpet shall sound, and the dead shall be raised incorruptible, and we shall be changed. For this corruptible must put on incorruption, and this mortal will be made into immortality, then it will be announced as prophesied, death is swallowed up in victory. O death, where is your sting? O grave, where is your victory? The sting of death is sin; and the strength of sin is the law. But thanks be to God Who gave us the victory through our Lord Jesus Christ. **1 Thessalonians chapter 4:13-17** tells us not to be ignorant, brethren, concerning those who are asleep, that you sorrow not, as those which have no hope. For if we believe that Jesus had died and rose again, even so those, who are asleep in Jesus, will God bring with Him. For this we declare unto you by the Word of the Lord, that we who are alive and remain until the coming of the Lord will not prevent those that are asleep. For the Lord Himself will descend from heaven with a shout, with the voice of the Arch-angel, and with the trumpet of God: the dead in Christ will rise first: then we who are living and remain in Christ will be caught up together with them in the clouds, to meet the Lord in the air: and we will be with the Lord forever.

John chapter 5:25 tells us that Jesus said, the hour is here, when those that are in their graves will hear My voice and they that hear will live. Don't be surprised that the dead will hear My voice: for the hour is coming, when all that is in the graves will hear My voice and will come out, they that have done good, unto the resurrection of life; and they that had done evil, unto the resurrection of damnation. **Revelation chapter 14:14,15** tells us that John saw an Angel that looked like the Son of man, having on His head a golden crown, and in His hand a sharp sickle (fork). And another angel came out of the temple, crying with a loud voice unto the Son of man, that sat upon the throne, saying, thrust in your sickle, (fork) and reap: for the time is come for you to reap; for the harvest of the earth is ripe.

God gave Satan, and humanity, and the earth six thousand years of probation. **Genesis chapter 18:20,21** tells us that the Lord destroyed Sodom and Gomorrah, because the cry of it was great, and because their sin was very grievous. **Jonah chapter 1:1,2** tells us that the Word of the Lord came unto Jonah the son of Amittai, saying, arise, go to Nineveh, that great city, and cry against it, for their wickedness is come before Me. **Revelation chapter 22:11** tells us that he that is unjust, let him remain unjust still: and he which is filthy, let him be filthy still: and he that is righteous, let him be righteous still: and he that is Holy, let him be Holy still. **Revelation chapter 6:17** tells us that the day of His wrath is come, and who will be able to stand?

Jeremiah chapter 25:33 tells us that the Lord will slay all the wicked in one day, from one end of the earth even unto the other end of the earth: they will not be mourned for, neither will they be heaped up nor be buried; but they will be like dung upon the earth. **2 Thessalonians chapter 2:8** tells us that the wicked will be made known, Whom the Lord will consume with the Spirit of His mouth, and He will destroy them with the brightness of His coming. **Revelation chapter 21:8** tells us that the fearful, and unbelieving, and the abominable, and murderers, and the greedy, and sorcerers, and idolaters, and all liars, shall have their part in the lake that burn with fire and brimstone: which is the second death. **Isaiah chapter 4:1** tells us in that day seven churches shall take hold of one man, namely Jesus Christ, saying, we will teach our own doctrine, and clothe ourselves with our own righteousness; only let us be called by Your name, to take away our shame.

The outpouring of His Holy Spirit renewed our conscience unto eternal life by means of which character perfection was reproduce in His once beloved church that slept for more than four thousand years before He came and set the captives free. Conscience over mind is obedience through faith. **Matthew chapter 22:37-39** tells us that obedience through faith is summarized as the Agape love of God, and Philia love is loving our neighbor as ourselves.

As the final grains of sand flows gently to the bottom of the hourglass and the cup of indignation becomes filled to the brim; it is clear unto those who have the discernment of the Lord's prophecy that the last days of judgment wherein we are called to preach the gospel as a witness unto the world is now. However, no one has the power to build a house without the necessary materials or tools thereof; even so faith without love is dead. We have all imagined life being easier, but often times we find ourselves being alone and that's when the Agape love of God becomes something that we are desperately in need of. Unfortunately, desperation will not produce the unconditional love of God; it will only promote Eros, which is *(Romantic love)* to nurture our pride.

We are all born with a sinful nature, and the desire to be self–seeking. And no matter how sincere we are as believers, sin will use our emotions against us. Anxiety is the spur of a moment, but impulsive decisions are without moral judgments. Eros, which is romance will first seem pleasant in the beginning, but in the end comes ignominy and reproach. We all have a general idea of how brutal mistakes can be, and with disappointments and regrets there are no easy fix. However, I thank God for His mercy and grace, whereby, if we continue in faith and prayer: praying always in the Spirit of truth, and persevering; we shall overcome every obstacle in the name of Jesus Christ our Lord and Savior. For only by making supplications through thanksgiving and praise will every good work be established in the name of Him that was, and still to come. Amen

Honor thy Father and thy Mother

Here in the west we believe in eating animals to make us strong, meanwhile in the east they believe in worshiping animals to make them wise. From my own personal experience, whenever my taste buds are satisfied the nutritional value is usually not there! Eating fish, poultry, and meat isn't necessarily a bad thing, especially when it's done in moderation. However, it takes about three to four hours for some of these foods to be digested, who has that amount of time to wait around for one meal to be transformed into energy?

The direct source of life is God Who created man in His Own Image and Likeness. Honor God the Father, and Mother Earth for longevity good health, vitality and stamina, which comes directly from the fresh air we breathe. The breath of life is simply H2O. I urge believers to exercise faith in God's health laws, which are: nutrition, exercise, water, sunlight, temperance, air, rest and trust. Faith is the Word of God, whereby we pray for His divine intervention, which is the indwelling of His Holy Spirit.

Proper nutrition starts with a balance diet: fish, fruits, herbs, meat, nuts, oil, poultry, and vegetables. Vegans and most vegetarians don't eat fish, poultry, and meat. However, our bodies need a daily-required amount of calories such as: fiber, minerals, oil, protein, and sugar, which are then broken down inside of the body for vitamins to maintain our immunity. Our immune system was designed to aid us in moderate illnesses. Proper nutrition is a requirement in order to stay healthy. Exercise is recommended on a daily basis to maintain youth, strength and flexibility of joints; meanwhile reducing anxiety and stress. <u>Exercise</u>, <u>water</u> and <u>oxygen</u> play a major part of our respiratory and lymphatic system.

The continual flow of fresh air throughout the body is priority number one. Furthermore, consuming small quantities of water throughout the day will keep the body hydrated, and eliminate the possibility of being dehydrated, which can cause nausea and fatigue. Dehydration can also cause morning sickness. Water also helps to purge the body of unwanted toxins, which can cause fungal infections to the digestive system. Some of the most common and deadly toxins are found in foods that aren't prepared properly. Furthermore, you have alcohol beverages, salt, smoke, and sugars from carbohydrates and starchy foods, which are detrimental to the heart, liver, and kidneys, because they deprive the entire body of water and oxygen. Without water and oxygen the body becomes constipated. Constipation is where the plumbing that operates our bowel movements becomes poisonous with toxins. Water and oxygen acts as a delivery system twenty-four-seven, whereby the entire body, soul and spirit is replenished.

Our bodies are maximized while we sleep with nutrients that were consumed during the day. However, in order to insure proper rest and rejuvenation of our bodies, meals that require more than an hour to digest should never be consumed before bedtime. The mind can become distorted from not getting enough rest due to poor sleeping conditions, whereby the inability of comprehension and thought processing becomes much more difficult for the individual. Notice the word rejuvenation, this happens when the body and mind becomes dormant, only then can harmony be achieved. Rest unites the body and mind as one living soul by means of which our spirit unites with Christ's Holy Spirit; therefore we are more alive while we sleep than when we are awake.

Sunlight is probably one of the most needed of the eight, but yet it's taken for granted simply because of its abundance. Without sunlight our planet would be covered in darkness and life would cease to exist. Temperance is a fruit of the Holy Spirit and can only be reproduced in those who have surrendered their lives unto Christ through faith. Amen

Health has become one of the largest issues of life due to the fact that we have made every effort to ignore our plant-based diet, which was given unto us by God. Man was created in the Image and Likeness of God, and he is held at a higher standard and accountability than any other creature that the Lord God made. **Genesis chapter 1:11** tells us that God said, let the earth bring forth grass: the herb producing seed, and the fruit tree producing fruit after his kind, whose seed is in itself, upon the earth: and it was so. **Genesis chapter 1:29** tells us that God said, behold, I have given you every herb producing seed, which is upon the face of all the earth, and every tree, in which the fruit of the tree producing seed; to you it shall be for food. **Genesis chapter 2:9** tells us that out of the ground made the Lord God to grow every tree that is pleasant to the sight, and good for food.

The health law doesn't require us to become vegetarians. However, the guidelines are very strict. **Genesis chapter 9:3-6** tells us that every moving animal that's alive shall be for food for you; even as the green herb have I given you all things, but the blood of the animals you must not eat. For certain, I say unto you, the life of every creature is in their blood, and I will require an account of every animal, man or beast whose life is taken by your hands. I will also require the blood of your life, for their life. And at the hand of every man's brother will I require the life of man. Whosoever kill a man, he must be put to death, because in the Image of God was man created.

Now that disease in animals is rapidly increasing, producing cancerous germs, we must choose the most nutritious foods for our bodies. **Leviticus chapter 10:8,9** tells us that the Lord spoke unto Aaron saying; do not drink wine nor strong drink, you or your sons. **Leviticus chapter 11:1-23** tells us that the Lord spoke unto Moses and Aaron, saying: speak unto the children of Israel, say unto them; these are the animals that you may eat of; animals with their hoofs divided and chew their foods mixed in with their saliva can be eaten. However, these you may not eat of; animals that have divided hoof, and chew not their foods mixed with their saliva: and also animals that chew with the saliva, but have not the divided hoof: the camel, and the rock badger they both chew with the saliva, but have not the divided hoof, also the rabbit even though he chews with the saliva, but he have not the divided hoof, the pig have the divided hoof, but he chew not with the saliva; these are all unclean. Any fish that doesn't have fins and scales should not be eaten. You must not eat the eagle, buzzard, vulture, osprey, kite, falcon, raven, hawk, ostrich, seagull, owl, crow, swan, pelican, stork, heron, bat and winged insects, except those that have jointed legs and hop. You may eat the grasshopper, locust and cricket, but all other insects are unclean. Our diet, make a statement about our love for God. Therefore, God must be placed first in all things we do. Amen

Basic Food Combinations

Fruits are broken down into four groups: sweet fruits, acid fruits, sub–acid fruits, and melons. Sweet fruits are best if eaten by themselves. Acid fruits, and sub–acid fruits combine well. Melons are best if eaten by themselves. Most fruits are easily digested in about one to two hours. However, melons digest faster than fruits and vegetables, and should be consumed by themselves.

SWEET FRUITS: bananas, plantains, dates, persimmons, figs, prunes, raisins, dried fruits. Do not combine with others.

ACID FRUITS: grape fruits, oranges, lemons, limes, kiwis, strawberries, cranberries, and pineapple, ok to combine with sub–acid fruits.

SUB–ACID FRUITS: apples, apricots, blackberries, plums, peaches, cherries, pears, raspberries, mangos, nectarines, grapes, and papayas, ok to combine with acid fruits.

MELONS: cantaloupe, honeydew, watermelon, casaba, christmas–melon, and crenshaw. Do not combine with others.

STARCHES: potatoes, carrots, parsnips, corn, winter squash, grains, barley buckwheat, dried corn, oats, rice, brown rice, wild rice, wheat, rye, pasta and bread. Starches combine well with legumes and vegetables only. Starches require about three hours to be digested.

LEGUMES: beans, peas, tofu and peanuts. Legumes combine well with proteins, starches, and vegetables only.

VEGETABLES: artichokes, broccoli, cabbage, cauliflower, celery, cucumber, green peas, green beans, red, yellow, and green peppers, kale, lettuce, spinach, sprouts, string beans, tomatoes and mushrooms. Vegetables combine well with legumes, oils, proteins, and starches.

PROTEINS: fish, meat, nuts, and poultry. Proteins combine well with legumes, and vegetables. Proteins require about four hours to be digested.

OILS AND FATS: avocados, coconuts oil, olive oil, safflower oil, and vegetable oil. Oils and fats combine well with vegetables.

High Acidic base foods are process foods like: dairy and other man made foods, which carry large quantities of preservatives. These types of foods are usually saturated with high fructose corn–syrup. Alkaline base foods are usually <u>natural or raw foods</u> like vegetables that are <u>high on antioxidant</u>, which helps to boost the immune and digestive system to work better. Taking a bigger bite out of life doesn't guarantee success or satisfaction especially if we can't digest what we are chewing on. The entire human race shares the same weaknesses when it comes to having patience and self–control. Animals have an instinct to do what is necessary to survive. It makes me wonder why we call them animals. The moral laws aren't always visible to the naked eye, but we know that they exist in our hearts and minds, and occasionally we get a glimpse of them manifesting themselves unto the glory of His name. Amen

"The Holy City of New Jerusalem"

Chapter 8

The New Earth

John chapter 14:27 tells us that Christ gave His peace unto us, "My peace I give unto you: not as the world give it, but I unto you. Let not your heart be troubled, neither let it be afraid." **John chapter 16:33** tells us that Jesus spoke these things, so that in Him we would have peace. However, in the world we would have tribulation, but be of good cheer; for I have overcome the world, says our Lord Jesus Christ. **Isaiah chapter 65:17-19** tells us that the Lord will create new heavens and a new earth: and the former shall not be remembered, nor come to mind anymore. But be glad, and rejoice forever in that, which I create: for, behold, I create Jerusalem for rejoicing, and her people will be a joy. For I will rejoice in Jerusalem says the Lord, and My joy will be in My people: and the voice of crying and weeping will not be heard in her anymore. **Isaiah chapter 66:22,23** tells us that the new heavens and the new earth that God will create will remain before Him. Furthermore, our children and our name will remain. And from one new moon to another, and from one Sabbath to another the entire congregation shall come to worship before Me, says the Lord.

Revelation chapter 21:1-5 tells us that John saw a <u>new heaven</u> and a <u>new earth</u>: for the first heaven and the first earth were passed away; and there was <u>no more sea</u>. John saw the Holy City, the New Jerusalem coming down from God out of heaven, prepared as a bride adorned for her husband. And I heard a great voice out of heaven saying, behold, the tabernacle of God is with men, and He will dwell with them, and they will be His people, and God Himself will be with them, and be their God.

And God will wipe away all tears from their eyes; and there will be <u>no</u> <u>more death</u>, <u>neither sorrows</u>, <u>nor crying</u>, <u>nor pain</u> will be there anymore: for the former things are passed away. And He that sat upon the throne said, behold, I make all things new. And He said unto me, write: for these words are true and faithful.

Revelation chapter 21:11-27, 22:1,2 tells us that the City of New Jerusalem have the glory of God, and her light was like unto a stone most precious, even like a jasper stone, clear as crystal; and the walls were great and high, and had twelve gates, and at the gates twelve angels, and the names of the twelve tribes of the children of Israel written on the gates. On the east wall there are three gates, on the north wall there are three gates, on the south wall there are three gates, on the west wall there are three gates. And the walls of the City were seated on twelve foundations, and in them the names of the twelve apostles of the Lamb were written. The City was laid out in a square; its length is the same as its width. It measured fifteen hundred miles along each side. And the walls were more than two hundred feet high. The walls of the City is made with green jasper, while the City itself is made of pure gold, clear as glass. The foundation stones of the City and its walls are made of all kinds of precious stones and countless colors: the first cornerstone was deep green made of jasper, the second rich blue made of sapphire, the third milky white made of chalcedony, the fourth bright green made of emerald, the fifth reddish pink made of sardonyx, the sixth deep red made of carnelian, the seventh bright yellow made of chrysolite, the eighth deep blue made of beryl, the ninth pale blue made of topaz, the tenth gold colored made of chrysoprase, the eleventh red made of jacinth, and the twelfth purple made of amethyst. Each of the twelve gates is made of one huge pearl, and the streets of the City are made of pure gold, as transparent glass.

In the City there is no temple to worship in, for the Lord God Almighty and the Lamb are the Temple of it. And the City had no need of the sun, neither of the moon, to shine in it: for the glory of God shines through it, and the Lamb is the light of it. And the nations of them that are saved shall walk in the light of it, and the kings of the earth do bring their glory and honor into it. And the gates remain open by day, for there are no nights there, and the Lord God and the Lamb shall bring their glory and honor of the nations in it. Furthermore, nothing that defiles, or profanes, or make a lie shall ever enter into it, but that which is written in the Lamb's book of life. And John saw a river as clear as crystal pouring out of the throne of God, where the Lamb sat. The river flowed alongside the street on both side, and the tree of life was on both side of the street that bear twelve different types of fruit each month, and its leaves were for the healing of the nations.

In the City of the New Jerusalem, the law of love is supreme. Furthermore, we have no desire to sin, no motive for earthly pleasure, and no pride for earthly things. For by His sovereignty all things are made wonderful, whereby the serenity of our peace is sustained by His righteousness; and by His love all things are made to give Him praise. The foundation of God's heavenly kingdom is obedience out of love. For even His Majestic City that was and still to come, displays His divinity, and Omnipotence from glory to glory without end, even so His Omniscient love shine from faith to faith. For His love that was and still to come, was not finite, and had no need of refinement to become perfect. Furthermore, our perfection was made complete by the glory of Him that is infinite. God's people are retroactive, having the ability to exercise free–will by faith; therefore, come now and let us sing songs of joy unto Him that is gracious and merciful, for we are the good citizens of the New Jerusalem. Amen

Prayer of Acknowledgment

Our Father, Who is in heaven, Holy is Your name. Your Kingdom come, let Your will be done here on the earth, as it is in heaven. Give us this day our daily command, and forgive us of our debts, as we forgive our debtors. And lead us not into temptation, but deliver us from evil: for Yours is the Kingdom, and the power, and the glory in the name of Jesus Christ forever and ever. For I acknowledge You as the creator of the earth, and I recognize that You are my provider. You have given me peace and made me whole. You have also raised Christ from the dead. O Lord, I ask in faith that You would grant me the capacity to be long-suffering in this mortal body, so that I may bring You much more honor and glory in the name of Jesus Christ. Amen

Prayer of Confession

I confess my sins unto thee O God, because You are just and merciful in judging me according to Your righteousness. Let not the Lord be angry because of my transgressions, even though they are many. The Lord God is wonderful, and purposely righteous in all things that You do. O Lord, my strength and my redeemer, please forgive me of my sins, not for my sake, but that the name of the Lord might be magnified, even upon the lips of those who have transgress Your law. For I have sinned against You, and only You alone have I sinned against. Forgive me O Lord for falling short with Your glory in the name of our Lord and Savior, Jesus Christ. Amen

Prayer of Thanksgiving

I thank You O God for the love that You have shown me, and the peace You have given unto me. I thank You for my health and my strength. I thank You for Your mercy and grace. I thank You for being a compassionate God. I thank You for Your many blessings and Your Son Jesus Christ Who died to save me. Amen

Prayer of Praise

I praise You O God, for keeping Your promises. I praise You for protecting me, and my love ones. I praise You because You are worthy to be praise. You are the heights of knowledge, and the depth of understanding. You are the God of wisdom, who is like unto You. For there is no other Rock apart from You O Lord; You are the Most High God: Jehovah by name. The King of kings, and The Lord of lords: Who sits on the throne of the everlasting Kingdom in the heavens. I give You praise in the name of our Lord and Savior, Jesus Christ. Amen

Prayer of Meditation

I will meditate upon the Lord's goodness, and His mercy and grace. For whosoever seeks after wisdom, knowledge and understanding seeks after the Lord. But whosoever seeks after pleasure, seeks after death and destruction of his soul. Learn to appreciate life and God will reward you with peace and joy, but a greedy person will inherit the wind. Call upon the name of the Lord, Jehovah-Jirah, Jehovah-Nissi, Jehovah-Shalom and He will grant you the fruit of His Spirit, and deliver you from the ways of sin. And if you continue to abide in Him, He will abide in you forever and ever. Amen

Persevering in the Lord

Ephesians chapter 6:10-18 tells us finally, brethren, be strong in the Lord, and in the power of His might. Put on the whole armor of God, that you may be able to stand against the wiles of the devil. For we fight not against flesh and blood, but against principalities, against powers, against the rulers of darkness of this world, against spiritual oppression in high places. Therefore, take on the whole armor of God; that you may be able to withstand the day of destruction, and having done all, to stand, make sure that you are anointed with truth, and having the breastplate of righteousness; and your feet made ready with the preparation of the gospel of peace; and above all the shield of faith to quench all fiery darts of the wicked, and the helmet of salvation with the sword of the Spirit, which is the Word of God. Praying always with all prayer and supplication in the Spirit, and watching with all perseverance and supplication for all saints.

The salvation of our Lord and Savior Jesus Christ was established from the foundation of the earth. Even though mankind chose not to believe in His hope and precious promises that were made unto them that labor not in love toward one another according to the commandment given unto them that heard it in the Garden of Eden before the deception of the world. The Almighty God, Who is the Father of creation and the universe, and love, and peace, and faith, and hope, chose not to abandon His creation. But the same Word brought forth righteousness in both: unto the first Adam who sinned, and also unto the second that came as a ransom.

Christ is the beginning of knowledge without end; whereby the Holy Spirit is given for the discernment of prophecies and judgment in every decision that is made. God will restore that which was lost by His Word. Let us be faithful in whatever we do unto the glory of His name. **Deuteronomy chapter 30:19,20** tells us that God has called heaven and earth as a witness before us, whereby He has given us free-will to choose life and blessings: by means of which His Word points toward salvation, that both you and I may live according to the Word of His prosperity that we may learn to love the Lord our God, and that we may obey His Word, so that we may holdfast to Him. For the Word of God is the strength of our life and the length of our days: that we may live in the land which the Lord made promise unto our forefather Abraham, and also unto Isaac, and Jacob by His Word.

The Truth about faith, hope and love is revealed in the divine attributes of Jesus Christ. Even though He was the only begotten Son, the Bible testifies of His lowly spirit, and His selfless Character; whereby He was found to be a faithful servant unto His Father in heaven. I must admit that I am very passionate about Christianity. And even though life has many wonderful things to offer, eventually clutter becomes the final result to every human trait; whereby love will turn to hate if not nurtured by the characteristics of Jesus Christ. It's never a simple application when it comes to making conscientious decisions, especially when other people who are involved don't share the same belief.

Life is a challenge and God has given us His Word. For He is my Rock and my salvation to Whom I belong. Whenever I am in distress, His Word fills my spirit with hope. Whenever I am weak His Word strengthens me from head to toe with the power to overcome the world. For whatever the need is, His Word never fails. His Word is everlasting throughout all generations. For even though the search might become tiresome the Agape love that is transpired from His Word is more than enough inspiration to overcome every obstacle. The empowerment of His Word enables us to call on His Majestic name by faith. **Ecclesiastes chapter 12:13** tells us that the fullness of the matter and the conclusion of the entire Word is Christ Jesus. Furthermore, love God and keep His commandments: for this is the whole purpose and duty of man. A man is made low so that God can establish him through His Word. For God will bring everything into judgment according to His Word: good and evil. Therefore, let us look forward unto the coming of our Lord Jesus Christ, Who is the author and finisher of our faith. Amen

Shalom

Thanks to a small group of people who have helped me on my spiritual journey: Alicia Pratt, Andrew Jones JR, Anthony Dobson, Atuanya Howson, Baron Smith, Brian Blake, Cordell Williams, Curtis Kiffin, Egerton Thomas, Everton Hunter JR, Evens Edouard, Fredrick Ganes III, Garth S. Thomas, Geneva Pratt, Gunzalis Smith, Ike Blake, John Fetkin, Kevin Grizzle, Kevin Fisher, Kroegor Daglobst, Lenford Fisher, Liseth Sergeant, Maud Forskin, Maxwell Reid, McCauley Blake, Miciah Sergeant, My father: Dainley Sergeant, My mother: Wilhelmina Forskin, My wife: Marva Dawes-Sergeant, Neil McIntosh, Parthenia Mungin, Paul Gordon, Pedro Tejada, Phillip Drummond, Phillippa Reid, Ralph Forskin, Sasha Smith, San J. Cole, Samantha Sergeant, Sheron Young, Stephenie Sergeant, Valerie Arrindell-Thomas, Wilder Domond, Winsome Sergeant, and Zelta Sergeant.

Special thanks to: Horse Guard Basic School and the teachers, Garlands Primary School and the teachers, and Maldon High School and the teachers, who taught me to read and write. My success did not come overnight, but with hard work and dedication. God has inspired me to thank you all for your efforts. Please exercise faith in Jesus Christ. Amen

Made in the
USA
Middletown, DE